Fair Play in Sport

Fair Play in Sport presents a critical re-working of the classic ideal of fair play and explores its practical consequences for current competitive sport. By linking general moral principles and practical cases, the book develops a contemporary theory of fair play. It demonstrates how, if pursued systematically, moral principles upon which most of us agree lead to a series of radical consequences for sport practice.

The book examines many of the key issues in the ethics of sport, including:

- fairness and justice in sport
- moral and immoral interpretations of athletic performance
- what makes a 'good competition'
- the key values of competitive sport.

The notion of fair play is integral to sport as we know and experience it, and is commonly seen as a necessary ethos if competitive sport is to survive and flourish. *Fair Play in Sport* provides an invaluable guide to the subject for all those with an interest in ethics and the philosophy of sport.

Sigmund Loland is Professor of Sport Philosophy and Ethics at The Norwegian University of Sport and Physical Education.

Ethics and Sport

Series editors

Mike McNamee
Cheltenham and Gloucester College
Jim Parry
University of Leeds

The Ethics and Sport series aims to encourage critical reflection on the practice of sport, and to stimulate professional evaluation and development. Each volume explores new work relating philosophical ethics and the social and cultural study of ethical issues. Each is different in scope, appeal, focus and treatment but a balance is sought between local and international focus, perennial and contemporary issues, level of audience, teaching and research application, and variety of practical concerns.

Also available in this series:

Ethics and Sport
Edited by Mike McNamee and Jim Parry

Values in Sport
Elitism, nationalism, gender equality and the scientific manufacture of winners
Edited by Torbjörn Tännsjö and Claudio Tamburrini

Spoilsports
Understanding and preventing sexual exploitation in sport
Celia H. Brackenridge

Fair Play in Sport

A moral norm system

Sigmund Loland

London and New York

First published 2002
by Routledge
11 New Fetter Lane, London EC4P 4EE

Simultaneously published in the USA and Canada
by Routledge
29 West 35th Street, New York, NY 10001

Routledge is an imprint of the Taylor & Francis Group

© 2002 Sigmund Loland

Typeset in 10/12 Garamond by
Steven Gardiner Ltd
Printed and bound in Great Britain by
The University Press, Cambridge

The publisher makes no representation, express or implied, with regard to
the accuracy of the information contained in this book and cannot accept any
legal responsibility or liability for any errors or omissions that may be made.

British Library Cataloguing in Publication Data
A catalogue record for this book is available
from the British Library

Library of Congress Cataloging in Publication Data
Loland, Sigmund.
  Fair play in sport: a moral nom system / Sigmund Loland.
    p. cm. – (Ethics and sport)
  Includes bibliographical references and index
  1. Sports – Moral and ethical aspects. 2. Sportsmanship. I. Title. II. Series.

GV706.3 .L65 2001
175 – dc21
                                                                2001034876

ISBN 0-419-26060-9 (hbk)
ISBN 0-419-26070-6 (pbk)

For Vetle, Vilde and Nina

Contents

Series editors' preface   ix
Preface   xi
Introduction: the fair play argument   xiii

1 Sport competitions: rules, goals, and social logic   1
  Sport and sport competitions   1
  Summary   15

2 A moral point of view   17
  Morality and ethics   17
  A moral point of view   21
  Norms   31
  Practical reasoning   33
  Norm systems   34
  Summary   38

3 Right sport competitions: fairness   41
  Fairness: a preliminary norm   41
  Formal, distributive and procedural justice   43
  Sport competitions as experiments   44
  Equality   46
  Inequality in sport competitions: athletic performance   65
  Unequal treatment and actual inequalities in sport competitions   83
  Summary   103

4 Good sport competitions: play   107
  Sport: play, work or war?   107
  Good competitions as the realization of intentional goals   109
  Utilitarianism applied   110

Preferences anong parties concerned   112
An argument at the critical level of moral thought   122
Good competitions as playful competitions   138
Summary   140

5 Fair play in sport competitions: a moral norm system   143
Fair play as a moral norm system   145
The moral goal of sport competitions   147

Notes   151
Bibliography   159
Index   167

Series editor's preface

The Ethics and Sport series is the first of its kind in the world. Its main aim is to support and contribute to the development of the study of ethical issues in sport, and indeed to encourage the establishment of Sports Ethics as a legitimate discipline in its own right.

Whilst academics and devotees of sport have debated ethical issues such as cheating, violence, inequality and the nature and demands of fair play, these have rarely been explored systematically in extended discussion.

Given the logical basis of ethics at the heart of sport as a practical activity, every important and topical issue in sport has an ethical dimension and often the ethical dimension is of overwhelming significance. The series addresses a variety of both perennial and contemporary issues in this rapidly expanding field, aiming to engage the community of teachers, researchers and professionals, as well as the general reader.

Philosophical ethics may be seen both as a theoretical academic discipline and as an ordinary everyday activity contributing to conversation, journalism and practical decision-making. The series aims to bridge that gap. Academic disciplines are brought to bear on the practical issues of the day, illuminating them and exploring strategies for problem-solving. A philosophical interest in ethical issues may also be complemented and broadened by research within related disciplines, such as sociology and psychology, and some volumes aim to make these links directly.

The series aims to encourage critical reflection on the practice of sport, and to stimulate professional evaluation and development. Each volume explores new work relating to philosophical ethics and the social and cultural study of ethical issues. Each is different in scope, appeal, focus and treatment but a balance is sought between local and international focus, perennial and contemporary issues, level of audience, teaching and research application, and a variety of practical concerns. Each volume is complete in itself but also complements others in the series.

Mike McNamee, Cheltenham and Gloucester College
Jim Parry, University of Leeds

Preface

In this book I present an updated, systematic and critical interpretation of what I consider to be the key concept in the ethics of competition: fair play. Many people have inspired and helped me in the process of writing it. Thanks are due to:

- the many competitors I have met in various sports over the years, who have taught me most of what I know about both fair and foul play;
- Mike McNamee and Jim Parry, editors of the series of which this book is a part. Their comments on content and language have helped me articulate and clarify whatever sound philosophical points the book may contain;
- Gunnar Breivik, my colleague and friend, for many good comments and interesting discussions over the last fifteen years;
- Jon Wetlesen, philosopher at the University of Oslo, who first encouraged me to start working with ethics in sport and from whom I have learnt a lot;
- my other colleagues, and students, at the Norwegian University for Sport and Physical Education, for providing an excellent working (and playing) environment in which topics of fair play are often discussed;
- The Philosophic Society for the Study of Sport, now The International Association for the Philosophy of Sport, for being an arena for serious and enjoyable discussions of sport philosophical issues.

Last but not least, there are people who mean much more to me than words can express. My 1989 doctoral dissertation on fair play, from which this book is developed, was dedicated to my mother and father who I consider to be ultimate fair players of life. I dedicate this work to my wife Nina and my children Vilde and Vetle who fill my life with value and joy. Without them, neither work nor sport would have much meaning at all.

In spite of having been inspired and helped in many ways by many people, the content of the book is, of course, my responsibility alone.

Oslo, March 2001
Sigmund Loland

Introduction

The fair play argument

How ought we to act in sport competitions? The question can be answered in many ways. The gymnast who dismounts the parallel bars with a well-balanced somersault acts according to norms for good technique; the football player who executes a penetrating 40-metre pass has 'an eye for the game' and makes a tactically correct choice of move. But by which criteria do we evaluate good and appropriate technique and tactics? Responses usually refer to the standards of excellence in the sport in question. In gymnastics and football, advanced somersaults and killer passes respectively, belong to the relevant technical and tactical skills. But, for the philosophically inclined sport enthusiast, these questions can be pursued further. Why do we exercise technical and tactical skills in competitions at all? What are the meanings and values of these practices? And, even more fundamentally, what is the role, if any, of sport in the broader framework of human life?

This book examines sport as a possible arena for human flourishing. More precisely, it suggests a re-articulation of a classic ideal for sport competitions, fair play, and argues that the realization of this ideal can make such competitions morally justifiable and indeed valuable activities in the broader perspective of human life. The claim is not that sport is a necessary part of human flourishing, but rather that, if practised according to fair play, sport can be one among the many activities that could contribute to such flourishing. What follows is an introductory outline of the argument.

Chapter 1, Sport competitions: rules, goals and social logic, performs the analytical task of presenting key terms in the argument and explaining how they are to be understood. Sport competitions are seen as social practices within which it is possible to identify what can be called structural, intentional, and moral goals. The structural goal of sport competitions is to measure, compare and rank competitors according to athletic performance. Individuals' intentional goals reflect individuals' reasons for engaging in sport and are, therefore, of a great variety. Finally, the moral goal of competitions is precisely what the rest of this book will attempt to articulate and justify.

I then give an overview of the historical roots and current understandings of what is traditionally seen as a moral goal for sport: fair play. The ideal is generally understood as having one formal and one informal component. Formal fair play demands adherence to the rules and prescribes what is considered morally right and just. Informal fair play refers to mutual respect between the parties engaged and to the ideal attitudes and virtues with which they ought to compete. I talk here of what is considered morally good.

To be able to examine this general understanding of fair play in a systematic way, we need criteria for the morally right and good. Such criteria are developed in Chapter 2, A moral point of view. The aim is not to develop a full-blooded ethical theory but, more pragmatically, to describe the basic premises and reflect upon the limits and possibilities of this work. I reject the idea of an absolute objective moral point of view but hold on to the possibility of rational discussion of ethical questions and of distinguishing morally sound norms and actions from morally unacceptable ones. My perspective is inspired by analytic and systematic studies of norms and values and their possible interconnections. I build on a version of ethical contract theory that searches for standpoints that cannot reasonably be rejected as a basis for unforced, informed general agreement (Scanlon 1984). These general criteria for the moral are specified in terms of a consequentialist norm inspired by utilitarianism and a non-consequentialist norm for justice that will serve as tools for thought or as backing norms in the further elaboration of fair play. In this way, I operate with what Frankena (1963) calls a 'mixed' ethical theory.

In Chapter 3, Right sport competitions: fairness, a first group of norms for fair play is formulated and elaborated. Sport competitions are social practices where two or more parties interact. I argue that if participation in sport is a matter of unforced choice, certain obligations towards the other parties arise. More precisely, if competitors are voluntarily engaged in a competition, they ought to act according to the shared interpretation of the rules among the practitioners of the sport in question, if this interpretation is just. A shared interpretation of the rules is called an ethos. This is a reconstruction of the idea of formal fair play and I refer to the formulation as a fairness norm.

With backing from the non-consequentialist norm developed in Chapter 2, considerable time is spent discussing the requirement for justice. First, norms are developed for equal opportunity to perform. I discuss how to deal with inequalities in external conditions, in person-dependent matters such as height, weight, sex, and age, and in the equipment and strength of support systems. Furthermore, a detailed normative interpretation is developed of the relevant inequality that all sports attempt to evaluate: athletic performance. Finally, I discuss what can be said to be a reasonable relationship between actual athletic performance and the distribution of advantages (rankings, points, goals, etc.) and disadvantages (penalties) in competitions.

Even if competitors follow the fairness norm, competitions may not necessarily be experienced as good. Two competitors may follow a shared, just ethos, but if they are uneven in performance potential and/or in attitudes, the competition might turn out as a negative experience for both. In

Chapter 4, Good sport competitions: play, I examine the intentional goals linked to people's engagement sport. The idea is developed that in good competitions, intentional goals among all parties concerned are realized to the greatest degree possible. With the help of the consequentialist, utilitarian norm sketched in Chapter 2, I weigh different intentional goals against each other and conclude that good competition is realized if competitors act according to what is called 'internal winning preferences'. Competitors ought to play to win within the framework of a shared, just ethos of the sport in question. Moreover, if agreement can be reached on the characteristics of good competition, it is rational to seek to maximize their number. Therefore, a set of sub-norms is developed which prescribes that competitors ought to be of similar performance potential and of similar preference strength. Here, I present a reconstruction of the idea of informal fair play. This becomes an additional obligation that arises when we voluntarily engage in sport. I talk now of a norm for play because it is directed at realizing experiential values, in the competitions themselves.

In Chapter 5, Fair play in sport competitions: a moral norm system, I argue that the fairness norm and the play norm constitute a moral norm system that is clear, simple, complete, consistent, and can be morally justified. The further argument is that the norms are not just consistent but that there are strong connections of meaning between them. The fairness norm makes just competition possible by prescribing that the participants adhere to a shared, just ethos. It secures equality of opportunity and a meritocratic distribution of advantages and disadvantages. The fairness norm represents predictability. The play norm prescribes that competitors should play (fairly) to win. It is designed to realize even competitions, openness of outcome, and unpredictability. By acting according to fair play, we can reach an optimal balance between fairness and play and between predictability and unpredictability, and so experience what (after Warren Fraleigh) can be called 'the sweet tension of uncertainty of outcome'.

'The sweet tension of uncertainty of outcome' should not be understood as a description of some kind 'essence' or 'substance' of good sport. The term refers to the phenomenological structure of the good sport experience, and can be interpreted and articulated in various ways in various socio-cultural contexts. Still, I argue that shared experiences within this structure unite people in morally valuable ways. In fair and good competition, participants join forces and strive together in ways that increase the joy for all. I argue that this is how sport can become an arena for the flourishing of human beings and one of many possible practices in a good life. The realization of 'the sweet tension of uncertainty of outcome' is therefore considered to be a moral goal in sport competitions.

Chapter 1

Sport competitions

Rules, goals and social logic

To be able to suggest a normative understanding of sport competitions as potentially meaningful and valuable human practices, we need a clearer grasp of what kind of practices we are talking about, and what traditionally have been their moral ideals. A focused normative analysis requires some conceptual groundwork.

SPORT AND SPORT COMPETITIONS

What do we mean when we talk of 'sport' and of 'sport competitions'? McPherson *et al.*'s (1989: 15) idea of sport as 'a structured, goal-oriented, competitive, contest-based, ludic physical activity' is quite representative of definitional efforts and captures common understanding and use of the term.[1] This definition includes a variety of activities. We talk of 'children's and youth sport', of 'recreational sport' such as leisure ball games in the local park, of 'amateur sport' such as college athletics, and of 'professional sport' and 'commercial entertainment sport' such as English Premier League football and the basketball played in the American National Basketball Association (NBA).

Moreover, activities we refer to as 'sport' develop, change, and sometimes vanish in relation to the social and cultural contexts of which they are parts. As Morgan (1994: 213) says, sport is '. . . a social rather than a natural kind'. The term 'commercial entertainment sport' would scarcely have had any meaning to the founding members of the International Olympic Committee (IOC) in 1894. The rise of women's sport in the latter half of the twentieth century was probably unthinkable to most sport leaders between the two world wars. Snowboarding and beach volleyball are new sporting activities that have developed over the last couple of decades.

Therefore, in such a socio-cultural setting, quests for 'objective', ahistorical definitions make little sense. My pursuit of clarification here is more modest. I propose an interpretation of fair play in what are traditionally seen as the core of sport practice, the competitions. In what follows, the term 'sport' refers to sport competitions unless otherwise indicated. Moreover, I shall discuss sport competitions as they are understood and practised today. To begin, here is a brief overview of what I consider to be their key characteristics.

Sport as a rule-governed practice

Sport competitions are rule-governed practices. The predominant view of the function of rules is that they structure and in fact define a practice, or at least that they define the framework within which the practice takes place. Searle (1969: 33) takes up the well-known Kantian distinction between constitutive and regulative rules and talks of 'constitutive rules' that '... constitute (and also regulate) an activity the existence of which is logically dependent on the rules':

> The rules of football or chess, for example, do not merely regulate playing football or chess, but as it were they create the very possibility of playing such games. The activities of playing football or chess are constituted by acting in accordance with (at least a large subset of) the appropriate rules.
>
> (Searle 1969: 33–34)

Regulative rules, on the other hand, regulate pre-existing activities that exist logically independently of the rules. Examples of regulative rules might be norms for proper conduct in social interaction, such as norms for how to engage in conversation, how to eat, or how to dress.

Constitutive rules stipulate a goal and the means, through prescriptions and proscriptions, by which this goal can be attained. In sport, the stipulated goal is usually given in terms of definitions of specific states of affairs to be attained, such as getting a particular kind of ball over a line drawn between two poles on a grass field, hitting another kind of ball over a net with a racket and making it bounce within certain lines drawn on a smooth surface, or jumping from a platform ten metres high into a pool while performing certain movements.[2] In addition, constitutive rules have as an integral part of them a description of the means by which these specific states of affairs can be reached, and how to rank competitors within this framework according to how they perform. Constitutive rules define what it means to win a sport competition. In football, winning means scoring goals by getting the ball over what is called the goal line more often than the opposing team without using the arm below the shoulder and without being in so-called off-side positions. Tennis players try to score more points, games and sets as defined by the rules of tennis than their competitors, and thus win the match. Divers jump from a ten-metre high platform while performing somersaults and twists in the best way possible according to certain well-defined criteria, so as to be awarded more points than their competitors. We can now see that constitutive definitions of winning demarcate one sport from another. In what follows, we shall talk of definitions of winning as sport-specific goals.

The constitutive rules of a sport define how to win but not how to compete successfully. Suits (1973) introduces a third category of rules, rules of skill. These are technical and tactical rules about how to perform well. In tennis we are told to keep our eye on the ball, and freestyle swimmers emphasize the importance of a 'high elbow'. But rules of skills are not constitutive rules. Sport can be realized in practice without actually adhering to them. A particular game of football can be a poor game but it is still football. We shall examine rules of skill in more detail in the discussion of athletic performance in Chapter 3. At this stage, the important point is that the constitutive rules of a sport by defining its sport-specific goal, provide a conceptual framework within which the sport can take place. In short, we can say that the constitutive rules stipulate what counts as play in a particular sport (Reddiford 1985).

Regulative rules, on the other hand, place constraints, restraints, and conditions upon activities that are logically independent of the process of competing. Usually, regulative rules are of secondary importance in the realization of a sport. Many of them serve to facilitate the realization in practice of the constitutive rules. Rules that define the appearance, size, and weight of the golf ball, or identify the profile of a ski jumping hill, are of this kind. A golf ball that is too heavy or too light would change the technical demands of golf and probably lead to changes in playing styles and equipment. If the profile of a ski jumping hill is different from what is stated in the rules, jumping could easily become more difficult and possibly more dangerous. In addition, Meier (1985) talks of 'auxiliary rules' that deal with matters that are outside the competitive situation, such as rules for eligibility (linked to age, sex, or performance), safety rules, or more or less arbitrary regulations linked to social, political, or commercial interests external to sport. Sometimes auxiliary rules override constitutive rules. Apel (1988: 230) uses an example from boxing to describe how a general moral principle for safety and non-harm from ordinary life [*Lebenswelt*] may be supervenient to the rules of the game-world [*Spielwelt*]: the attending medical doctor may consider a boxer's injuries so serious that the fight is called off.

The distinction between constitutive and regulative rules serves for analytic purposes but it is not absolute. Regulative rules can be seen as extensions of the constitutive ones – they depend upon constitutive rules. Regulative rules necessarily presuppose a practice to regulate. Moreover, the various kinds of rule overlap. Do the rules that define the size of basketball courts or stipulate a maximum number of five players on the court at any one time, belong to the constitutive or the regulative rules of basketball? Is a two-against-two pick-up game in the local park still basketball?

In the present context, a clear answer here is not really important. My aim is to establish moral norms for competitions in which persons mutually agree upon, and compete according to, what are considered the constitutive rules. The norms at which I arrive should be relevant to both highly formalized elite basketball games and for the pick-up game in the local park. What is of interest now is that sport competitions are made possible by what are deemed as their constitutive rules, and that regulative rules are, among other things, designed to facilitate the realization in practice of the constitutive rules.

The social logic of sport

According to, Suits (1973), Meier (1988), and Morgan (1987, 1994: 211ff.) among others, the understanding of goals and means in sport sketched above implies there is a particular social logic in these practices. 'Winning' in a sport is logically dependent upon using only the means defined in its constitutive rules. Morgan (1987) talks of the inseparability of goals and means. We cannot win unless we compete in accord with the constitutive rules. Moreover, according to Suits (1973), when we reflect on the nature of such rules we see that they seem always to prescribe the use of less efficient means towards the state of affairs that counts as winning rather than more efficient means. Instead of walking up to the net and smashing the ball straight down and out of reach of the opponent, a tennis player is given only two serving attempts from the base line. Instead of grabbing the ball and running with it, players in European handball are restricted to carrying the ball a maximum of three steps then bouncing or passing it. Instead of going straight down the slope, slalom racers are required to cross with both skis the imaginary line between the two poles of every gate of the slalom course. More precisely, a sport can be understood as a kind of game with a particular social logic that entails inseparability of means and goals and a voluntary attempt to overcome what Morgan (1994) calls 'gratuitous difficulties'. This logic, the argument goes, serves to demarcate sport and games from non-games.

A more detailed example can illustrate how the logic works. Traffic control is a rule-governed practice. The goal of traffic control can be said to be the efficient transport of people and things from A to B with least risk of injuries and material damage. In short, the goal of traffic control is efficient and safe transportation. Typical traffic rules point to what are considered the most efficient means to reach this goal. Realizing this goal does not require that the rules are always adhered to. Though some people run red lights in the middle of the night in towns devoid of people, or a bicyclist may ride on the wrong side of the road where there are no cars around, they still manage to move from A to B in a safe manner. The rules of traffic control are regulative rules and have only instrumental value in reaching a goal that is independent of the rules.

Imagine I compete with a friend to discover who is the faster cyclist by having a race from the restaurant in which we have had lunch back to the university, without breaking traffic rules. We agree that taking short cuts on the wrong side of the road and racing through an intersection on a red light, even if there are no cars around are not allowed. Now the social logic of the practice changes. Or rather, we now engage in a different practice. We are no longer engaged primarily in efficient and safe transportation but rather in an attempt to see who, according to a shared set of rules, is the fastest and smartest cyclist. The normal traffic rules take on the characteristics of constitutive rules upon which we have specifically agreed for our purposes. We cannot reach the goal of our practice without keeping to them. Our cycling amounts to something like a competitive game in which motor skills are of significance to the outcome – what we can call a sport competition.

The idea of sport's particular social logic must not be taken as an empirical claim about the actual understanding of sport among parties concerned. Some subscribe to the logic of the game and compete for fun or as a challenge. Others are engaged for instrumental reasons such as profit and prestige. The assumption is that, however various the goals of the participants may be, sport has built into its structure of rules the possibility for a non-instrumental, 'gratuitous' logic of overcoming 'unnecessary' obstacles to reach specific goals. A further assumption is that it is precisely by grasping this possibility that sport becomes joyful, challenging, interesting, and exciting – which, in Morgan's (1994: 211) words, is '... after all, the main point of sporting endeavors'.

The assumption that sport has a particular social logic seems to have strong standing both among philosophers who deal with these topics and the general public. However, it is not unproblematic. I shall weigh alternative interpretations of sport against one another below (Chapter 4). For now I shall proceed by looking more closely at some critical comments on the understanding of rules suggested above.

The formalist position

In D'Agostino's (1981) view, the idea that a set of constitutive rules defines a sport and that the means described in the rules and the goal of winning are inseparable, represents a formalist understanding of social practices. A game or a sport can be defined only by reference to its constitutive rules, and sport competitions, the formalist would claim, are realized only if the constitutive rules are adhered to completely in all aspects.

D'Agostino is critical of this position. An immediate objection is that it seems counter-intuitive and against common-sense understanding. If we take the position seriously, a formalist would have to say that we do no longer play a game G 'if a rule of G is violated during an alleged instance of G' (D'Agostino 1981: 9). But, as D'Agostino demonstrates with an example from basketball, rule violations seem to be an unavoidable part of most sport competitions. An actual instance of the game of basketball without intentional body contact (which in fact is proscribed by the rules) would seem meaningless to most players. A similar example can be taken from European handball. The way the game is currently played includes regular rough body checking of attackers by defenders that leads to so-called nine-metre throws. Although a nine-metre throw is in principle a penalty, it is considered an acceptable part of current handball technique and tactics. Handball as it is played today is inconceivable without it.

According to D'Agostino, the formalist's mistake is to overlook the important real life-distinction between acceptable and non-acceptable rule violations. Moreover, the formalist perspective makes it impossible to distinguish between competitions of various degrees of fairness, and unfair competitions (Loland 1998). Indeed, in real life we talk of a fair result of a game of basketball or handball even if rule violations occurred, as long as they do not seem to have been decisive for the outcome.

The core problem for the formalist is that rules are always of a certain generality, and their implementation must therefore be based upon interpretations. As Wittgenstein (1953: §201–202) points out, a rule cannot determine its own application. Formalists end up here in a constant quest for new rules for the interpretation of older ones, a process becomes an infinite regress. Rule interpretation is a logical necessity. But, no system of rules can define completely the full variety of possible actions within the practice it constitutes. No competition, or no piece action in a particular competition, is ever identical with other competitions and actions. Empirical surveys, among others by Heinilä[3] and Nilsson (1993), show that the interpretation of the rules of football varies with level of performance, age and the socio-cultural context in which the game is played. For instance professionals, to a greater degree than young and amateur players, accept rule violations that serve efficiency and team interests. Indeed, Nilsson (1993) found significantly different understandings of rules among football clubs in the same geographical area and at the same level of performance, findings he explains by reference to local culture and club traditions.

Few if any people interested in sport, hold to the hard-core formalist position. The position is just unreasonable. Still, a statement and critique of formalism is helpful as a step towards a clearer understanding of sport competitions as a social practice. The inadequacies of the formalist position indicate that sport is best understood with reference to the social and cultural context in which it takes place.

The ethos of sport

A contextualist approach is based on the insight that no rule or rule system speaks for itself, and that human interaction in rule-governed practices must build on shared norms for interpretation of such rules among the parties concerned. According to Newcombe *et al.* (1966: 221ff.), norms are shared if they satisfy two requirements.

First, there must be a certain amount of common knowledge among the parties concerned about how the basic rules are to be understood. To play tennis, both players must agree upon interpretations of what it means to serve, to score a point, and to win games, sets, and finally the match. To play football, all players must agree upon what it means to score goals and that it is forbidden to handle the ball. Such knowledge provides a necessary condition for sport competitions to be realized at all.

Second, competitors must mutually recognize their common knowledge of basic rules and act upon it. This calls for communication between them. Each competitor has to demonstrate in words and actions observable to others his or her acceptance of certain norms for rule interpretations. Then all competitors can recognize that each competitor has accepted a certain interpretation of the rules that they also accept, and each competitor can become aware of this recognition on his or her own part. We can now understand competitions as advanced forms of cooperation. Tennis players demonstrate their mutually recognized consensus by following, without question or discussion, the prescribed counting of points, games and sets, and by moving and behaving on the court accordingly. Football players demonstrate the same thing by moving away from the ball when the other team is given a free kick, and if the free kick results in a goal, by lining up again together with their teammates on their own half of the pitch for a new kick-off.

On this understanding, norms are shared when two or more parties are aware that they are consenting to an interpretation of the basic rules. That is to say, there exists a consensual perception of the consensus, or a consensus of a second order, among the participants. This does not mean that sharing norms requires perfect agreement. Among tennis players, we find disagreements about players' conduct and responsibilities when a referee makes a mistake and calls a good ball out. Should the player who gained the point correct the referee, or should she not? Among football players, there is disagreement about the moral status of the so-called 'professional foul', where a player is fouled openly to serve the interests of the team. Every sport, and every particular sport competition, can be seen as a verbal and embodied discourse in which shared norms for the interpretation of the rules are challenged, negotiated and adjusted (Loland and McNamee 2000).

It has to be noted, however, that even if norms for the interpretation of rules are social norms in constant change, major sports such as track and field athletics and the most popular ball games have a history of few radical rule changes and relatively few dramatic changes in rule interpretations. Most sports can be said to be relatively stable social practices.

We can now return to D'Agostino's critique of formalism. His solution to the formalist challenge builds on a similar idea to that of shared norms by introducing the idea of the ethos of a game. Such an ethos consists of '... conventions determining how the formal rules of that game are applied in concrete circumstances'. He is talking here of the '... unofficial, implicit, empirically determinable conventions which govern official interpretations of the formal rules of a game' (D'Agostino 1981: 7, 13).

The ethos approach does not include the distinction between constitutive and regulative rules, for this, to D'Agostino, is a typical expression of formalism. The very idea of constitutive rules is linked to an understanding of the inseparability between rules and goals, to which contextualism claims to represent an alternative. Inspired by Morgan (1987), however, I hold the distinction between constitutive and regulative rules to be a *prima facie* one. In practice, players seem to distinguish between more and less important rules along these lines. To be able to play basketball or handball, (regulative) rules about air pressure in basketballs and handballs are not really crucial. What does count here are shared norms for interpretation of the (constitutive) definitions of 'winning' in the sport in question, or of what I earlier called the sport-specific goal. In the discussion that follows, therefore, an ethos should be understood as a set of shared norms for the interpretation of the sport-specific goal of a sport among a group of people.

This idea of an ethos has many attractions. It takes seriously the diversity of interpretations of the same set of written rules in different socio-cultural settings. Although Heinilä[4] and Nilsson (1993) demonstrate great diversity in the interpretation of the rules of football among different groups of players, we still say that they all play football. Moreover, the formalist picture was found wanting with respect to rule violations. In D'Agostino's ethos approach, we are able to draw distinctions between permissible acts that are in accordance with the rules, acceptable rule violations that are considered 'part of the game', and rule violations that are considered unacceptable and perhaps immoral. It is still possible to play basketball in spite of a shared norm that allows for body contact. Rough bodily encounters in European handball that lead to nine-metre throws can be part of the game as long as all parties engaged mutually accept that they are.

However, the ethos-approach has weaknesses as well as attractions. Perhaps the most important criticisms concern its apparent relativism (Morgan 1987, 1994: 225ff.; Loland 1998; Loland and McNamee 2000). Is any kind of rule violation acceptable as long as it is commonly accepted among the participants? There is no doubt that the development of a violent ethos would be problematic for most sports. Moreover, if the ethos of a sport tolerates a high number of rule violations, its rule system may lose clear meaning and no longer serve as a conceptual framework for a practice at all. Finally, competitions between groups of competitors each of whose ethos has radically different content become very hard if not impossible. There would be few shared norms and the sport in question may degenerate or even die. Sometimes, as in the well-known controversies in England in the nineteenth-century over the rules of football, which led to the distinction between rugby and football, the solution can be differentiation in terms of new sport-specific goals and indeed new sports.

Hence, even if we ought to accept diversity in the interpretation of rules in a sport, the ideal must still be to minimize the number of accepted rule violations. I shall return to criteria for morally acceptable kinds of sport ethos in Chapter 3.

The structural goal of sport

An ethos of a sport is a social construction. As with any set of shared social norms, it is a more or less clear expression of human interests and goals. What are these goals? And how can they be articulated?

Let us start with the most obvious category. We have already seen that the constitutive rules define the sport-specific goal or what it means to win in a particular sport. Shared interpretation of 'winning' is a necessity for meaningful competitions to be possible at all. The question is whether one general understanding of 'winning' can be elaborated in a way that makes sense in all sports and can serve to demarcate sport as a social practice.

We can seek an answer by looking at practical examples. In power-lifting each competitor is given three attempts to lift as much as possible in each of the three events: the squat, the bench press, and the dead lift. In running, the goal is to reach the finishing line as quickly as possible. In the slalom, skiers pass through the gates that make up the course as quickly and efficiently as they can. Football teams try to score more goals than their opponents. All kinds of sport competitions seem to deal with the measuring of what can be called the relevant athletic performance.

We do not, however, define one single athlete's performance as a competition. A cross-country skier may demonstrate good technique but we know little of the quality of her performance until she has raced against other skiers. A point won for one tennis player is always a point lost for another. A handball team cannot practice its sport without another team to play against. We understand sport competitions as social practices in which we do not just measure but also compare performances among competitors.

During competitions, measuring and comparing athletic performances is an ongoing process. In a boxing match, we measure and compare tentatively the whole time by counting punches, hits, points, and rounds. The marathon runner's performance is constantly evaluated in terms of time and space differences with respect to other runners. After the last round, a boxer's points are counted and compared with those of his opponent to rank the two boxers accordingly. After all marathon runners have crossed the finishing line, we rank them according to time taken for the complete distance. So measuring and comparing performances leads to a final ranking of competitors according to performance.

A relevant question here is what counts as 'a competitor'. Does a swimmer's race against a seal, or a climber's struggle to 'defeat' a mountain, or a 10,000-metre runner's attempt to beat the world record count as sport competitions? Can people compete with animals, or abstract entities like records, or with non-humans? These activities are no doubt competitions in a common usage of the word, but they are hard to categorize as sport. The basis for an understanding in such cases is that sport competitions are constituted by an ethos, that is, a shared interpretation of the basic constitutive rules that define what it means to win. Shared interpretations require a communicated consensus between all parties engaged. Therefore, we should understand sport competitions as social practices that arise and are realized in a process of communication between persons.

In spite of great diversity in sport-specific goals, then, it is possible to formulate a general goal that characterizes sport competitions as such: the goal of sport competitions is to measure, compare and rank two or more competitors according to athletic performance. This goal seems to be common to all sports, however diverse their ethos. It defines sport's characteristic social structure, and I shall therefore call it the structural goal of sport competitions.

Intentional goals among competitors

I consider the structural goal to be a core element in the shared understanding of sport. However, it should not be confused with competitors' individual goals linked to their particular engagement. I am now speaking of individuals' subjective reasons for engaging in sport, what I shall call their intentional goals.

Intentional goals are many and various. Some compete in pursuit of goals that can be realized within the practice itself, such as excitement, tension, a feeling of community, challenge, and mastery. Others are more focused on possible outcomes of competitions that are not internal to them, such as establishing friendships and social networks, or, at high levels of performance, prestige and profit.

Intentional goals are shaped and influenced by many factors. Psychologists point to the significance of the social-psychological climate in sport settings, such as the social reward structure and coaching styles (Weinberg and Gould 1999: 93ff.). Within the same social group we find individual differences related to the particular personality and background of each participant (Weinberg and Gould 1999: 25ff.). In the larger framework, individuals' intentional goals are best understood in relation to the historical and socio-cultural contexts in which they find themselves. The ancient Olympic Games were part of a religious cult, and we may assume that at least some of the participants understood their engagement as worshipping the gods. Today's Olympians may have ideas of serving their country, their race, their ideology, or even their God. Still, secular goals of performing well, of winning, and of attaining fame and fortune are probably more common. During China's Cultural Revolution, the slogan was 'friendship first, competition second'. Before a competition began, McIntosh (1979: 171) tells us, participants would sing and practice together, and share their knowledge of their sport. After the competition was over they would gather and, at least according to the official version, reflect upon whether the ideal of friendship taking precedence over competition had been realized. This is in clear contrast with the Western high-performance sport mentality expressed in telling slogans such as that attributed to the Green Bay Packer American football coach Vince Lombardi: 'Winning isn't the most important thing, it's the only thing!' or baseball player and coach Leo Durocher's 'Nice guys finish last!' The aggressive, competitive individualism of the market seems predominant there.

Most of us have mixed intentional goal structures. We are motivated by both internal and external goals. Indeed, there are probably as many different intentional goal structures as there are sport competitors. It seems hard to come up with any general formulations of content here. All we can say at this stage is that we understand individuals' participation in sport competitions as expressions of intentional goals of various kinds linked to their engagement in sport.

The moral goal of sport

Sport competitions can be described in terms of sport-specific goals, the general structural goal, and the intentional goals of the parties engaged. But sometimes these goals can conflict. The intentional goal of some athletes to play according to a relevant basketball ethos can contradict other athletes' goal of winning at almost no matter what cost. The structural goal of measuring, comparing, and ranking competitors according to performance can be overruled by intentional goals among commercial interests aiming at producing attractive TV entertainment. Which goals should provide direction in situations where conflicts occur? Is it possible to allocate priorities among conflicting interests? Can we reach a systematic ordering of the goals of sport competitions, according to moral relevance and value?

Reflection on specific goals of particular actions and practices leads to reflection on more general and fundamental goals. It seems impossible that we choose everything for the sake of something else. If this were the case, deliberation over goals would go on infinitely. It seems as if something must, somehow, be of value in itself – of ultimate value – and provide final answers to our questions. Aristotle's solution is to see the ideal of all action as striving towards the fulfilment of human nature, in its proper functioning. For him, this is a virtuous life of reason in which we develop and exercise to the full all our powers and capabilities. The ultimate good toward which we strive, is *eudaimonia*, happiness, or human flourishing (Cooper 1975: 89–143).

Aristotle's logic here is dubious. His premise that all human actions strive towards something good does not necessarily entail the conclusion that there is an ultimate good towards which all actions strive (Føllesdal *et al.* 1996: 214). In modern pluralistic societies there are many different ideas of 'the ultimate good', and there seems to be no absolute Archimedean point from which we

can judge one particular idea as uniquely right or clearly better than another. However, in Chapter 2, I shall argue in favour of the claim that rational deliberation over questions of fundamental norms and values is possible. In fact, Aristotle's contention that our actions and practices are better understood if we reflect upon them in the larger framework of human life is in any case fertile in the questions it raises. Why do sport competitions exist? What is their *raison d'être*? Is it possible to for sport competitions to become valuable and meaningful to all parties engaged and thus contribute to human flourishing in general? If so, how? These will now be considered.

Fair play: historical background

Moral ideas of the value and meaning of sport are as old as sport itself. Finley and Pleket (1976) provide vivid descriptions of the ideals of sport in the ancient world. These were closely linked to a warrior ethos, with an emphasis on honourable and just conduct. Like the warrior, the Olympic athlete strove for victory and honour in front of his gods. Moreover, the very idea of ranking athletes according to performance required a certain equality of opportunity. In chariot races, there were relatively sophisticated starting procedures to ensure such equality. In the running events, starting before the signal could result in public flogging and competitors who accepted bribes were heavily fined. The concern for equal opportunities seems close to ideas we today would call 'fairness' (Wischmann 1962; McIntosh 1979).

Still, Liponski (1988) argues that the fair play ideal as we know it today has Roman–Celtic roots. The Roman occupation of England brought with it certain elite legions manned by members of the nobility and sons of affluent citizens who pledged to act in accord to a rigid moral code. Honourable and just conduct in battle was held as a basic characteristic of a good soldier. According to Liponski, their warrior ideal left a deep impression on the Celts who came under Roman influence. After the Roman withdrawal from England in the fifth century AD, romanized Celts kept the tradition alive. This is the tradition of the so-called *eques cataphractarius*, the knight errants of the Middle Ages. The development of norms for conduct in medieval tournaments and later in sport competitions was at least in part based on these ideals (Wischmann 1962; Guttmann 1987).

The concept of 'fair play' gradually developed as a standard reference for morally right and good behaviour in competitions. 'Fair' has been used in English to define what is 'impartial' and 'just' in books of homilies dating from 1175. The expression 'fayre game' is found in English poetry from the fifteenth century and 'foul play' in tournament rules from 1467. Shakespeare used 'fair play' in his historical drama *The Life and Death of King John*, written in the last decade of the sixteenth century (Wischmann 1962; Liponski 1988). We can assume that the oral tradition started earlier.

The passage of the term 'fair play' into everyday language is linked to the growth of sport in nineteenth century English public schools, such as Winchester, Eton, Harrow and Rugby, and also to sporting life at the universities of Oxford and Cambridge. *The Sporting Magazine*, published from 1792 and the first sport periodical in the world, used 'fair play' regularly (Liponski 1988), but nineteenth-century Britain was the age of the ideal of 'the gentleman amateur'. Through sport, young men were taught physical and mental toughness, and loyalty to their team and school. Practising 'fair play' was regarded more as a personal virtue than a formal norm of rule-adherence. Competitors should aspire to follow 'the spirit of the rules', not just the letter, and play with style. As it was expressed in a Harrow song: 'Strife without anger, art without malice' (Holt 1989: 99). The general educational ideal of the time later came to be called 'muscular Christianity'. Sport was used, for better and for worse, as a means to realizing what was seen as an ideal masculine, moral and Christian upbringing (McIntosh 1979; Mangan 1981).

The increased significance of fair play ideals has sociological explanations. To the middle and upper classes of Victorian Britain, use of an amateur ideology was an effective way of keeping their sport to themselves and resisting interference from the expanding working class. For instance, so-called amateur rules were framed on the premise that manual labour led to 'unhealthy' instrumental attitudes towards sport and spoiled 'natural grace' and talent (Holt 1989). Professional sportsmen were excluded, because they were thought not to compete with the 'correct' attitude and respect for the intrinsic values of the game. The gradual inclusion of the middle class, who shared with the upper classes the view that there was no need for 'new games' despite structural changes in society, only strengthened the regulative functions of amateurism and the (partial) fair play ideal (Guttmann 1987). Elias (1986) also notes, that the need for competitions that were impartial and fair grew considerably with the increased popularity of gambling. Interest in putting money on a horse or a dog depended upon whether gamblers could rely upon an impartial and just result.

Given this historical background, how is the ideal of 'fair play' commonly understood today?

Fair play: current understandings

According to the dictionary, 'fair' has its origin in the old English *foeger* and can mean among other things (1) 'attractive', 'beautiful', (2) 'unblemished', 'clean', (3) 'blond' (as in fair hair), (4) 'clear and sunny', (5) 'easy to read' (a fair hand), (6) 'just and honest', and (7) 'according to the rule'.[5] The understanding of 'fair play' as certain attitudes or virtues (as expressed in the English ideal of the gentleman amateur) can be derived from interpretations (1) and (2). Fair actions in competitions can be considered attractive, unblemished and clean in that they do not merely serve self-interest but are performed from an impartial sense of the common good and from a sense of obligation. Interpretations (6) and (7) point to more formal understandings of 'fair' in that they refer to conceptions of justice and what counts as acting in accordance with a rule.

These dictionary definitions cohere with official declarations from sport organizations and institutions. The International Council of Sport Science and Physical Education's (ICSSPE) declaration on fair play, endorsed by the United Nations Educational, Scientific and Cultural Organization (UNESCO) and the International Olympic Committee (IOC), provides a representative text (Hahn and Remans 1988). The emphasis is on conformity to rules, respect for officials and their decisions, and respect for fellow competitors. In addition, 'fair play' is associated with showing generosity in play, modesty in victory and graciousness in defeat. These obligations are deemed valid for all who participate in sport, be they competitors, parents, coaches, officials, leaders, or supporters.

Declarations on fair play usually do not include justifications of the ideal. In more academically oriented studies, such justifications are elaborated and examined. There is a series of works in the (sport-) philosophical literature that deals explicitly with fair play. So Keating (1964) understands fair play as adherence to the letter and the spirit of equality before the rules of sport. McIntosh (1979) examines both the historical roots and possible philosophical understandings of fair play, among them utilitarian and Kantian interpretations. Loland (1989) develops an extensive and detailed interpretation of the idea of fair play, upon which the present book is built. Simon (1991: 35, 43) construes fair play as 'commitment to the principles supported by the idea of ethically defensible competitions', that is, competitions understood as 'a mutual quest for excellence in the intelligent and directed use of athletic skills in the face of challenge'. Lenk distinguishes between 'formal fair play', which refers to rule conformity, and 'informal fair play', which refers to attitudes towards the game, to other competitors, and to officials (Lenk 1964, 1993; Lenk and Pilz 1989). In Gabler's (1998) overview, emphasis is put on the interpretation of fair play as adherence to rule, equality of opportunity, and respect for opponents as person and partners. Tuxill and Wigmore (1998) demonstrate how the idea of fair play can be based on general ethical ideas to do with 'respect for persons'. Gerhardt (1993) discusses fairness as the constitutive virtue of competitors and as a condition *sine qua non* for competitions to arise. Butcher and Schneider (1998) combine MacIntyre's concept of the internal goods of a practice with empirical studies of the experiential qualities of autotelic practices, and suggest an interpretation of fair play as 'respect for the game'.

Lenk's analytic distinction between formal and informal fair play seems to cover, in one way or the other, most of the interpretations of the ideal and so may serve as our normative point of departure. In what follows, formal fair play should be understood in terms of norms for rule conformity and justice that express what is considered morally right. Informal fair play should be seen as prescribing that players compete with a certain attitude or with certain virtues linked to the values and 'internal goods' of sport itself, and is tied to ideas of the morally good.

SUMMARY

In this chapter I have sought to provide a detailed interpretation of sport competitions. Sport competitions are social practices subject to change. Here I have discussed what we find to be reletively stable elements of these practices, as we understand them today. Let me now sum up.

Sport competitions are given a conceptual framework by a set of constitutive rules. Constitutive rules define their goals and the means with which to pursue these goals, that is, they define what it means to win. Such definitions of the rules of a sport express its sport-specific goal. Further, competitions can be understood as having the social logic of games. Games are characterized by inseparability of means and goals and by a social logic described by Suits (1973) as 'the voluntary attempt to overcome unnecessary obstacles'. The idea common to authors such as Suits (1973), Meier (1988) and Morgan (1994) is that sport at its best is realized when such logic is taken seriously.

This assumption is not unproblematic. Constitutive rules are open to a variety of interpretations, among which the logic of games described above is just one. Still, for competitions to be possible, there is a need for shared norms for interpretating these rules in practice. Shared norms are based on a consensus on the part of two or more participants who are aware of being consensual and express and communicate their consensus in their actions. A set of shared norms for interpretation of the sport-specific goal among a group of practitioners of a sport is called the ethos of that particular sport among that particular group of practitioners.

The ethos of a sport is influenced by the socio-psychological and socio-cultural context in which it is practised. Hence it is a social construction that again is a more or less clear expression of human goals. Such goals are of many kinds. Sport-specific goals define what counts as winning in a particular sport, and they distinguish one sport from another. In spite of the diversity of sport-specific goals, however, I have proposed that it is possible to articulate a shared common goal that is relatively stable and can serve to distinguish the social structure of sport competitions from the social structures of other practices. What I call the structural goal of competitions is to measure, compare, and rank competitors according to athletic performance.

In addition, I have discussed intentional goals among competitors. I am speaking now of more or less clearly articulated subjective reasons for engaging in sport. Some people take part in sport to realize values internal to the activity itself, whilst others are engaged because the competitions are seen as a means to external goals such as fame and fortune. Most of us have mixed intentional goal structures and there are probably as many different goals and goal structures as there are competitors. At this stage general formulations of content seem impossible.

I ended by asking questions linked to the moral goals of sport competitions. Why do competitions exist at all? What are their potential meanings and values? Can these practices contribute to human flourishing and the good life, and if so, how? Answers are often linked to the ideal of fair play. A traditional interpretation is to distinguish between formal fair play and informal fair play. Formal fair play prescribes rule conformity and refers to ideas of what is morally right and just in sport. Informal fair play is linked to certain attitudes and requirements of respect for competitors, officials, and for the game as such. The idea of formal fair play will serve as my normative point of departure in the discussions that follow on fairness and justice (Chapter 3), while informal fair play will serve the same function in the discussion of what makes sport competitions morally good (Chapter 4).

Chapter 2

A moral point of view

We have seen that the shared understanding of sport competitions varies in different historical, cultural and social contexts. We have also seen that intentional goals among competitors are greatly varied. The aim of this book is to develop a moral norm system of fair play to guide conduct in competitions in general. This is an ambitious aim. A degree of scepticism is in order. Why should we practise sport in one way instead of another? And, if we consider one mode of practice as morally superior to another, what are our arguments for doing so? How can we justify such a claim?

Scepticism often raises fundamental philosophical questions. And even the most concrete questions can lead to metaphysical puzzles if properly pursued. Here, moral norms seem to presuppose that individuals actually can freely choose between alternative courses of action and that they can be held responsible for their choices. But is this presupposition reasonable? If it is, what are the characteristics of a free or voluntary choice? Moreover, if we can be held responsible for our actions, it seems reasonable to assume that we can be challenged on our justifications. But is it possible to give a particular choice of action a 'true' moral justification? Are there moral facts and moral properties that exist 'out there', independent of our moral beliefs and attitudes, that can be known? If there is such a moral knowledge, what kind of knowledge is it and how can we obtain it?

I cannot, of course, deal satisfactorily with these questions here (could anyone?) Still, in a work on practical ethics a description and a brief justification of basic premises can serve to demonstrate both the possibilities and the limitations of the approach adopted here. Clarification of a normative framework can make the analysis more systematic and better focused, and so lead to insights than could otherwise easily be overlooked in everyday discussion of morality. Let us start, therefore, by clarifying some key concepts.

MORALITY AND ETHICS

The word 'ethics' is derived from the Greek *éthos* (with a short e), which refers to 'habit' or 'custom', and *êthos* (with a long e), which refers among other things to well-established or institutionalized practice. When ancient Greek philosophical terms were translated into Latin, *éthos* was rendered as *mos* (pl. *mores*), custom(s). The terms 'morality' and 'ethics' are used interchangeably even today, though some nuances have emerged (Crane 2000 a, b).

Morality can be understood as a sub-class of social norms and values of a group of people. Moral norms and values regulate interaction in situations in which what are considered basic values are at stake; in cases of conflict they usually override other social norms (Beauchamp 1991: 16ff). For instance, they prescribe how we should act so as to do good to others, how significant goods and burdens should be allocated, and how people should relate to one another in matters of promises and contracts. Breaking moral norms leads to internal sanctions such as guilt, and/or external sanctions such as blame.

Ethics on the other hand is commonly understood as the philosophical study of morality. In ethics, we do not just seek empirical descriptions of the moral norms and values of a given group of people but attempt to reflect critically and systematically upon their nature. The conclusions of these reflections include suggestions for modification and change or, as in the case of Nietzsche, in the rejection of traditional moral systems as a whole. When terms such as 'morality' and 'ethics' are used here, meaning is more or less in accord with these common understandings.

Ethical questions typically start from practical questions. Should an athlete use a forbidden drug, as other competitors do, to enhance performance, or should she not? Is it right or wrong to commit the so-called 'professional foul', in which a player fouls an opponent on the football field to prevent a clear opportunity to score a goal?

A first step towards answering could be to examine the commonly held views and beliefs about these dilemmas. Studies of the morality of individuals or social groups constitute empirical or descriptive ethics. Historians, social anthropologists and sociologists have described a variety of norms and values in sport, both past and present. From the past come examples illustrating the origin of fair play norms and the ways the ideal has been interpreted. An example from the present is the Canadian Dubin report, which found that in certain social groups, shared norms have developed that allow for the use of performance-enhancing drugs (Dubin 1990).

Descriptive ethics often provides important insights for normative reflection. Knowledge of commonly held views on, and experience with, performance-enhancing drugs is directly relevant to the ethical debate over doping. But this kind of knowledge is not sufficient to reach normative conclusions. Even if the majority of athletes in a group accept doping, this does not necessarily entail that doping is morally justifiable. There is a need for some kind of critical criteria here. So we now need to move on to ethical theory, into the field of normative ethics.

Normative ethical theories specify criteria for distinguishing the good and determining what is morally right. Usually they also set out ways of reasoning that can lead to justifiable decisions about moral dilemmas. As illustrative examples, let me briefly sketch three familiar theoretical positions.

Aristotelian ethics deal with how human beings can realize their true nature and attain their *telos*, the goal towards which all human beings ought to strive. In Greek this goal is called *eudaimonia*, usually translated in English as 'happiness', or 'human flourishing' (Cooper 1975: 89–143). For Aristotle, human flourishing means living a life of reason in which we develop and exercise all our powers and capabilities by acting in accordance with virtue. The key question is 'what kind of person ought I to be?' A virtue-based ethics has been revived in our time in the writings of philosophers such as Alasdair MacIntyre (1984).

Such neo-Aristotelians present a critique of, and an alternative to, predominant ethical theories that emphasize rational justification. The focus in these latter theories is not on the person and the socio-cultural context in which we live, but rather on the search for universally valid answers to questions such as 'how ought I to choose?' or 'what ought I to do?' The central doctrine in utilitarianism, for instance, is that we ought to choose our actions solely according to the total amount of good (or bad) they will generate. In its classic form, the utilitarianism of Bentham and Mill prescribes the choice of that action which, when compared to alternatives, '... contains the greatest net balance of aggregate human pleasure or happiness or satisfaction' (Scheffler 1988: 2).

Utilitarianism is an example of a consequentialist ethical theory, a theory that says we should judge the morality of things by their consequences. The rightness of actions and policies depends upon the goodness of their results. Non-consequentialist theories, on the other hand, prescribe right actions independent of, or based on criteria prior to, utility maximization. Ideas of what is right have standing independent of ideas of the good (Rawls 1971: 30).[1]

Kant's ethics is the standard example. According to Kant, an action is considered right if, and only if, it conforms to a moral rule that a rational person would follow if this person acted in accordance with pure reason, as opposed to more or less contingent desires. The appeal to reason places obligations on everyone independent of social context and individual differences. As with utilitarianism, Kantian morality applies universally. Further, the condition for any action to be morally good is that the agent acts with a good will. Kant sums up his view in the categorical imperative: 'Act only according to those maxims that can be consistently willed as a universal law!'

When discussing ethical theories, the question often arises of how we are to choose between different theoretical traditions, such as consequentialism and non-consequentialism. Can normative ethical theories be compared and critically assessed?

These are meta-ethical questions. Meta-ethics examines the fundamental assumptions, basic concepts and methods of justification of normative ethics. Ontologically, realists, those who believe there is an objective moral reality and that ethical truth exists, have argued against relativists and constructivists who reject the possibility of such truths. Epistemologically, non-cognitivists have criticized cognitivists for their view that moral statements can be characterized as true or false, and that it is possible to articulate such a thing as moral knowledge (Beauchamp 1991: 21ff.; Jamieson 1993).

In recent decades, it seems as though the interest in these traditional questions has decreased. One line of this development has led to a more pragmatic, linguistic approach that deals primarily with (semantic) analyses of the way we use ethical words and expressions (Hare 1963), another with the logic of moral arguments, so-called deontic logic (von Wright 1963). A third line has led to scepticism towards ethical theorizing as a whole. So Williams (1985) has argued that rational, critical ethical analyses say little of what morality is all about. We should be more concerned with examining and articulating 'thick ethical concepts' – the substantive basic moral understandings and beliefs that guide action in everyday morality.

In another sense, such a shift of interest has indeed taken place. Fifteen years ago, Singer wrote:

> To an observer of moral philosophy in the twentieth century, the most striking development of the past twenty years would not be any advance in our theoretical understanding of the subject, nor would it be acceptance of any particular ideas about right and wrong. It would, rather, be the revival of an entire department of the subject: applied ethics.
>
> (Singer 1986: 1)

The focus in applied ethics is on particular moral questions and on the formulation and justification of moral norms and values of social practices and institutions. Most work here is characterized by a pragmatic attitude towards established theory – it is invoked when and where it helps in the analysis. In applied ethics, theoretical insights become significant 'tools for thought' that help structure and sharpen the discussion. Here, when examining equality and inequality in sport in Chapter 3, non-consequentialist theories of justice will play a key role. In the discussion of good competitions in Chapter 4, consequentialist theories, in particular utilitarianism, are helpful. However, this is a work in practical ethics, and so is concerned not with the 'blind' application of established ethical theory but with developing moral norms for a practice inspired by insights in theory.

This clarification of the various levels of ethical enquiry can serve as an outline of the main argument here so far. My starting point was the question of how we ought to act in sport competitions. In Chapter 1, I described key characteristics of these practices and how a traditional moral ideal, fair play, has been interpreted in different historical and socio-cultural contexts. That exercise in descriptive ethics prepared us to enter the realm of normative ethics which is the concern of this chapter: to establish a moral point of view and suggest a more detailed interpretation of the concept of fair play. So the

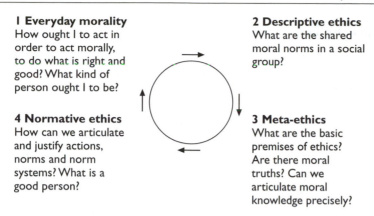

I Everyday morality
How ought I to act in
order to act morally,
to do what is right and
good? What kind of
person ought I to be?

2 Descriptive ethics
What are the shared
moral norms in a social
group?

4 Normative ethics
How can we articulate
and justify actions,
norms and norm
systems? What is a
good person?

3 Meta-ethics
What are the basic
premises of ethics?
Are there moral
truths? Can we
articulate moral
knowledge precisely?

Figure 1 The levels of ethical inquiry

general sequence is that I start with sport as a practice, use ethical theory to conceptualize and sharpen my analysis of that practice, and arrive at a standpoint on fair play in the practice of sport that I contend is morally justified.

It is important to note that the levels of ethical inquiry sketched in Figure 1 are not meant to be taken as absolutely distinct. Moral reasoning is hardly ever a strictly, deductive process. As philosophers of the neo-Aristotelian tradition point out, the distinction between the descriptive and the normative, or between fact and value, is questionable (MacIntyre 1984: 77ff.). Neither sociological accounts of everyday morality nor meta-ethical analyses can be said to be free of normative foundations. To examine some questions in favour of others always involves choice and hence criteria for choice, while studies of descriptive ethics influence us in our normative deliberations. Still, the distinctions can serve as useful heuristic devices, illustrating how different questions in ethics are posed with different intentions, and how they can be interrelated in a systematical ethical argument.

A MORAL POINT OF VIEW

I shall now try to make clear more specifically the normative premises for my interpretation of fair play. First, I present a sketch of how we should understand human agency and of the role of moral reasoning in such agency. Three general norms are then formulated upon which the subsequent argument will build. Taken together, these norms and the argument elaborating them constitute the moral point of view of this book.

Voluntary choice

I have said that ethics is the critical and systematic philosophical study of morality. Normative ethics is also prescriptive – it is supposed to have action-guiding force. For normative ethics to have such force, then, requires some kind of understanding of human agency as based on choices, for which the people making these choices can be held responsible. Can such an understanding be provided, and if so, how?

Let us first look at the question of human freedom. A minimum conception says that we can be held responsible for our actions if we could have chosen otherwise. Let us call this the idea of 'practical freedom' (Young 1993). On this conception, acting freely is basically a matter of doing what we want to do. A person acts voluntarily (from the Latin *voluntas*, 'will') when that person chooses (wills) a particular action from at least two alternatives and when there are no direct obstacles effectively preventing the person from acting in that particular way. Voluntary action is unforced.

The idea of 'practical freedom' in no way solves the deeper philosophical problems involved. Even if there are no obvious external constraints that prevent us from acting the way we want, we may act as we do because of dispositions that we have acquired and internalized, for instance during a rough childhood. Though we act immorally, it might be argued that we really cannot be held responsible for these acts. The deeper question, then, is not simply whether we can do what we want to do, but whether we are free to choose the will that we would want to have (Young 1993).

Some strong determinists would deny such a possibility and say that we are determined in our actions either by our natural dispositions or, in Locke's famous phrase, because we are from birth a *tabula rasa* that is inscribed solely by environmental influences. Whether we realize it or not, our actions are in a fundamental sense parts of strict causal relationships that we cannot change. Indeterminists deny these claims. Radical indeterminists, such as the existentialists, claim that there is no such thing as human nature and that social determinism is mistaken. We are 'doomed' to be free and have no choice but to choose our own interpretations of the right and the good, if we are to live 'authentically'.

I cannot pursue these complex, metaphysical questions here. My aim is to state the general premises upon which my particular argument will build. All moral arguments are founded on an interpretation of human freedom and responsibility. A minimum interpretation is that we have the potential for unforced choice among alternative actions. This interpretation retains the idea of practical freedom, but does not necessarily entail an individualistic understanding of action. As has been emphasized in the above discussion of various kinds of ethos in sport, we are social beings who communicate over and so can agree upon norms for interaction. Neither does it preclude the possibility of individual responsibility. As we shall see, it is precisely in social communication over values, norms and actions that our potential for unforced choice and individual responsibility can be developed and cultivated. This can be clarified with the help of an example.

Imagine a boxer who has been socialized into a morally problematic ethos that includes hitting below the belt when the officials cannot detect this violation of the rules. In competitions there is no room for dwelling on more or less complex psychological and sociological explanations of action. The idea is to reward individuals and teams as their actions merit. Hence, there is a need to eliminate wrongdoing or compensate for its consequences by penalties. Athletes' actions must be judged 'at face value', so to speak, which means there and then. And this seems to make perfect sense to the parties engaged. In most sporting communities, the idea of athletes' responsibility for their actions takes the character of a shared norm. Without awarding points for a good punch, and without imposing penalties for blows below the belt, boxing ceases to exist as a competitive sport.

The ideas of unforced choice and individual responsibility can be justified above mere pragmatic concerns. In his first encounter with a different ethos of the sport, the boxer with the problematic ethos might be penalized for his internalized dispositions and therefore for states of affairs for which he cannot be held fully responsible. But, an ethos of a group is a more or less dynamic system of shared norms and values. The group members negotiate with each other, and with members from other groups with different kinds of ethos, and with officials who represent the official ethos of their sport. Even if a first penalty might be harsh for the boxer who is not prepared for it, it can lead to reflection on, and in fact adjustments of, his actions and the ethos of the group to which he belongs. Through reflection and in social discourse, there is always the possibility of challenging and changing beliefs and conduct, and in this sense we can be held responsible for them.

However, a voluntary choice is not, of course, always a moral choice. A boxer can continue to hit below the belt even if he knows that this is against the shared norms of the practice and that it is morally wrong. He may act for subjective reasons. In ethical discussions, we deal with why we ought to act in certain ways rather than others. Arguments are built on the premise that some kind of objective or moral reason has a role to play. Does this premise hold water?

Moral reason

This is another classic philosophical question, which accordingly has received various answers. The Kantian tradition sees reason as an autonomous source of ethical norms that is capable of motivating behavior independently of desire and aversion. Pure practical reason, free of contingent desires and emotions, is the ground of the categorical imperative mentioned above: 'Act only according to those maxims that can consistently be willed as a universal law!' Choice of goals and actions according to such maxim expresses our nature as free, rational, moral agents.

An alternative tradition from Hume sees reason primarily as 'slave of the passions'. Although reason is used in consequential ways to disclose important facts and to find the most efficient means for dealing with the world, in terms of morality reason is 'perfectly inert'. For Hume morality is founded not on reason but on the affections; it springs from what he calls our 'moral sentiments', such as empathy and benevolence, that constitute our 'moral sense'. Although admirable from a moral point of view, morality itself is not the product of any kind of objective reason but, ultimately, of our passions and desires.

My position draws on both traditions. Socialization, norm internalization and choice of action are complex processes that involve the whole human being – passions, desires, emotions, and reason. Moral conduct is learned primarily through social interaction in a morally intelligible environment. When moral education is successful, the many and complex factors that influence our choices and actions are unified. We act morally based on coherent inner motivation. The main concern of this book is to find sound moral reasons for choosing particular goals and courses of actions over others in sport. The norms at which I arrive in the course of this search should be understood as possible goals of a good socialization process. But the practicalities of how moral education should proceed in order to bring together the many factors that influence action and internalize such norms, though one of the key topics in the psychology and the pedagogy of sport, is beyond the scope of this book.

With that distinction clarified, I can now proceed by examining more closely the characteristics of moral reason, or as I shall call it, moral rationality.

Rationality as the maximization of self-interest

The possibility of choice based on reason refers not only to actions on the playing field, but to intellectual choices as well. In an ethical discourse, a series of theoretical possibilities is open to us. In my search for norms for fair play I should examine systematically and critically in what way various theoretical alternatives can be of help to us. As Hare (1981: 228) says, 'Our freedom consists in that we are free to be rational'. Rationality is itself a normative notion. For any choice, if it is more rational than its alternatives, we ought to choose it. But criteria of rationality vary.

Being rational is often associated with being prudent, with acting according to self-interest. Thomas Hobbes, perhaps the most famous proponent of this view, considered the basic rationale for human action to be self-preservation. The misery of the anarchistic 'state of nature' where life was 'solitary, poor, nasty, brutish, and short' resulted in the establishment of a social contract, whereby individuals agreed on norms of peaceful interaction based on rational self-interest, that is, on knowledge of what in fact is better and worse for them. Such a solution is expected to make everyone better off.

However, this expectation is problematic (Elster 1989: 52ff.). Imagine that a rational egoist has framed intentional goals with regard to a sport competition. The egoist knows that this competition is arisen from a shared interpretation of the constitutive rules: an ethos. If the egoist's intentional goals are to be realized, it is rational to subscribe with other participants to a contract about acting in accordance with the ethos. Nonetheless, promises, contracts, or for that matter a shared ethos in the group of which we are part, do not really count at all. They are purely pragmatic devices to realize competitions, as long as the egoist takes pleasure in them. There is no argument here against ethos violations in principle. The egoist will cheat if this would be effective. For cheating to be effective, others must keep to the rules. Egoistic actions are in this sense 'parasitic' on moral actions. The egoist is a 'free rider', who benefits from others' cooperative efforts without contributing his or her share to those efforts.

The moral possibilities of rational egoism cannot be sufficiently discussed here, but the position does not seem capable of conceptualizing sufficiently what is commonly held to be the realm of morality. If we were all rational egoists, cooperation and common interpretation of rules would become mere strategic means, and social practices such as sport would become extremely fragile. Are there other accounts of rationality that are more promising?

Consequentialism and utilitarianism

The rational egoist's position is an example of what is called consequentialism. Consequentialism refers to a particular structure of ethical arguments (Scheffler 1988: 1 ff.). First, we have to make clear what is intrinsically valuable or what is valued as good in itself. Second, we evaluate how actions, practices and institutions contribute to what is considered intrinsically good. What is right in dilemmas of choice always depends on what maximizes the good.

What, then, is of value in itself? Midgley (1985, 1991) is critical of what she calls the myth of the Hobbesian social contract: that human beings are by nature pleasure-seeking individuals with little concern for the common good. She points to biological and anthropological studies that provide evidence at odds with the rational egoist's assumptions. Active sympathy for and empathy with others, shared consideration, shared joy, and shared sorrows are commonly found among higher animals and in almost all human societies. An alternative and more plausible theory of the origins of social norms contends that human beings come to agreements with one another because they are simply disposed by nature to like and communicate with each other. Our natural dispositions for empathy and sharing norms seem at least as strong as those for rational egoism. Indeed, the most influential consequentialist theories include concern for others as a key element.

These theories come from the utilitarian tradition, in which happiness or well-being is considered intrinsically good and this is combined with the universalistic idea that any one person's happiness is as important as any other's. Substantive utilitarian theories, such as the classic Benthamite hedonistic position, Mill's eudaimonian utilitarianism, or Moore's idealistic utilitarianism, consider 'the good' to be an actual mental state, such as pleasure or happiness. In the theories of most modern utilitarians, the good is defined formally, for instance in terms of the satisfaction of preferences. In moral dilemmas, the right choice results in at least as much preference-satisfaction as any alternative choice. In Chapter 4, I shall replace the term 'intentional goals' with 'preferences' and use a utilitarian approach to arrive at norms for good competition. Accordingly, following comments will concentrate on the preference-utilitarian approach.

Utilitarianism is in many ways a strong and intuitively appealing theory. Scheffler (1988: 1) suggests that the core idea of utilitarianism is 'to make the world the best possible place to live'. The point of defining the satisfaction of preferences, or individual well-being, as intrinsically good, and thereafter judging all actions as right or wrong accordingly, is simple and corresponds to a certain extent with common sense. In everyday moral reasoning, if pressed on our views, we usually end up by pointing to the consequences of the various alternatives.

However, counter-arguments come easily to mind. To most of us, it is unreasonable to allow preferences of any kind count without considering their content. Some preferences may be grounded in false beliefs and mis-understandings; some might be anti-social, evil and/or dangerous; some are simply expressions of mental disorders. In sport, it seems unreasonable that one competitor's egoistic desire to win by any means should count as much as another competitor's desire for a just and good game. A proper question here concerns the critical criteria for what preferences a utilitarian calculus should accept. Is it possible to 'launder' preferences so as to end up only with well-informed, rational ones?

John Stuart Mill's distinction between higher and lower pleasures is a move in this direction. In a celebrated passage, Mill argued that

> It is better to be a human dissatisfied than a pig satisfied; better to be a Socrates dissatisfied than a fool satisfied. And if the fool, or the pig, is of a different opinion, it is because they only know their own side of the question. The other party to the comparison knows both sides.
>
> (Mill 1863: Chapter II)

Within a utilitarian framework, however, such a moderating strategy is hard to defend. The distinctive mark of the utilitarian approach, as specified by

Bentham, is that 'everybody (is) to count as one, nobody for more than one' (Hare 1981: 4). Moreover, in most cases of utilitarian reasoning, or reasoning 'in the world as it is' (Hare 1981: 146), there seems to be no need for preference-laundering. Bizarre, evil or confused preferences usually 'drown', for they are very few compared to the reasonable preferences of most parties involved.

Another criticism of utilitarianism is that applying the theory in practice to find what is the right choice is very difficult. In most dilemmas of choice, we act under uncertainty and usually under limited access to information. Should we or should we not accept the use of a newly developed performance-enhancing drug in sport? Questions of fact immediately arise. Is the drug dangerous to health? How strong is its potential enhancement of performance? Will everyone get access to the drug if it is allowed? Lack of relevant knowledge of alternatives and their consequences should modify strict demands for maximization of preference-satisfaction. What can be asked for may be only the maximization of expected preference satisfaction among all parties concerned.

An additional problem with classical utilitarianism is that it prescribes the maximization of overall sum of net utility resulting for all parties concerned. This does not include consideration of how utility is distributed among the parties. For instance, a large number of sport competitors whose individual preferences are satisfied only to a very small extent and who are therefore generally unhappy would easily outweigh a much smaller number of competitors who each enjoy a very high degree of individual preference-satisfaction. But it seems unreasonable to prefer a population of many unhappy competitors over a population of a few happy ones.

Such an outcome could be avoided by changing the criteria from maximizing total utility to maximizing an average of the overall sum of utility separated for each member of the group, that is, the overall sum of net utility divided by the total number of affected individuals.[2] With this modification, we can formulate a more precise utilitarian consequentialist norm:

> Maximize expected average preference satisfaction among all parties concerned.

The question now becomes whether this general norm is sufficient for discussions of morality in sport competitions. Does it provide the necessary grounding to establish and justify more detailed norms for fair play in sport?

The need for an alternative to the utilitarian approach

Even if we accept a formal definition of the good in terms of preference-satisfaction and introduce average utility measures, the utilitarian approach is still problematic. It provides no well-developed conception of unforced, voluntary choices, or of what it is to be person, or of persons as moral agents with rights and duties. Persons become collections of more or less complex preference structures, just 'occasions' or 'sites' where preferences are satisfied. What counts is the accumulation of preferences among all parties concerned. As Rawls (1971: 27) sums up this shortcoming, '. . . utilitarianism does not take seriously the distinctions between persons'.

Moreover, given its one-sided quest for preference-satisfaction, critics argue that utilitarianism cannot in principle distinguish between different kinds of moral norms – distinction that seems to be crucial common-sense understanding of morality. For example, there are supererogatory acts, acts that are over and beyond the call of duty, and also obligations that represent what is considered the minimum requirement of acting morally. Utilitarianism does not take seriously such diversity and complexity in moral life.

Modern utilitarian theories such as Hare's 'universal prescriptivism' seem to put to shame some of this criticism. Hare (1981) distinguishes between two levels of moral reasoning. In everyday morality, people's conduct is based on commonly accepted moral norms and values. There is no need to question such everyday morality, if it is uncontroversial and functions well. This argument is a 'rule-utilitarian' one – it prescribes acceptance of general norms of conduct as long as they seem, by and large, to lead to high average preference-satisfaction among all parties concerned.

However, in moral dilemmas when established norms conflict, or where there are no established norms, this strategy does not work. In a given situation, for example in shot-putter X's dilemma before the World Championships whether to use banned drugs and probably be ranked among the top competitors, or not use banned drugs and probably not reach the top rank, X might be in doubt regarding what is the right thing to do. Drugs are banned and use implies rule violation. At the same time, most competitors use drugs without being caught. The rules may appear to be unfair. So we need to turn to a second, critical level of moral thinking. The decision procedure now is one of 'act utilitarianism'. With access to the relevant facts, we should seek the solution that can be expected to maximize average preference satisfaction among all parties concerned. Then X can choose the morally right course, and resume training with a justified norm that can serve him and others in similar dilemmas in the future.

Hare engages with traditional views of morality, including non-consequentialist ones, but only at the first level of moral thought. Whenever we are in doubt about what is morally right, we need to turn to the critical level of act utilitarianism. But even then, the two level-theory is still open to the criticism presented above.

Utilitarianism seems to cover only a narrow range of what we understand as the realm of morality. In a moral theory that claims to be comprehensive, it seems unreasonable not to include broader notions: of persons as somehow having value in themselves independent of preferences, of intrinsic features of actions such as fairness and justice, or of what it is to be a (good) person.

A non-consequentialist norm

Non-consequentialist theories, it should be remembered, prescribe right actions independently of utility comparisons. In acting rightly, we operate within what are called 'non-consequentialist constraints', such as the Kantian idea of the infinite worth of persons within, or the neo-Aristotelian emphasis of the moral relevance of the virtues. By including non-consequentialist constraints, some of the unfortunate aspects of utilitarianism can be remedied. According to Frankena (1963), a mixed ethical theory, in which the maximization schemes of utilitarianism are combined with concerns for persons as moral agents and for justice, represents a workable synthesis. As we saw in Chapter 1, notions of justice have particularly strong standing in sport. What, then, is justice?

In philosophical dictionaries, justice is said to involve the distribution of significant goods and burdens among persons. In more precise terms, justice typically deals with situations in which 'person p is accorded ... benefits or burdens due or owed to p because of p's particular properties or situation' (Beauchamp 1991: 342). One of the classic conceptual frameworks for this subject is found in Aristotle's (1976) *Nichomachean Ethics*, Book Five, Chapters iii–v. First, Aristotle suggests, we should look at what should be held equal among parties; second, at what are the morally relevant inequalities that can qualify for unequal treatment; and third, at what are the non-relevant inequalities that should be eliminated or compensated for (Wetlesen 1986: 121ff.). A formal norm for justice can be formulated as follows:

> Relevantly equal cases ought to be treated equally, cases that are relevantly unequal can be treated unequally, and unequal treatment ought to stand in reasonable accordance to the actual inequality between cases.

This formal norm has no direct action-guiding potential. When I come to develop substantial norms for the distribution of goods and burdens in sport competitions (Chapter 3), I need access to relevant information about the practice under discussion. At this stage, the norm stands as a backing norm in need of elaboration.

The consequentialist and the non-consequentialist norms now formulated seem to complement each other. This does not necessarily mean that they constitute a complete moral point of view. I have not yet said anything of the relationship between them and their role in my subsequent argument.

A meta-norm for unforced, informed general agreement

The idea of formal justice from Aristotle is uncontroversial. In fact, although in different ways, philosophers from Kant to Popper have regarded the idea of treating equal cases equally and distinguishing cases according to relevant inequalities as a basic mode of perception and cognition, an *a priori* norm that characterizes our rational faculties in general. Discussions of justice usually become more problematic when we seek to establish substantive norms in concrete practices. In sport, for example, the relevant inequality that is used as a basis for the distribution of goods and burdens is athletic performance. Other inequalities are eliminated or compensated for. But how are we to define 'athletic performance'?

Here, consequential norms can be of relevance. Faced with several definitions, we ought, perhaps, to choose the definition that can be expected to maximize average preference-satisfaction among all parties concerned, or maybe the one that can be expected to maximize joy in sport. But what do we do if such a solution contradicts non-consequentialist ideas of persons? Imagine that the joy among spectators during the gladiatorial contests of ancient Rome outweighed the sufferings of the gladiators and their victims. It would still be ethically difficult to justify the practice. Individuals are sacrificed, literally speaking, to please the masses. How should we decide precedence between consequentialist and non-consequentialist norms in cases of conflict?

I subscribe to a view of persons as moral agents with the potential of using reason in choosing their actions. Further, I assume that as such persons we are social beings with dispositions for empathy and for understanding each other's joys and sorrows. These premises open the possibility for the shared norms that can be found in the ethos of various sports. At a more general level, the possibility of norms that are shared among all parties concerned is a key idea of what is called non-consequentialist ethical contract theory.

Contract theories have a long history in moral philosophy (Kymlicka 1993). Consequentialist versions may be derived from the Hobbesian tradition, whereby self-interested parties bargain to reach solutions of mutual advantage. These cohere with a view of persons as rational egoists. Other versions are based on the Kantian idea that morality arises from an ideal agreement that people would adopt if they met as an assembly of equals to decide collectively on norms to govern their relations. Their decisions must be based on access to all relevant information and without favouring particular interests. The authority of the norms is derived from the fairness of the procedure for deciding on them. These non-consequentialist versions build on similar premises as the ones sketched above.

The leading contemporary representative of the non-consequentialist social contractual tradition is John Rawls. To secure impartial and rational outcomes in questions of social justice, Rawls (1971: 136–137) describes a hypothetical contractual situation, the so-called 'original position'. Here free and rational persons concerned to further their own interests choose principles for their future cooperation from behind a 'veil of ignorance' they do not know the particular facts about themselves, such as their sex, race, intelligence, special talents or handicaps, and so cannot choose based on informed self-interest. At the same time, the parties are in command of all general information relevant to their choices, such as general facts about human societies, and theories of social organization and of human (moral) psychology. In this setting, the argument goes, the parties will reach solutions that are impartial and morally right. The original position is considered a paradigmatic example of fair circumstances. Although Rawls aims at a theory of social justice, he hints that conditions of fairness like those of 'the original position' can be the starting point for norms that prescribe what is morally right in general (Rawls 1971: 17).

I subscribe to the idea of moral norms as based on some kind of unforced, informed agreement that gains authority by the fairness of the procedures by which they arise. However, my ambition is somewhat different from that of Rawls. The more limited goal in this book is to develop a theory of fair play in sport. I have presented sport competitions as social practices that are realized through some kind of shared interpretation of the rules among participants, what I called an ethos. An ethos of a sport arises, and is negotiated and developed, in concrete social settings by full-blooded persons with the capacity to make voluntary choices. I have allowed for the possibility for more than one ethos of a sport to be morally acceptable. Consequently, the understanding of the contract procedure I have proposed is not of rational decision-makers seeking full consensus behind a veil of ignorance, but, rather, of persons searching for a set of norms that can readily be accepted, or at least that cannot reasonably be rejected, as a basis for rational agreement. I shall now argue in line with Scanlon (1985), who has formulated a slightly different version of a contractualist criterion of choice:

> Choose norms that no one can reasonably reject as a basis for unforced, informed general agreement.[3]

This formulation will function as meta-norm in subsequent discussion. It will be the main criterion of choice in possible conflicts between consequentialist and non-consequentialist arguments, and serve as the final test of moral justification in articulating norms for fair play.

NORMS

Moral norms are sub-classes of social norms. They are shared prescriptions for action in situations of interaction where what we consider to be significant benefits and harms are at stake. They often have an overriding function in relation to other social norms, and violations usually incur sanctions of guilt and shame (Elster 1989: 113ff). Later, I shall consider norms for fair play with different kinds of justification and different levels of generality. For now, more precisely, what can be said of their validity? And what, if any, are the connections between the different kinds of norms?

An initial distinction can be made between norm statements and so-called value statements. Norm statements are statements that prescribe that something ought to, or may, or must, not be done (von Wright 1983: 67ff.; Eckhoff and Sundby 1988: 45ff., Elster 1989: 113ff.). They express obligations, permissions and prohibitions, such as 'competitors ought always to play to win'. Value statements include value predicates that rank state of affairs as good or bad, best or worst, or possibly neutral, such as 'this was a good game'.

Value statements and norm statements are interconnected. Value statements like 'this was a good game' can be justified by referring to commonly accepted norms for a good game in a sport. On the other hand, norm statements are often justified by referring to what are considered important values, such as 'one ought to play according to the standards of a good game because then games can become meaningful and joyful to all'. The discussion here concentrates on norms but I shall return to the discussion of values in the final chapter, Chapter 5.

Rawls (1971: 108ff.) distinguishes between two kinds of moral norm for individuals: natural duties and obligations. Natural duties are general norms that apply to all human practices. As examples we can point to (consequentialist) norms that proscribe exposing others or oneself to unnecessary harm, or in their stronger version, prescribe the maximization of average preference satisfaction among all parties concerned, or again to (non-consequentialist) norms for acting fairly and justly. In contrast to natural duties, obligations arise when individuals choose voluntarily to participate in rule-governed practices. As we shall see in the discussion of fairness, the content of an obligation is defined within the framework of natural duties that cover all human practice.

Both natural duties and obligations incur negative sanctions if violated. There is another kind of norm, however, that does not lead to such responses. Supererogatory norms prescribe admirable but not obligatory actions – actions that are beyond the call of duty. They are encouraged by morality but not required by it. For instance, if a cyclist stops during a race to help a fellow competitor with a flat tyre, for many this is an admirable act. But assuming there is a shared norm among cyclists in competition that they should be able to fix a flat tyre themselves, there would be no blame attached if the cyclist had continued the race without stopping to help. If, on the other hand, a fellow competitor is badly hurt after a crash and needs help, stopping to help is commonly considered a moral obligation, based on the natural duty of not exposing others to unnecessary harm.

Norms for sport competitions have the status of obligations that obtain when we voluntarily engage in rule-governed practices. I have said that natural duties override obligations linked to particular practices. But how can we decide precedence between natural duties, or obligations, when these conflict? This will depend on whether the norms are seen either as absolute and ordered in a hierarchical system, or rather as guidelines that may conflict and so must be weighed against each other in concrete circumstances (Eckhoff and Sundby 1988: 90ff.).

Statements of norms involve operators such as 'ought', 'should', and 'must'. They also usually involve a qualifier ('if . . .') that indicates the conditions for a norm to be applicable, followed by a prescription ('then one ought to . . .'). Even if a norm has many specific exceptions, it may have absolute validity within its range of application. Choices within this range either comply with or violate the norm. Absolute norms have separate areas of application that do not conflict.

Norms for fair play should have the character of guidelines. I noted that the general consequentialist and non-consequentialist norms formulated above complement each other and together express moral rationality. I need to deal with both natural duties and specific obligations linked to particular practices. Obligations can conflict with other obligations, and natural duties with natural duties. As in the discussion of possible conflicts between con-sequentialist and non-consequentialist norms, I must carefully weigh the claims of each and find solutions that, according to the contractualist meta-norm, 'cannot be reasonable rejected as a basis for unforced, informed general agreement'. Such a weighing procedure will take on the character of practical reasoning.

PRACTICAL REASONING

With the growth of practical ethics in the second half of the twentieth century, there has been increasing interest in practical reasoning. Work in the deontic logic, the logic of obligation and permission, has clarified the structure of normative discourse through the use of methods and techniques drawn from formal logic (von Wright 1963, 1983). However, though the argument here aims at a systematic ordering of norms, it proceeds less formally and is more closely linked to traditional practical reasoning than to the deontic logic approach.

In Book Six of the *Nichomachean Ethics*, Aristotle (1976) discusses the differences between theoretical, practical and technical rationality. In the case of practical rationality, which deals with choice of goals and actions (*phronesis*), he takes as a satisfactory starting point for argument commonly received opinions (*endoxa*) – claims or positions that are known and acknowledged by competent parties. Competence, according to Aristotle, can derive from wisdom, conviction, or simply the fact that one is part of a decision. I start out with commonly accepted descriptive and normative premises. In Chapter 1, I outlined a basic understanding of sport competitions, and in this chapter I have sketched three basic norms that are constitutive of my moral point of view. In working out norms for fair play, I shall fill out these bare formations with relevant information and appropriate knowledge to do with sport.

In this process I shall argue *pro et contra* case by case. Modern decision theory has developed such for-and-against reasoning in a critical and systematic way. In dilemmas of choice we set up an overview of alternative choices, then try to evaluate them, among other things, by examining their consequences and probabilities. I shall use this approach directly in the (utilitarian) discussion of good competitions in Chapter 4.

In the discussion of justice in Chapter 3, I shall adopt more of a casuistic approach. Casuistry, Miller (1996) argues, can serve to develop our powers of moral perception. It cultivates our moral sense and 'liberates' the discourse from the formal restrictions of traditional ethical reasoning. The key is to distinguish morally relevant features of the cases under discussion and to articulate more precisely the moral dilemma in each particular case. In Chapter 3, I seek to do this by drawing on parallel cases and analogies, and by constructing taxonomies. For instance, I shall distinguish between what I call non-relevant inequalities, which ought to be eliminated or compensated for in sport, and relevant inequalities (in athletic performance), which need specific evaluation. I can do this by differentiating between external conditions, factors specific to the individual athlete, and factors linked to the systems of material, economic, technological, and scientific resources that support athletes and teams.

NORM SYSTEMS

The practical reasoning I set out will issue in the formulation of a series of norms. My goal is to establish a system of moral norms that articulate a theory of fair play. What are the requirements that such a system has to meet? Indeed, what are the characteristics of normative systems?

Internal requirements

To a certain extent, we can place similar requirements on a system of moral norms to those we place on scientific theories in general. These usually include insistence on clarity, simplicity, completeness, and internal consistency.[4]

A system of norms should be clear. The terms used should be understandable by everyone, and if there are any technical terms at all, they must be explained in a clear and straightforward way. Further, the norms should be un-ambiguous. In particular, there should be no doubt about the conditions on which a norm is to apply, what kinds of action it prescribes or proscribes, and what sanctions are to be imposed if the norm is violated. Qualifiers and contigent consequences must be clearly formulated. Chapter 1 sought to clarify our understanding of the practices of 'sport competitions'. Chapter 3 and Chapter 4 will seek similar clarity in formulating moral norms for these practices.

A system of norms should be simple. The demand for simplicity applies both to single norms and the system as a whole. If the system consists of many very specific and detailed norms, its action-guiding potential may become problematic. Simplicity improves overall understanding and facilitates practical implementation. The norm system for sport competitions developed in this book consist of two groups of norms that relate to common understanding of formal and informal fair play, and to the general consequentialist and non-consequentialist norms formulated above.

The demand for simplicity should not overshadow the demand for completeness. The norm system ought to be able to guide choice in all moral dilemmas encountered in sport, or at least in as many as possible. The realm of morality is the realm of 'the right' and 'the good'. My theory of fair play in sport will include norms prescribing what is considered right, just and fair, and norms for the good. Hence, I shall argue that it can provide guidelines for all kinds of moral dilemma in sport and that in this sense it satisfies the criterion of completeness.

Finally, to attain the status of a system, a group of norms must be internally consistent. By internal consistency I mean that a norm and its negation are not both found within the same system. We are working here with guidelines that in certain situations may come into conflict. As we shall see in Chapter 5, however, the norms for fair play satisfy not only, the demand for consistency demand, in that there are no contradictions between them. Beyond that, they are strongly related. They complement and mutually support each other through more or less strong interconnections of meaning. The aim is that the norms for fair play should constitute a coherent whole and express a unified conception of the moral goal of sport competitions.

External justification

If the norms developed here seen as a whole satisfy these internal requirements, they can be said to constitute a system of norms or a normative theory. However, my goal is a system of *moral* norms. Internal requirements alone are not necessarily indicators of moral justification. The requirements of clarity, simplicity, completeness, and consistency say nothing of moral substance. There can be well-constructed normative systems that are immoral, or even evil. The egoistic competitor is acting consistently in cheating whenever it seems to pay off, but we would not characterize such conduct as morally acceptable. How can a system of norms be shown to be morally justified?

A standard requirement of a scientific theory is that it is open to logical and/or empirical falsification. We cannot justify a system of moral norms in the same way. Good ethics depend on well-established facts but cannot be guided solely by such facts. I seek here to avoid both relativism, the claim that there are no critical criteria of the ethically right and good, and naive realism, the belief in absolute, complete and ahistorical schemes of moral truths. I accept as one of my premises that indeed there are certain moral insights in which we do have strong confidence and in which we can firmly believe, for example that it is morally wrong to hurt people for pleasure, or that it is morally wrong to lie and to cheat other people for pure egoistic reasons. These are what we may call first-order moral beliefs. Another premise adopted here is that it is possible to reason systematically and critically within consequentialist and non-consequentialist schemes, and on rational grounds to propose morally acceptable solutions and reject morally unacceptable ones.

Taking these two premises together, I conduct my search for a theory of fair play in sport in a particular way. In the course of my argument, theoretically derived general norms will be weighed against actual practice and first-order moral beliefs. If a general norm entails practices that clearly conflict with such beliefs, we must re-examine those norms and perhaps revise and adjust them. For instance, a situation could arise in ice hockey where the public 'wants' more violence and, based on consequentialist reasoning, the officials accept assaults and hazardous play in order to increase spectator satisfaction, but this conflicts with most people's first-order beliefs about fairness and respect for persons. On due reflection, and with backing from non-consequentialist perspectives, such official acceptance based on considering spectator satisfaction might well be modified or perhaps abandoned entirely. On the other hand, systematically developed general norms can shed light on morally problematic facets of traditional beliefs and practice, leading to their revision. The great inequalities in support systems in modern high performance sport seem to be more or less tacitly accepted by the athletes, the support systems, and the public. As we shall see in Chapter 3, however, upon reflection these inequalities may come to seem indefensibly unjust, and we may decide our beliefs ought to be adjusted.

Methodologically, the aim of this mutual adjustment process is to reach something similar to what Rawls (1971: 19–22, 48–53) calls a 'reflective equilibrium'.[5] Through mutual adjustments, fair-play norms and first-order moral beliefs are brought into accord with one another. Such equilibrium is considered a sign of the reasonableness of our conclusions. This places me within a coherence tradition of justification (Jamieson 1993). General norms serve as hypotheses that are tested in practice and against first-order moral beliefs, and current practice and beliefs are critically reviewed with the help of more general norms. The various levels of moral reasoning mutually influence each other. Here, the critical criterion in this weighing process is the contractualist meta-norm I formulated above, which prescribes choice of

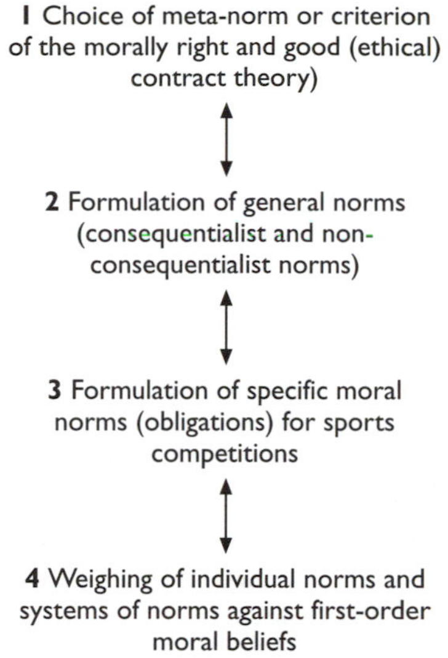

1 Choice of meta-norm or criterion
of the morally right and good (ethical)
contract theory)

↕

2 Formulation of general norms
(consequentialist and non-
consequentialist norms)

↕

3 Formulation of specific moral
norms (obligations) for sports
competitions

↕

4 Weighing of individual norms and
systems of norms against first-order
moral beliefs

Figure 2 Practical argumentation – an overview

solutions that 'no one can reasonably reject as a basis for unforced, informed, general agreement'.

In this way, I propose what we may call a soft moral realist standpoint. I contend that it is possible to find reasons for judging some choices to be morally better, and by assumption to have a better claim to be morally true, than other choices. However, as in other quests for knowledge, there is never complete certainty here. Claims to moral truth are always coloured by the language in which they are stated, by the particular attitudes and beliefs of the individuals and groups that make them, by the actual historical and socio-cultural context in which they are articulated, and so forth. Such claims and our acceptance or rejection of them can never attain absolute validity. In this way, practical ethics becomes a continuous and open-minded search for moral truth within the historical, social, and cultural setting we find ourselves living and in which we must act.[6]

This line of reasoning is illustrated in Figure 2.

I start from a chosen meta-norm based on ethical contract theory. In step 2, I use relevant knowledge and understanding of ethical theory to formulate general norms to guide the subsequent argument, such as the consequentialist and non-consequentialist norms stated above. In step 3, norms for fair play in sport competitions are formulated. Then in step 4, with access to the relevant facts, I engage in a weighing process involving between general norms, first-order moral beliefs and current practice in the search for an internally consistent moral interpretation of fair play.

As I shall argue in Chapter 5, because of the strong internal connections of meaning between the individual norms, the system as a whole can be considered an expression of a single goal, which I shall set out (at the end of the book) as the moral goal of sport competitions.

SUMMARY

In this chapter I have attempted to make clear the basic assumptions of the argument of this book, the better to understand its scope and limitations. A first assumption is that people have the possibility of choosing freely, in a restricted, practical sense of the term. I talked of voluntary choice – choice that is unforced in the sense that in a situation in which we could have chosen otherwise, there are no external constraints that determine our choice in a particular direction. I have assumed as well that if we have this possibility of choosing freely, we can be both held responsible for our choices and be challenged on their justification.

Human agency is a complex product of both non-rational and rational factors. I have further assumed that moral reason has the potential to illuminate human agency, and that the description and use of moral reason is the key task of ethics.

I continued to search for a clear general understanding of a justifiable moral point of view by discussing criteria of moral rationality. More specifically I sought norms to back a systematic and critical examination of the idea of fair play in sport. I looked at the egoist position and contrasted it with a view of humans as primarily social beings with natural dispositions to empathy and mutual understanding. I argued that answers to ethical questions are best sought in communication between informed and reasonable persons who can choose in unforced ways and who have mutual respect for each other's potential as moral agents. This coheres with the non-consequentialist contractualist tradition in moral philosophy. Inspired by Rawls (1971), and in particular by Scanlon (1985), I formulated a meta-norm for my project. This meta-norm guides both theoretical and practical choices and is the most general expression of my moral point of view. In what follows, it will be referred to as norm I:

> I Choose norms that cannot be reasonably rejected as a basis for unforced, informed general agreement.

I have examined other basic concerns of moral arguments that should be included in moral reasoning as well. When challenged on our actions and moral views, we often refer to their consequences. Consequentialist theories say we should judge things morally in just this way: the rightness of actions and policies depends upon the goodness of their results. The primary consequentialist theory is utilitarianism. I formulated a consequentialist, utilitarian norm, henceforth called norm II:

II Maximize expected average preference satisfaction among all parties concerned.

Consequentialism in general and utilitarianism in particular has been subjected to severe criticism. Critics point to its lack of an adequate concept of persons as moral agents, and to its failure to acknowledge the diversity of human interaction. Non-consequentialist theories, on the other hand, prescribe right action as independent of, or based on criteria logical prior to, utility maximization and utility comparisons. Ideas of the right have standing independent of ideas of the good. I therefore developed a norm for justice (norm III). Following Aristotle, this can be formulated as follows:

III Relevantly equal cases ought to be treated equally, cases that are relevantly unequal can be treated unequally, and unequal treatment ought to stand in reasonable accordance to the actual inequality between cases.

The consequentialist and non-consequentialist norms II and III represent two important and complementary perspectives in ethical reasoning. They will serve as premises for our subsequent discussion of specific norms for sport competitions. They are to be seen not as absolute norms but rather as guidelines that can overlap and conflict. In case of conflict, the critical criterion of choice is meta-norm I.

Finally, I discussed how to reach my goal of an interpretation of fair play in terms of a system of norms. Such a system has to satisfy internal requirements of clarity, simplicity, completeness, and consistency. Further, I suggested an external justification inspired by a coherentist scheme of justification and characterized by what is called reflective equilibrium. In reflective equilibrium, theoretically derived norms and first-order moral beliefs about the substantive matters to which the norms apply are seen to cohere and support each other. I proposed what I called a soft realist position, which holds that it is possible to distinguish rationally between morally acceptable and morally un-acceptable standpoints, and claims that the acceptable ones express some kind of moral truth. However, I noted that such moral truths are expressed in varying degrees in various ethical and moral positions, and can be articulated in a variety of ways in different historical, social and cultural settings. So I described the challenge for ethics as being to search continuously for the best possible articulations in the particular contexts in which we find ourselves living and acting.

Chapter 3

Right sport competitions
Fairness

Questions of fairness and justice arise regularly in sport as in other areas of life. Was this a fair competition? Did the football team deserve that goal? Did the better competitor win? Sometimes, we hear claims that the best team actually lost, that the game was unfair and that the loser was the 'moral' winner. What do we mean by such claims? How is fairness and justice in sport to be understood?

The fair play ideal is associated with ideas of justice. 'Formal fair play' prescribes keeping to the rules or, according to the understanding developed in Chapter 1, keeping to the socially shared interpretation of the rules in terms of the ethos of the sport in which we are engaged. But these ideas need elaboration and specification.

To do this, I first suggest an interpretation of the concept of 'right' in terms of ideas of 'fairness' and 'justice', then formulate a preliminary fairness norm. I shall proceed by relating the preliminary norm to sport and developing norms for just competitions. I conclude by formulating a complete fairness norm for sport competitions.

FAIRNESS: A PRELIMINARY NORM

In contemporary philosophical literature, and in particular in Rawls (1971: 11–17, 108–14, 342–50), fairness is understood as certain impartial procedures in dealing with questions of justice. As we have seen in Chapter 2, Rawls suggests the possibility that 'the original position', which is considered a paradigmatic example of fair circumstances, can serve as a source for deriving norms for the morally right in general. Ideas of the morally right include 'natural duties', such as norms for upholding justice, norms for non-injury and non-harm, and obligations such as that on fairness (Rawls 1971: 113ff.).

Initially, Rawls characterizes the formal conditions for choosing morally right actions as conditions that are fair. Then he discusses a norm for fairness that is established under these conditions. How is this to be understood?

Rawls seems to interpret fairness on two levels. First, fairness characterizes the conditions that have to be met in order to articulate and justify norms for the right. I have interpreted these conditions in terms of meta-norm I, which prescribes solutions that no one can reasonably reject as a basis for unforced, informed general agreement. Second, Rawls understands fairness as a more specific norm:

> when a number of persons engage in a mutually advantageous cooperative venture according to certain rules and thus voluntarily restrict their liberty, those who have submitted to these restrictions have a right to a similar acquiescence on the part of those who have benefited from their submission.
>
> (Rawls 1971: 343)

In short, it is wrong to benefit from the cooperation of others without doing one's fair share. According to Rawls, fairness constitutes the first obligation that arises from voluntary participation in rule-governed practices.

This interpretation of fairness has a non-consequentialist basis. Its origin is a Kantian idea of respect for persons as moral agents with the potential for making voluntary choices based on reason. However, the obligation of fairness does not arise unconditionally. The first condition to be met is that we are voluntarily engaged. This means that we have chosen participation over non-participation without external force of any kind. Moreover, there are general moral norms or 'natural duties' that are valid for all human inter-action. One of these is to uphold justice. If goods and burdens are distributed in arbitrary or autocratic ways, there is no clear definition of what is our fair share and no clear idea of what each of us should contribute in, or receive from, our cooperation. An unjust practice does not take seriously the idea of persons as moral agents. The very idea of fairness is undermined.

Can we now formulate a fairness norm for sport competitions? Rawls (1971: 113) explicitly mentions games to illustrate the fairness idea: 'We acquire obligations by promising and by tacit understandings, and even when we join a game, namely, the obligation to play by the rules and to be a good sport.' In Chapter 1, I construed the idea of voluntary choice of engaging in sport as being based on intentional goals of various kinds. Goal realization depends upon the cooperation of the other competitors. All, or at least most, of the competitors must keep the shared ethos of the practice if the practice is to be realized at all. Thus it seems intuitively right to give other competitors the same possibilities for intentional goal realization that they give us through their cooperation. We can formulate a preliminary fairness norm as follows:[1]

1 Parties voluntarily engaged in sport competitions ought to act in accordance with the shared ethos of the competitions if this ethos is just.

The parts of the preliminary fairness norm 1 that deal with voluntary engagement and 'a shared ethos' should be easy to understand from what was said in Chapter 1 and Chapter 2. But the third requirement of justice has not been specified. Precisely when is a sport competition just?

FORMAL, DISTRIBUTIVE AND PROCEDURAL JUSTICE

I turn now to the general interpretation of justice given in norm III:

> III Relevantly equal cases ought to be treated equally, cases that are relevantly unequal can be treated unequally, and unequal treatment ought to stand in reasonable accordance to the actual inequality between cases.

Norm III is formal and merely provides a framework for the elaboration of distributive justice. Local distributive norms vary greatly (Walzer 1983; Elster 1992). Substantive criteria of what is to be considered equal, and what is to be considered relevant inequalities that qualify for unequal treatment, have to be formulated with reference to the various goals of each particular practice or institution.

Let us take some examples.[2] Imagine that a certain amount of money is to be distributed among a number of people. We could choose a perfect egalitarian norm: each person gets exactly the same amount of money. We could distribute the money meritocratically, according to each person's objective performance: for example, as a reward for a record set in a competition. A third alternative would be to distribute the money based on effort. The athletes who demonstrate the most willingness to do their best are rewarded independently of objective results. Fourth, goods and burdens could be distributed according to need, to position in a particular group or society, or to legal right (as in the European Middle Ages, when one-tenth of all income was supposed to go to the church). In real life we often find combinations of such norms.

Distributive justice norms constitute ideal schemes of distribution. Such schemes require procedures to carry them out. Like Rawls (1971: 85–6), we can differentiate between perfect, imperfect, and pure procedural justice.

Perfect procedural justice is characterized by a procedure which guarantees that a given distributive norm is realized to its full extent, without exceptions. Rawls' (1971: 85) example concerns a number of people who are to divide a cake in a fair manner. Suppose they all have an equally strong desire for the cake. The solution, then, is to have one of them divide the cake and let that person take the last piece, the others choosing their piece before him. The best strategy for that person would be to cut the cake in equal pieces.

Imperfect procedural justice has the characteristic that although there is an independent criterion for the outcome, there is no established procedure that

Formal norm for justice	Local norms for distributive justice	Procedures
	Egalitarian Meritocratic According to effort According to need According to position or legal entitlement Combinations of the above norms	Perfect Imperfect
	Pure procedural justice	

Figure 3 Overview of norms and procedures of justice

can guarantee it. The Norwegian progressive taxation system is a good example. The intention is that each person or household pays according to ability. Those with the largest resources pay the most, those with the least pay the least. Realizing this ideal in practice, however, is extremely difficult. To find any exact measure of what people really need, and how much they ought to contribute to the community are both problematic. No one would maintain that the Norwegian procedures for collecting tax are perfect.

Pure procedural justice is characterized by the fact that there is no independent criterion or no distributive norm to define a just distribution. The procedure itself guarantees a just outcome. The paradigmatic case is a lottery. If the participants are voluntarily engaged, if they all know and accept that goods are to be distributed by lots chosen at random, and if the choosing of lots is conducted in a fair way, the outcome will be just regardless of who wins the prize.

Reading Figure 3 from left to right indicates the sequence for what follows. The general formal norm for justice, norm III, is the point of departure. By adding information I seek to formulate particular local norms of justice for the case of sport. We know of the social structure and the various goals relevant to sport, we know of the history of sport and its role in society, the various kinds of ethos that can be found among competitors, and so on. So now I shall seek solutions that can satisfy the requirement set by meta-norm I.

SPORT COMPETITIONS AS EXPERIMENTS

The structural goal of sport competitions is to measure, compare and rank two or more participants according to athletic performance. In a sense, competitions represent the pursuit of a particular kind of knowledge. In Fraleigh's (1984: 41) terminology, competing is a search for knowledge of '... the relative abilities of the participants to move mass in space and time within the confines prescribed by an agreed-upon set of rules'. This idea inspires an analogy which, although it has its limitations (that we take part in sport with various intentional goals, of which the quest for knowledge is just one), can help focus my discussion of justice.

Imagine that sport competitions are scientific experiments in which we want to measure, compare and rank participants based on the 'variable' of athletic performance. The first part of norm III prescribes that relevantly equal cases ought to be treated equally. In order to make our performance evaluations as precise as possible, we must insist on reliability. In the terminology of scientific methodology, reliability concerns how the measurements are carried out; it requires, among other things, a certain intra-subjectivity and inter-subjectivity (Galtung 1969: 28–9). Requirements of intra-subjectivity are designed to ensure that repeated observations of the same responses by the same observer yield the same data. Requirements of inter-subjectivity imply that repeated observations of the same responses by different observers yield the same data. According to my analogy, we suppose that we are seeking similar 'objective' evaluations in sport competitions.

The second part of norm III allows for unequal treatment based on relevant inequalities. Discussions of equality bring us closer to a more precise articulation of what is the relevant inequality in sport: athletic performance. This, then, becomes the dependent variable in our experiments. The concern for evaluating relevant inequalities in performance mirrors the concern for validity in the experiment: 'Data shall be obtained of such a kind and in such a way that legitimate inferences can be made from the manifest level to the latent level' (Galtung 1969: 29). We must measure only that which is relevant to our interests: manifest actions in a competition that count as the 'athletic performance' that represents the latent level. Consequently, we must eliminate and/or compensate for non-relevant factors or 'sources of error'. Such elimination and/or compensation procedures are what discussions of equality in sport are all about.

Finally, the last part of norm III prescribes a reasonable accord between unequal treatment and actual inequality. The criterion for unequal treatment is inequality in athletic performance. Typically, in sport we ask questions about who is the faster, stronger, has greater endurance, or is technically and tactically the most-skilled competitor. We treat competitors unequally by distributing unequally what we may call competitive advantage, such as rankings, points, goals, and the like. Rankings, points and goals become the operationalizations of the dependent variable 'athletic performance'. The demand for reasonable accordance is analogous to concerns for reliability and validity in the experiment. Measurements and distribution in terms of advantages of various kinds should reflect accurately the actual inequalities in performance.

Generally, then, we can say that if 'the experiment' to measure, compare and rank two or more competitors according to athletic performance satisfies requirements of reliability and validity, it will also satisfy requirements of justice. The measuring, comparing and ranking are solely based on, and are in a reasonable accord with, the actual inequalities in question. Against this background, let us now move on to examine the implications of the justice norm III in sport.

EQUALITY

The first part of the formal justice norm III is as follows:

III.1 Relevantly equal cases ought to be treated equally.

What should be equal in sport competitions? As we have seen in Chapter 1, the distributive norm for competitions is meritocratic. Individuals are rewarded according to relatively precise definitions of athletic performance. Still, norms of equality are also important. If we are to measure the relevant inequalities in performance, we must standardize some conditions. Our experiment must be controlled in order to yield the relevant knowledge, that is, in order to be valid. At the start of and during the process of competing, non-relevant inequalities should be eliminated. Elimination is not always practically possible. For instance, complete equality in climatic conditions in outdoor sport is a utopian ideal. The task, then, is to compensate for what are considered non-relevant inequalities in the best way possible. We must strive to give all participants equal opportunity to perform.[3] Based on III.1 we can say:

III.1.1 All competitors ought to be given equal opportunity to perform through eliminating or compensating for non-relevant inequalities.

Equal opportunity is a necessary condition for measuring inequalities in performance. The history of the norm is as old as sport itself. In chariot racing in ancient Greece, for example, some chariots were given a flying start if they had the longer lane turning the first corner (McIntosh 1979: 7–8). The development of English sport in the eighteenth and nineteenth centuries showed, among other things, increasingly advanced standardization techniques. In running, there was great concern about equivalent surfaces and tracks, at official arenas and for accurate measurement of distances. New technology such as the stopwatch improved accuracy. In ball games such as football, rules were elaborated in detail and codified, and among them were strict specification of the number of players on each team and for the changing of sides, and so on (Mandell 1984: 132 ff.). Indeed, Guttmann (1978) lists standardization as one of the defining marks of modern sport.

Today, norms to secure equal opportunity are many and detailed. I shall first look at how norm III.1.1 for equal opportunity should be applied to regulate external conditions at the start of and during competitions, and then examine inequalities in person-dependent matters and in access to resources.

Equality in initial external conditions

By 'external conditions' I mean primarily climatic conditions during competitions, such as wind, sun and precipitation, and material conditions linked to the competitive arena, such as the surfaces of running tracks, football pitches and alpine skiing courses. But I shall also discuss competitors' subjective experiences of inequalities in external conditions where this is relevant.

The challenges of varying external conditions differ to a certain extent with the way competitions are organized. I shall make an initial distinction between direct and indirect competitions (Patriksson 1982: 33–5; McPherson *et al.* 1989: 16). When participants compete at the same place and at the same time we may characterize the competition as direct. Examples are the 1500-metres race in track and field, the 400-metres freestyle in swimming, and competitions in different ball games. In indirect competitions, participants compete indi-vidually and partly or totally separated in time and space. The long jump, the high jump, the javelin, and alpine skiing are all organized as indirect competitions.

Direct competitions

In a scientific experiment we calibrate the measuring instruments before the test begins. In sport competitions initial conditions ought to be equal for all. In ball games, each half of the arena is to be of the same quality, and goals and baskets have identical dimensions. In swimming, all participants take off from identical starting platforms with identical height over the water. In the 100 metres race, all sprinters start from the same line using the same kind of starting block.

Nevertheless, initial external conditions are rarely if ever completely identical. In direct competitions, separate positions in space can cause certain inequalities. In the 100-metres race with eight runners, there are eight lanes of which the middle lanes are considered the better ones. Running in the middle makes it easier to see the positions of other competitors. In the last seconds before the start of a 10,000-metres race where no lanes are assigned, competitors manoeuvre in order to get a favourable position as soon as possible. In sailing, boats try to avoid the lee side of other boats and thereby not 'lose wind' at the start.

Is it possible, or even desirable, to compensate for such inequalities? Let us first look at a 100-metres race. In such a direct competition, starting in separate lanes is a physical necessity. The procedure most often chosen is based on meritocratic norms. The best lanes are allocated to the competitors who have performed best in the past. During events such as the Olympic Games and the World Championships in athletics, lane allocation is based on results from qualifying heats. Why do we choose this procedure? Why do we not allocate lane as in a lottery?

One good reason is this. Often 100-metre races are won by tenths or hundredths of a second. Marginal inequalities in conditions can be decisive for the outcome. If the presumed lesser performers gain an advantage from being assigned the presumed best lanes, they can end on top in the final ranking due to inequalities in external conditions and not due to superior performances. When the presumed best sprinters are assigned the presumed best lanes, time differences over the presumed lesser sprinters may increase, but the ordinal ranking of runners will gain validity. Moreover, because the middle lanes are almost identical in terms of equality of opportunity, the validity of the ranking within the two- to four-person group of presumed best sprinters increases as well.

Let us now look at the examples of the 10,000-metres and sailing. What can be done to increase equality of opportunity in initial external conditions for long-distance runners? One possibility is to reduce the number of runners, or to widen the track so there will be one lane per runner. Another possibility is to keep the current procedure and to say that initial positioning at the start is part of the relevant tactical skills of a runner. Not all runners go for the inner lane from the start. Sometimes the best runners prefer to start well back in the field and then work their way up during the race. If such positioning at the start is considered to be a tactical skill of the sport, inequalities here are parts of the relevant inequalities we want to evaluate. Similarly, sailing is an outdoor sport with constantly changing conditions and it is practically impossible to eliminate inequalities at the start. They are usually due to a combination of luck and skill (or the lack of it) and can be considered relevant inequalities. (Interestingly, in sports such as long-distance running and sailing, competitions actually seem to start before the official start signal is given.)

Let us now consider inequalities due to controllable conditions that work systematically in favour of one competitor and against another.

Another problem of equality of opportunity linked to initial external conditions is that competitions seldom take place on neutral ground for all competitors. During the 1984 Olympics in Los Angeles, fans at the stadium supported and cheered Carl Lewis, whereas his British rival Linford Christie received almost no support at all. At the 2000 Australian Open in tennis, the home favourite Lleyton Hewitt had thousands of supporters backing him, whereas opponents like the Russian Yevgeny Kafelnikov got limited support. Medal statistics from the Olympic Games illustrate how the host nations often do better than might be expected (Kamper and Mallon 1992). In ball games, it has been shown that the home team has a 60–40 home-court advantage (Weinberg and Gould 1999: 83). How can such inequalities be eliminated or compensated for?

The procedures chosen in most sports are designed to give all competitors the same number of competitions home and away. In track and field and in tennis, there are races and tournaments in different places during a season, and most performers get to compete on, or close to, their home ground at least once. In series and leagues for ball games, teams compete against each other twice and end up with the same number of matches home and away. Most of the time the inequalities that non-neutral ground bestows are shared equally between participants. But in events such as the Olympic Games, which are held every fourth year, this is impossible. Most athletes never have the chance to compete in the Games on their home ground. However, the very fact that possible advantages of home ground are so rare among athletes makes such inequalities within the range of the acceptable. Again, the solution is based on imperfect procedural justice.

The most problematic inequalities in initial conditions in direct competitions are probably climatic changes in outdoor sports, for these cannot be controlled and are hard or impossible to eliminate or compensate for. Classic examples are the football team that has the advantage of the wind at their backs, or the tennis player who has the disadvantage of the sun in her eyes. How are we to deal with these inequalities?

There is a radical solution. We could stop competing outdoors and so gain complete control over all conditions in laboratory-like indoor facilities. And indeed, to meet requirements for equality and to increase spectator comfort and TV coverage quality, there is a tendency for more sports, even traditional outdoor sports such as skiing and windsurfing, to move indoors. Here, however, the discussion moves to consider somewhat different matters than equality. Elsewhere (Loland 1996) I have argued on eco-philosophical grounds that in some sports, competing in close proximity to the nature environment, and interacting with the natural elements such as the sun, wind, rain, and snow, increases the complexity of skill tests and the joy of competition. This is not the place for a detailed discussion of these matters. I shall simply take it as an accepted premise that outdoor competitions have values that should not necessarily be overridden by a single-minded concern for equality. As long as the external conditions are not of an extreme kind, such that competitions turn into games of chance (strong wind and heavy rain, for instance), I suggest that outdoor sports are acceptable despite the problems with equality of opportunity. For my purposes here, I shall concentrate on seeking consequent norms and procedures that to the greatest possible extent secure equal opportunity to perform.

A more moderate solution, then, is that when we face more or less uncontrollable climatic inequalities, starting positions ought to be determined by drawing lots. In this way the possibility of competitors being affected unequally is distributed randomly. In football and tennis, starting positions (who plays in which half or serves first) are distributed by flipping a coin or spinning a racket. We operate by pure procedural justice, as in a lottery. Nonetheless, we should continuously look for new ways to enhance equality of opportunity. As we shall see in the next section, inequalities in initial conditions can be compensated for during the activity by changing positions. Football teams change sides in the second half, tennis players change sides after every other game. Norm III.1.1 ought to be realized in practice through the procedure that to the largest possible degree provides equal opportunity to perform.

Indirect competitions

What can be said about inequalities in initial external conditions, in indirect competitions, in which participants compete either totally or partially separated in time and space? How can norm III.1.1 for equal opportunity to perform be realized in such competitions?

There are more problems here than in the case of direct competitions. In outdoor competitions in particular, this is due to the fact that competitors start at different points in time. In jumping and throwing events in track and field, changing winds can have a significant effect on performance, and evaluations can become inaccurate. In downhill skiing, strong winds can make races both unfair and dangerous. Most outdoor sports have defined more or less precise limits of acceptability when it comes to such inequalities. Stormy weather may make track and field competitions and the downhill skiing impossible. In such conditions display of the relevant technical and tactical skills becomes unreliable, which again usually leads to cancellation or abandonment of the events.

Still, the rule-defined range of acceptability of inequalities in external conditions usually allows for a degree of inequality. Once in a while, marginal inequalities arise that are decisive for the outcome. A chance weak head wind can give the discus extra lift. A sudden gust at his back gives the long jumper the extra centimetre to win. As long as we accept the idea of outdoor sport, such inequalities are uncontrollable. They do not exert systematic influence on performance. We never know beforehand who will gain an advantage or a disadvantage, and we cannot use any particular distributive procedure to satisfy the norm for equal opportunity to perform. Therefore, the starting order is drawn by random lot. Again, we follow a principle of pure procedural justice like that of a lottery.

In other indirect competitions, we use mixed procedures. This is the case when we can partially control non-relevant inequalities. In alpine skiing, skiers start according to ranking points based on earlier performances, and only for the seeded group of presumed best skiers is the starting order drawn by lot. For this group, the course is still in a good condition, so the best skiers have more or less equal opportunity to finish high on the ranking list. In cross-country skiing, the presumed best athletes (the 'seeded' group) start last. They thereby have a tactical advantage in that they can choose to 'push ahead' based on the results of the skiers who started before them.

Why do we use mixed procedures here? Why do we allow the presumed best participants to start under the most favourable conditions? Are these the procedures that best compensate for non-relevant inequalities in initial conditions, for 'sources of error' in our 'scientific experiment'?

This problem is similar to the allocation of lanes in the 100-metre sprint. One justification of the adopted procedures is that if the presumed best competitors perform under less favourable conditions than the presumed weaker competitors, they may finish behind them due to non-relevant inequalities. The ranking based on the variable 'athletic performance' would lose validity. The counter-argument is that this starting procedure might increase the time differences between the presumed best skiers and those of presumed lesser performance potential. We thereby lose reliability at the interval level of measurement. But, as suggested above, this cost seems to be worth the increase in validity of the final ordinal ranking. In addition, as in the 100-metre sprint, time differences in sports such as cross-country skiing are often marginal, so we can expect an increase in validity of ranking within groups of competitors of similar performance potential.

Sport competitions are about the measurement, comparison, and ranking of the performances of all participants, both the presumed best and the presumed second and third best. The ideal towards which we ought to strive is norm III.1.1: equal opportunity to perform for all. Even if the mixed procedures sketched above are imperfect, under the circumstances they seem to be those that come closest to the ideal.[4]

Equality in external conditions during competitions

How can norm III.1.1 for equal opportunity be followed when it comes to external conditions during competitions?

We can start again with what I call direct competitions. Let us keep to the example of the 100-metre sprint. Suppose the starting gun has gone off and the sprinters are on their way to the finish line. Each competitor runs under nearly the same conditions. A sudden gust of wind or a low evening sun in the eyes will affect everyone alike. Except for the inequalities already discussed in the allocation of lanes and running on away-tracks versus home-tracks, it seems that the equality norm is realized.

However, in other sports equality problems may arise during the process of competing. For example, in motor-cross the leading motorcyclist churns up the track for those who follow. If the track is wet, mud and debris will spray up and hamper their vision. In a field with many runners in a cross-country race, a mud area will be tougher to pass for a runner who is far back in the field than for the leading group. Are we dealing here with non-relevant inequalities that ought to be eliminated or compensated for?

Hardly. It can be argued that for the motor-cross driver, athletic performance means mastering all conditions encountered on the track, while the cross-country runner gains a deserved advantage if she runs tactically well and quickly from the start. A degree of variation in external conditions represents relevant inequalities if the impact of the variation is connected to performance of relevant technical and tactical skills.

In other direct competitions, such as the martial arts, in boxing, and in the netball and ball games, competitors compete face to face. Here, inequalities in climatic conditions may arise, but such inequalities can be compensated for if competitors change position at regular intervals. Still, changing of positions can control such inequalities only in part. Uncontrollable inequalities in weather conditions may make it difficult. In football, a wind can blow up in the second half. The team with the wind at their backs gain an advantage. A low sun can be a handicap in a decisive game for a tennis player, but by the time the other player takes the same position it may have set. Obviously, changing position has the status only of imperfect procedural justice; we have a distributive norm III.1.1 that prescribes equal opportunity to perform, but no perfect procedure.

What can be said about the equality norm when it comes to external conditions during indirect competitions? Again, the fact that participants compete at different points in time leads to problems. Variation in wind, light, and temperature can lead to large inequalities. If variation in conditions is within the defined range of acceptability, pure procedural justice seems to be the best strategy. The starting line-up is drawn by random lot.

Finally, inequalities in external conditions may be due not only to weather changes and position. As with direct competitions, changes in the competitive arena itself can cause problems. But to a certain extent, such inequalities can be controlled. In alpine skiing, the course is soon worn down and easily becomes full of bumps and holes and must be repaired regularly. Fast and efficient skiing becomes increasingly more difficult. In speed skating, the ice wears down after each pair competes and must be watered at regular intervals. As a rule it is an advantage to compete in the first pair, or in a pair skating soon after watering.

As long as we accept outdoor competitions in close interaction with natural elements, inequalities of this kind can hardly be eliminated. But because they affect in negative ways the validity and reliability of our measurements, they ought to be compensated for. The ideal is identically prepared snow and ice surfaces for all. What are the procedures here that are the least unjust?

In sports such as skiing and speed skating, what usually happens is that first, and before the competitions take place, representatives from all affected parties meet and decide the intervals within which arena conditions should be repaired. Then the start list is drawn by random lot. In this way each competitor is exposed to the same risk of ending up in the worst-off position. In this case, we have in fact a situation close to Rawls' 'original position'. The decision-makers pursue their own interest behind 'a veil of ignorance', where they have all relevant information except knowledge of their own position in the upcoming contract. This situation ensures that decisions on repairing are taken impartially.

Two norms for equality in external conditions

I have argued that complete equality between competitors in external conditions is hard to realize in practice. Perfect procedural justice cannot be attained. But in order for our evaluations to be reliable and valid, norm III.1.1 of equal opportunity must be followed as closely as possible.

I can now specify some implications of norm III1.1. A first specification deals with uncontrollable inequalities, such as inequalities in external conditions in outdoor sport.

> III.1.1.1 Uncontrollable inequalities in external conditions ought to be distributed by the drawing of competitors' positions.

The second specification deals with inequalities that can be fully controlled, such as inequalities in the surface of different running lanes, or partly controlled, such as inequalities in snow conditions in an indirect skiing competition, or in wind conditions during a football match.

> III.1.1.2 Controllable inequalities in external conditions ought to be eliminated, while partly controllable inequalities in external conditions ought to be compensated for by mixed procedures that to the greatest possible extent realize equal opportunity to perform.

Equality in person-dependent matters

The structural goal of sport competitions is to measure, compare and rank competitors according to athletic performance. Athletic performance, the relevant inequality that is to be evaluated, depends upon a series of factors. Performances are the complex outcomes of genetic predispositions in inter-action with the environment, together with situational factors in the competition in question. In the section on inequality that follows, I shall discuss this in more detail. At this stage I am interested in person-dependent inequalities that ought to be regulated by norm III.1.1 for equal opportunity to perform.

Among the premises of my moral point of view is the idea that persons can choose voluntarily and that they can be held responsible for such choices. On the other hand, if we are talking of inequalities that are not due to voluntary choices, for instance certain outcomes of the natural genetic lottery that cannot be influenced by an individual, we cannot properly hold people responsible for them. This coheres with the regulative principle, agreed upon in most ethical theories, that it is unreasonable to treat persons unequally in essential matters based on inequalities that they cannot influence in any significant way (Rawls 1971: 74; Beauchamp 1991: 372). To what extent do inequalities in person-dependent matters exert an influence when it comes to the devel-opment of athletic performance, and to what extent is there a need for elimination or compensation here?

Body size: height and weight

Let us first take a look at one of the outcomes of the genetic lottery that we have limited scope to affect: the size of our bodies in respect of height and (to a lesser extent) weight. Height is genetically determined and can be manipulated scarcely if at all, if except by special medical treatment at an early age. Though we can influence our weight, body composition is based on genetic pre-dispositions and there are clear limits here. Weight is closely related to height (Bouchard *et al.* 1997: 149–72, 173–219). Should norm III.1.1 for equal opportunity to perform come into force when it comes to inequalities in body size? Are inequalities in body size relevant or non-relevant inequalities in sport competitions?

The critical question is to what extent this affects measurements of relevant inequalities in 'athletic performance'. In some sports, body size does not seem to be of decisive importance. Top football players may be between 160 and 210 centimetres tall, and so can good sprinters, long-distance runners, and tennis players. In a particular duel in the air the taller footballer has an advantage, and in a 60-metres sprint it might be advantageous for a sprinter to be smaller, but the complex skill requirements of these sports make body size less significant. The shorter footballer may have an advantage in being quicker in turning and more agile in feints. A bigger sprinter is stronger and may have more power to accelerate and keep up speed over 100 metres. Although inequalities in body size may once in a while be of significant influence in particular situations, they do not exert a systematic influence on performance. Such inequalities do not create genuine measurement problems in our 'experiment'. So we can accept the pure procedural justice that in this case is 'the natural lottery'.

In other sports, however, body size matters more. According to Norton and Olds (2000), elite athletes have generally become taller and heavier, and the rate of increase has outstripped the trend in the general population. In some sports, body size exerts both a significant and a systematic influence. Boxing is a good example. The constitutive rules of 'the noble art of self-defence' provide criteria for what counts as the relevant skills. Punches with a closed glove to the head and body are awarded points. Punches with an open glove or punches below the belt are forbidden. However, usually a boxer with a body weight of 100 kilograms will have an easy contest against a boxer of 70 kilograms, even though the smaller boxer may display superior technical and tactical skills. Boxing matches are decided if one boxer is rendered defenceless for at least ten seconds (or less according to the judgement of the referee), that is, who is hit with such an impact that he or she cannot continue the match. The bigger boxer has a longer reach and a heavier punch, and so could win by knockout even with relatively primitive skills.

Differences in body size thus cause large non-relevant inequalities in boxing. These inequalities weaken the validity of the evaluation of performance. We are no longer measuring what we set out to measure. How are we to tackle this problem? Of course, there is no one-to-one relationship between body size and performance. Once in a while small boxers defeat taller and heavier opponents. The challenge is to find the break points where inequalities in body size exert significant and systematic influence. In boxing, classes are distinguished at intervals of three to five kilos. Although classification is based more on experience and tradition than on critical statistical analysis, it seems that equality of opportunity is reasonably secured. Again, we end up with imperfect procedural justice.

We find similar solutions in other sports in which inequalities in body size have significant and systematic influence. Weight classes can be found in all combat sports: wrestling, fencing, judo, karate, and tae-kwon-do, and also in power sports such as weight lifting. But there are some sports where in-equalities in body size seem to be equally important for performance but where no attempt is made to eliminate or compensate for them. In basketball and volleyball, for example, height is of decisive importance. Studies of the relationship between body size and financial rewards in the American NBA underline the point. Larger players have longer careers and they earn more. On average, NBA players of the late 1990s made about $31,000 per kilogram body weight and $43,000 per centimetre height per year. However, the tallest NBA players made an additional $15,000 per year per additional kilogram body weight and an astonishing $45,000 per year with each additional centimetre height (Norton and Olds 2000). In the shot putt, mass velocity is decisive for the length of the throw. A 60 kilogram shot putter will have little chance if she competes against a 100 kilogram opponent, even if there are great differences in technique in favour of the lighter competitor. Obviously, the reason is that mass velocity is crucial for performance. In gymnastics, body size is of great significance as well, but in the opposite manner. Due to the need for rapid and well-coordinated body movements on the gymnastic apparatus, relatively low body height is preferred. A female competitor of 180 centimetres has little likelihood of competing successfully. Should we require elimination or compensation for inequalities in body size in these sports?

The only reason not to eliminate or compensate must be that such inequalities are considered relevant parts of the variable 'athletic performance'. Let us look systematically at the argument. Are inequalities in body size relevant inequalities in, say, basketball, volleyball and the shot putt? We now have general knowledge of the structural goal of sport, and of the variety of intentional goals held by participants. We have particular knowledge of the significance for performance of body height in basketball, volleyball, and gymnastics, and of body weight in the shot putt. If inequalities in body size were to be considered relevant, only these with body height and weight considerably above (for basketball and volleyball) or below (gymnastics) average would benefit from the solution. Many participants would be handicapped at the very outset by virtue of the rules. However, it is irrational for a group of people to agree on something that would disadvantage the majority of them. This solution cannot satisfy meta-norm I, for it cannot be reasonably accepted as a basis for unforced, informed, general agreement. We ought, therefore, to regard inequalities in body size as non-relevant inequalities.

How can this conclusion be implemented in practice? In basketball, volleyball and gymnastics, we could have leagues: for instance, two leagues for men with the critical limit on body height of 180 centimetres and two leagues for women with the critical limit of 170 centimetres. In addition we could make some changes in external conditions to ensure that players meet the same relative demands. Basket and net height and the gymnastic apparatus could be adjusted in relation to the critical height that defines the class. Similarly, in the shot putt we could have two classes for each sex, with average body weight among women and men as the differentiating criterion.

There are, of course, many possible objections to this. One objection could build on general scepticism to extensive classification systems. The world of sport is diverse. Some sports favour small, light athletes, while other sports are more or less designed for the tall. Each individual can choose what suits his or her talent and interests. There is no need for more classifications than already exist.

However, if we take the sceptic's view as a general norm, we ought not just to resist more classification, but abandon classification altogether in boxing, weightlifting, and other sports in which there is long traditions of it. The rationale for classes in these sports is just as strong (or, for the sceptic, just as weak) as for classes in basketball. Obviously this will make sports like boxing less complex. We would probably end up with just the heavyweight classes and their style of boxing. Moreover, the suggestion that each of us can choose a sport to which our body size is suited, does not necessarily correspond to the way our interests in and motivation for sport work. In spite of being short, a person can have a particular talent for the technical and tactical demands of volleyball. But in the current situation, brilliant technique and an excellent 'eye for the game' are hardly enough to enable the player to make the best teams. Being short might exclude her in favour of less skilled but taller competitors. Again, according to norm III.1.1 for equal opportunity to perform, this seems unjust.[5]

A second objection goes in another direction. If we are to classify for inequalities in person-dependent matters that exert significant and systematic influence on performance, we could end up classifying for almost anything: from inequalities in genetic pre-dispositions to inequalities in the social and cultural environments in which we are born and raised. I shall discuss this in more detail in the next section. Here, it suffices to say that this objection overlooks an important element in the supporting norm that prescribes the elimination of or compensation for inequalities that we cannot influence in any significant way. To a certain extent, individuals can influence the development of their strength, endurance and speed. We can train and improve. Limited natural talent from genetic predispositions can be compensated for by the strength of our own efforts. Moreover, even if the environment influences to a large extent what we become and what we can achieve, we may still hold on to the conception of persons as moral agents with the potential for unforced choices based on reason. Problematic social and cultural backgrounds can be fought against and overcome. Extended and detailed classification systems based on all kinds of individual differences, including those we can influence by own efforts, seem unreasonable.

Sex and age

In most sports, competitors are divided into classes according to sex. Men compete with men, and women compete with women. Moreover, along with the development of sport for children, youth and older persons, competitors have been classified according to age. Children and teenagers often compete in classes with one- or two-year intervals. From around the age of twenty to approximately thirty-five, competitors are expected to reach their peak performance period; in most sports there is no classification according to age here. After that age, competitors are placed in senior, masters or 'old boys' and 'old girls' classes with five- to ten-year intervals. What can be said of classifications of competitors according to sex and age? Are they in accordance with norm III.1.1 for equal opportunity to perform?

The rationale for sex and age classification is the assumption of genetically and biologically based human development over the span of life. Men, women, young, and old are considered unequal when it comes to predispositions for performance. Hence, if there were no classification, competitors would gain or lose based on inequalities that they cannot affect in any significant way, and for which they therefore should not be held responsible. Still, the classification systems of sport ought to be further examined to see if they can meet the requirements of norm III.1.1 for equal opportunity to perform.

Let us look at sex classifications first. Biological distinctions between females and males are not as clear-cut as many seem to believe. There are many grey areas. Some women who are defined psychologically and socially as men, are, genetically speaking, similar to women, and *vice versa*. Variations in pre-dispositions to develop athletic performance within each sex are greater than the mean variation between the sexes. Some of those who are classified as women no doubt have a stronger potential for developing performance than many men. The many traumatic histories from the International Olympic Committee's (IOC) sex testing regime demonstrate how classifications are often based on sexist prejudices – on ideas of some kind of merely assumed biological inferiority of women compared to men (Skirstad 2000; Schneider 2000).

What are the consequences of this? The radical solution suggested by (among others) Tännsjö (2000) and Tamburrini (2000: 104ff.) is to abandon sex classification altogether. Is such a 'gender equity programme' in sport well justified? Although it is true, as Tännsjö (2000) points out, that classes based on statistical differences can lead to injustice in individual cases, it might be the case that greater injustice will be done if sex classification were abandoned. The critical question is whether sex-determined inequalities really have significant and systematic influence on performance.

Again, there is a need to differentiate between sports. In the 100-metre sprint, in which speed is crucial, and in power lifting, where results depend to a large extent on explosive and maximum strength, biological and physiological inequalities between the sexes seem to exert significant and systematic in-fluence (Bouchard *et al.* 1997: 311ff.). Women experience disadvantages for which they cannot be held responsible. Sex classification in these sports seems reasonable. Other sports, such as football, golf, archery, and shooting, pose different requirements on their competitors. What Bompa (1994: 259ff.) calls the basic bio-motor abilities, such as speed, endurance and strength, are no more the foundation of performance. Superior ability in one or a few of these areas is not enough to ensure success. What really count are technical and tactical skills. In football, players have to be able to control the ball and to move in relation to their teammates and opponents in ways that generate advantages. Top players such as Pele and Diego Maradona might have performed only at the average level when it came to endurance, but extraordinarily in the technical and tactical domains. In golf, technique and tactical choices are essential. Simon (1994: 20) cites the case of the female golfer Patty Sheehan, who had one of the best swings in the world and could no doubt have competed successfully with most elite male players. In shooting disciplines, fine-grained motor and mental skills are decisive factors. Tamburrini (2000: 104) describes an event at the 1992 Olympic Games in Barcelona, Spain, where the fourteen-year-old Chinese shooter Zhang Shan was the first woman ever to win an Olympic cross-sex competition. She set a new Olympic record in winning the skeet shooting. Due to the complexity of these sports and the less predominant role of basic bio-motor abilities, women can do just as well as men. Classification according to sex contradicts norm III.1.1 for equal opportunity to perform, is thus unjust and so ought to be abandoned in such sports.

Can we reason in similar ways when it comes to age? It is a physiological fact that, statistically, our potential for performing well according to absolute standards when it comes to bio-motor abilities such as strength, speed and flexibility, decreases after we reach the age of 35 (Bouchard *et al.* 1997: 311ff.). Classification seems justified. But again, statistics can become 'the tyranny of the average'. As between the sexes, there are great individual differences. Moreover, studies such as Conzelmann's (1998) demonstrate the general underestimation of performance potential among older persons. A 60-year-old cross-country skier may compete with and indeed beat a 20-year-old opponent. A 75-year-old runner may perform better than her 50-year-old competitor. The English football legend Stanley Matthews played professionally for 33 years, retiring at the age of 50. Still, there is reason to believe that when it comes to sports where basic bio-motor abilities have significant and systematic influence on performance, more competitors would suffer injustice if age classes were abandoned than if they were kept. The idea of 'old boys', 'old girls' and 'masters' classes seems justifiable. In sports such as golf, archery and shooting, on the other hand, classification according to age seems rather meaningless unless we are talking about people, above 70 years of age, say. As with inequalities between the sexes, low performances are probably due more to socio-cultural norms and values and limited possibilities for activity than to genetic and biological factors.

Children and adolescents constitute a somewhat different case in all sports. Maturation from newly born to old age is a process that involves development of all our dispositions – bio-motor, mental, social, and moral ones. Age dif-ferences cause large inequalities. For instance, Hoare (2000) has studied what he calls 'the relative age effect' in Australian basketball. There seems to be a skewed distribution in the birth dates of athletes selected in representative teams. Those born early in the year (January–March) are over-represented. At junior age, one year's difference in maturation can be of crucial importance. It seems as if younger participants have a greater tendency to drop out in spite of having potential for performance similar to their older counterparts. Classification according to age among children and adolescents is therefore seen as necessary, and moreover should be relatively fine-grained.

These tentative conclusions beg a series of questions concerning implementation. There is a need to examine further the premise that there are *de facto* significant and systematic inequalities when it comes to predispositions for developing certain bio-motor abilities between the sexes and among different age groups. Moreover, there is need to evaluate continuously what kinds of sport ought to have sex and age classes, and what kinds of sport ought not to. In these discussions, we are operating along a continuum. At one end we could have shooting, equestrian sports, archery, and sailing, in which only a degree of classification according to age among children and the elderly seems justifiable. At the other end, we could place the 100-metre sprint and power lifting, as sports where a systematic sex- and age-classification seems necessary because of the significance of bio-motor abilities for performance.

Two norms for equality in person-dependent matters

We can conclude this discussion of equality in person-dependent matters with the formulation of two norms. I started with a premise similar to the one expressed in norm III.1.1.3:

> III.1.1.3 Competitors ought to be differentiated in classes only in cases where inequalities in person-dependent matters that they cannot influence in any significant way and for which they cannot be held responsible have systematic and significant influence on athletic performance.

Based on the discussions of body size, sex and age, this can now be further specified:

> III.1.1.3.1 Where inequalities in body size, sex and age exert significant and systematic influence on athletic performance, such inequalities ought to be eliminated or compensated for by establishing reasonably standardized weight, height, sex, and age classes.

Access to resources

This final section of my discussion of equality widens the perspective. As noted above, athletic performance is a result of complex interaction between genetic predispositions and environmental influences from the moment of conception to the moment of performance. What are the consequences of norm III.1.1 for equal opportunity to perform when it comes to inequalities in environmental influences?

In general, we know that great inequalities exist among individuals and groups when it comes to access to material resources such as sports arenas and equipment, human resources such as coaches and psychological and medical support systems, and last but not least, the necessary economic resources to practice and compete in sport competitions. Let us examine these factors systematically, and start with inequalities in material resources.

In many sports, access to equipment and facilities is crucial. In tennis, skiing and other winter sports, specialized equipment and/or environment are the absolute necessities for performance at any level. Typically, elite tennis players come from the middle and upper socio-economic classes of the developed part of the world, in which such facilities are accessible. Skiing performance depends upon access to technology and facilities, as well as special climatic conditions. Some years ago, Sweden's alpine team was dominated by competitors from Tärnaby, a small region in northern Sweden with good, stable snow conditions and extensive alpine facilities. Norwegian bandy players (bandy is a team ball game played on ice skates, with a stick to hit a ball) all come from the central south-east region. Elsewhere in the country there are neither the facilities nor traditions of playing the game.

To the degree that performers have the possibility of unforced choice between alternatives, there is hardly any reason to eliminate or compensate for such inequalities. In sport competitions at a local level, we compete with people from within the same geographic area. We have relatively equal access to sport facilities, equal possibilities to participate in organized training, and so on. In general, we can say that most competitors are able to meet the economic burden that comes with training and competing. Most of us can afford to participate in fifth division football or amateur bicycle races. Access to resources is primarily a question of our own priorities – so inequalities here are not unjust.

At regional, national, and international levels of performance, however, inequalities in access to resources are distributed in other and more problematic ways. Almost twenty years ago, Heinilä (1982: 235–54) described what he calls 'the totalization process' of high-performance sport. Athletic performances are developed within large 'systems' of material, technological and scientific resources, including facilities and equipment, trainers, medical and administrative apparatus, exercise scientists, technologists, and so on. Given all this, the public admiration of the winning athlete or team appears to be based on false premises. We do not just measure, compare and rank competitors according to skills; rather, we are measuring the strength of whole systems. Interestingly, Heinilä (1988) talks about 'the hidden validity' of high-performance sport.

There seems to be empirical support for Heinilä's claims. Statistics for medal distribution at several Olympic Games show clearly how competitors from capitalist, competitive Western countries and former Eastern Bloc countries take most medals (Kamper and Mallon 1992). Indeed, the Soviet Union dominated the Games from its first entry in the summer Games in 1952 and the winter Games in 1956, up to the late 1980s, challenged only by the German Democratic Republic and the US (Riordan 1999: 57ff.).

Current development indicates that in some sports at least, state-sponsored sport programmes are becoming less significant. However, this does not necessarily mean that inequalities have decreased. Sport is heavily influenced by market forces operating in the international entertainment industries. The financial situation of the sport system to which an athlete belongs is becoming decisive for success. European football is a paradigmatic case. Successful teams such as Manchester United and Chelsea (England), Bayern München (Germany), Juventus and Milan (Italy), and Barcelona and Real Madrid (Spain), have immense economic resources and can buy the best players on the market. Teams with fewer resources cannot compete equally with the wealthy ones.

Should norm III.1.1 for equal opportunity regulate inequalities in access to resources in high-performance sport? Are such inequalities to be considered sources of error in our evaluation of athletic performance? Should they be eliminated or compensated for?

If inequalities in system strength are accepted as relevant, competitors from weaker sport systems will have a disadvantage in developing performance from the very outset. In the most resource-demanding sports such as skiing, sailing or motor racing, they will have no chance at all. At the same time, the system we belong to is not a matter of voluntary choice and is hard to influence by individual effort. So individuals cannot reasonably be held responsible for such inequalities. From a moral point of view, we can say that inequalities in access to resources in terms of system strength ought to be eliminated or compensated for.

This idea is by no means new. Its historical origins can be found in ideas of amateurism in English sport in the nineteenth century. 'Amateur' (from the Latin *amator*, 'lover' or 'friend', and *amare*, 'love') describes a person who loves a particular subject or practice, in this case sport. Based on that etymology, an 'amateur' can be understood as a person who takes part because of experiential values to do with the activity itself – the person has a love of sport for sport's own sake. External goals, such as prestige or money, are considered insignificant. In the twentieth century, the idea of amateurism has had its strongest expression in the ideology of the Olympic movement. The revision of the IOC's views on amateurism demonstrates how the idea has evolved over these years.

Originally all forms of 'professionalism', defined variously as income directly or indirectly tied to sport, as work within sport (for example as a coach or physical education teacher), as compensation for lost income from work, or as acceptance of advertising money, meant disqualification (Glader 1978: 129–68). However, along with the professionalization and commercialization of high-performance sport, the rules on amateurism gradually softened. The word 'amateur' itself disappeared from the Olympic Charter in 1974. In 1986, the IOC left it to the international sport federations to decide whether to allow professional athletes into Olympic competitions. In the 1988 Winter Games held in Calgary, Canada, professional ice hockey players took part. In the 1992 Barcelona Games, all rules against professionalism of athletes were in practice abandoned. The International Basketball Federation (FIBA) allowed the multi-millionaires of the American NBA to compete against teams from poor countries such as Angola, Puerto Rico and Lithuania, and to win gold medals without losing a single game.

Today, traditional rules on amateurism seem rigid, paternalistic and rather unrealistic. Their history demonstrates clearly that enforcement of rules that regulate athletes' lives outside the competitive context can be very difficult. Amateur rules were used in unjust, discriminatory ways and for political purposes by excluding competitors from the so-called working class (Glader 1978; Holt 1982; Guttmann 1992).

Currently, then, except for the ban on doping, there is almost no regulation of competitor preparation that is intended to eliminate or compensate for obvious inequalities. Are there other procedures than rules on amateurism and the like that could realize norm III.1.1 for equal opportunity to perform to a higher degree?

One alternative might be to regulate the competitive situation itself in a way that eliminates or at least reduces to a minimum the influence of inequalities in system strength. Let us take a few examples.

In cross-country skiing, strong systems include ski-preparation experts and people who provide competitors with tactical assistance immediately before the race, and with information about position in relation to competitors during the race. Skiers in weaker systems have little or no support of this kind. In important championships, the US national track and field team have a large staff of trainers, doctors, physiotherapists, and masseurs to support them, whereas runners from Third World countries must operate pretty much by themselves. In order to compensate for these inequalities, one suggestion is that individual competitors or teams should to the largest possible degree be left to themselves immediately before and particularly during competitions. No external assistance should be allowed immediately before, and in particular during, a competition. Or, if we accept external assistance, it should be in such a way that all competitors can enjoy its benefits equally.

Steps should also be taken to reduce systematic and significant influence from inequality in technology. One solution is increased standardization. In some sports the standardization of equipment has a long tradition. In the shot putt, the javelin, and the discus and the hammer throw, the equipment is identical for all competitors. In fencing, there are strict equipment standards. In sailing, boats are divided into classes where there are quite precise specifications on hull and sail. But in other sports such as skiing, there is little or no effort to standardize. So, under certain conditions, the skier with the best skis and the best preparation team wins. Can these inequalities be eliminated or compensated for?

Traditionally, the skills of preparing and waxing skis have been considered part of the tactics of skiing and therefore as relevant in the evaluation of athletic performance. If we apply norm III.1.1, however, all competitors ought to have equal access to skis, preparation expertise and preparation material. Again, a solution to eliminate or compensate for possible inequalities would be standardization. But we should standardize with care, based on insight into the sport in question. In skiing for instance, it is of crucial importance to choose skis with the right cut, stiffness and length. These are choices connected to athletes' insights into their individual technical and tactical skills, and can be seen as part of the performance to be evaluated. Inequalities here ought not to be eliminated or compensated for. Inequalities in the quality of the ski base and its preparation, on the other hand, are the product of technologists and experts, and not of the athletes themselves. Since ski-base quality can be decisive in competitions, inequalities ought to be eliminated or compensated for.

In other words, all skiers in all disciplines ought to compete using skis with identical bases and identical preparation. Representatives from the skiing industry claim that to produce an identical base on two pairs of skis is impossible. Given today's high-tech ski production, this is hard to believe. However, if it is true, we ought to deal with it in line with the way we deal with uncontrollable inequalities in external conditions relevant to norm III.1.1.1. We should produce skis with as equal a base as possible, and then distribute them to skiers based on pure procedural justice via random lots.

It is worth mentioning another original procedure intended to secure equal opportunity in terms of equipment. This is found in the so-called 'public races' ('folkerace'), motorcar rallies with participation open to all. Large inequalities in car quality are eliminated through applying the following rule: after the race all participants can demand to buy the winner's car for a specified low sum of money. The consequence is that all participants tend to compete with cars that are not worth much more than any other. However, if a competitor prized the victory highly, he or she may choose to compete with an expensive car. The pay-off for the losers, or at least for one of them, is the chance to get a good car for practically nothing after the race. In addition, the problem for the winner is that the victory will not be considered a genuine one and will probably earn little social prestige as well. Usually, equality of opportunity is secured.

What, then, can be done about economic inequalities among competitors that have significant and systematic influence on performance, as in the case of European football? Again, standardization efforts could be of interest. For instance, football federations such as UEFA (Union des Associations Européennes de Football) and FIFA (Fédération Internationale de Football Associations) could define a maximum amount per year which teams are allowed to spend on buying new players. The skills and strategic thinking of the club would become more important than its financial situation. Should a team buy three players with a good level of performance or one star player? Is the strategy this year to invest in young talent or in regular, mature players? In a system with controlled resources, coaches and managers would have to prioritize. Moreover, the whole football culture would become more un-predictable and more dependent upon skills. More football clubs could have the chance to gain international success. Another positive side effect would be that the enormously increasing wages paid to individual players, considered problematic by most coaches and administrative leaders of the sport, would come under a degree of control.

I have sketched a few examples of the application of norm III.1.1 for equal opportunity to perform when it comes to external resources.[6] Let me now conclude this section by formulating a more general norm:

> III.1.1.4 Inequalities in access to resources that are not subject to voluntary choice, and that exert significant and systematic influence on athletic performance, ought to be eliminated or compensated for by regulation of the competitive situation, and/or by relevant standardization procedures.

INEQUALITY IN SPORT COMPETITIONS: ATHLETIC PERFORMANCE

In the preceding discussion of equality we moved closer to ideas of what should be considered the relevant inequality to be evaluated in sport competitions, or by analogy, what should be the 'dependent variable' in our 'scientific experiment'. I shall now set out in more detail what I contend is a morally justifiable interpretation of the very basis for the measurements, comparisons and rankings of competitors: 'athletic performance'.

I have construed sport as constituted by practices in which we interact based on shared norms for interpretation of the basic rules: an ethos. I discussed how the shared understanding of sport varies according to historical, social and cultural contexts. Sport is a 'social' and not a 'natural kind', that is, it is a cultural practice that is a more or less clear expression of human interests and goals. These interests and goals are of many kinds. I distinguished between the intentional goals of individuals, the structural goal of sport competitions, and their moral goal. My aim here is to develop an interpretation of the moral goal. More specifically, we can say that a moral interpretation of athletic performance is of key significance as it signals basic ideas of what sport competitions ought to be all about.

Let me start this discussion by turning to the second part of the general norm on formal justice that deals with inequality norm III, and formulate norm III.2:

> III.2 Cases that are relevantly unequal can be treated unequally.

In sport, the relevant inequality and the primary ground for unequal treatment is athletic performance. Inequalities in athletic performance give rise to unequal treatment in the distribution of competitive advantage. The fastest sprinter builds up a lead and has a shorter distance to the finish than the competitors. The football team scores a goal and so gains an advantage that might be decisive in the final ranking.

But advantages based on performance are not the only cause of inequalities. Sometimes competitors break the fairness norm 1 and violate the shared, just ethos, which may lead to unfair advantages. A sprinter who gets away with a false start gains an advantage without truly performing the relevant skills. The performance of a golf player who in an illegal way moves the ball to a better position cannot properly be compared with that of competitors who play fairly. Inequalities due to ethos violations are non-relevant inequalities and ought to be eliminated or compensated for. Below I shall discuss more closely how advantages in competitions can be distributed in just ways. At this stage, I shall concentrate on an interpretation of athletic performance. We can formulate norm III.2.1 as follows:

> III.2.1 In sport, unequal treatment ought to be based upon inequalities in athletic performance.

The rules of competitions specify which actions are allowed, which actions are forbidden, and how advantages and disadvantages are to be distributed. They provide a framework for the interpretation of athletic performance. Here, each sport is different. Each has its own sport-specific goal that distinguishes it from other sports. In the marathon, the runner who runs 42,195 metres over the agreed course and crosses the finishing line first is considered the best performer. In tennis, the winner is the one who in accordance with a shared, just ethos takes the most sets.

At the same time, as the very existence of the term 'athletic performance' indicates, ideas of performance in different sports seem to share some common ground. In daily conversation and in the mass media, there are endless discussions about who is the athlete of the year, who is the best athlete ever, what was the greatest sport performance of all time, and so on. In standard works on sports science, for instance in Martin *et al.* (1991: 24ff.), we can find more systematic and critical descriptions and explanations. Here, I first describe a common understanding of the basic elements of athletic performance and then examine four possible interpretations of it from a moral point of view. My aim is to suggest an interpretation that is in accordance with meta-norm I – an interpretation that cannot reasonably be rejected as a basis for unforced, informed general agreement. In the last part of this section, the relevance and action-guiding potential of my interpretation will be tested by applying it to one of the major moral dilemmas in contemporary competitive sport: the use of various bio-chemical substances and performance-enhancing techniques known as 'doping'.

Athletic performance: a description

The now-retired Norwegian long-distance runner Grete Waitz has become a paradigmatic example of a great performer in her sport. She had tremendous stamina. Mentally, she was strongly motivated and had among other things the long-distance runner's special ability to endure fatigue and pain. Overall, she was able to perform well in long-distance races both technically and tactically: she could pace herself superbly and consistently come up with strong finishes.

Similarly, the Canadian ice hockey player Wayne Gretzky is a legend in his sport. Gretzky's fast skating and skilled handling of the puck demonstrated advanced technical coordination. His tactical understanding of the game is considered pre-eminent. His moves and passes were often both surprising and effective in neutralizing competitors and scoring goals. He was able to concentrate and play at his best in important matches where stress and mental strain are at their maximum. And, like most good athletes, Gretzky was strongly motivated and able to train intensively and at a high standard.

What, more precisely, are the basic elements of athletic performance? On what factors are performances built? Athletes demonstrate a wide variety of human abilities and skills. Advanced performances can be seen as paradigms of human functioning at its most complex. According to Dreyfus and Dreyfus (1986: 30), performances at the expert level are best understood as non-analytic, creative and intuitive. It seems impossible to capture fully their open-ended holistic character. To be able critically to discuss different interpretations of athletic performance and to draw lines between morally acceptable and unacceptable ones, however, requires that some basic distinctions be drawn.

Athletic performances are the results of a high number of relevant genetic and non-genetic factors (Bouchard et al. 1997: 3ff., 384). In sport, genetic predispositions to develop good performance are often called 'talent'. Non-genetic factors may be referred to as 'environmental influences'. We are speaking now of influences from the very first nurturing and psycho-social stimuli, via influences from the general physical and socio-cultural environment, through to sport-specific influences from training, access to facilities, equipment, coaching, and other kinds of expertise.

In the earlier discussion of inequality in sport, I examined inequalities in environmental influences and argued that reliable and valid evaluations of performance depend upon all competitors being given equal opportunity to perform. I proceeded using the regulative principle that inequalities which significantly and systematically influence performance, but which individuals cannot affect in any significant way and for which they therefore cannot reasonably be held responsible, ought to be eliminated or compensated for. I developed norms to regulate inequalities in external conditions, in person-dependent matters such as body size, sex and age, and in system strength (strength of material resources, of finance, and of general and sport-specific expertise). What I am interested in now is a series of inequalities of relevance to athletic performance that can be compensated for, or strengthened, by individuals themselves.

Basically, there are two kinds of these inequalities. A first kind is linked to the more or less genetically based development and maturation of all human beings. I am speaking here of general abilities. A second kind is the result of learning by experience and of specific environmental stimuli, or what I shall refer to as 'skills'. Let us take a closer look at both kinds.[7]

Talent and the development of abilities

I have understood talent as genetic predispositions to develop performance. Abilities are genetically programmed to develop in all human beings. There are many ways of categorizing them (Schmidt 1991: 127ff.; Martin *et al.* 1991: 24ff.). In the present context, a rather simple general overview will suffice.

Athletic performance depends upon the development of what I have called bio-motor abilities (Bompa 1994: 259ff.). To be somewhat more specific, I am speaking of:

- strength: the force exerted by muscle groups during a single maximal muscular contraction;
- endurance: local muscular endurance and cardiovascular endurance;
- flexibility: suppleness of movement at a joint;
- speed: reaction time, frequency of movement per unit time, speed of travel over a given distance; and
- coordination: the ability rationally to solve movement problems, which in part depend upon coordination of the nervous processes in the central nervous system.

The successful exercise of bio-motor abilities includes, of course, the functioning of certain general mental abilities, such as those linked to:

- sensation: experiences associated with simple stimuli through the senses of vision, hearing, smell, taste, and various body senses;
- motivation: factors that energize behaviour and gives it direction and goals;
- emotion: strong mental states, usually involving high energy and excitement, that give rise to feelings and passions such as fear, anger, joy;
- cognition: perception, memory, reasoning, decision-making, problem solving; and
- personality characteristics: (distinctive patterns of thought, emotion and behaviour that define an individual's interaction with the environment, such as extraversion, neuroticism, sociability, and emotional stability.[8]

Abilities develop to a certain extent according to genetic programming in all 'normal' human beings. This genetic programming can be 'read' from the genome; the total set of genes in the nucleus of a cell. Genes are units of hereditary information with a fixed position (locus) on a chromosome. More particularly, they are codes for the production of various enzymes (catalysts of biochemical processes) and structural proteins (building blocks of cells and tissues) in the cells of all living organisms.

But even if the development of phenotypes (the manifestation of traits resulting from the expression of relevant genes and non-genetic influences) such as the bio-motor and mental abilities is genetically programmed in all human beings, the process is characterized by great diversity and variability (Bouchard *et al.* 1997: 384). The moment of conception represents the random realization of one of hundreds of millions of possible unions of sex cells. In addition, each possible union represents a particular arrangement of perhaps as many as one hundred thousand genes encoded by three billion chemical pairs of DNA. No wonder this is referred to as 'the natural lottery'. Furthermore, genes never operate alone or in isolation. At a very early stage of development, cells in complex organisms such as humans differentiate and specialize, for instance into muscle cells, cells in the brain and the nervous system, cells that build up the cardiovascular system, and so forth. Differentiation and specialization of cells results from complex interactions between genes and between genes and the environment. Hence, what I have called a genetic predisposition is impossible to observe in its pure form. Or rather, it exists in its pure form only at the moment of conception. Likewise, human conduct can never be understood as pure expressions of environmental influences, either. Although to varying degrees, human (and non-human) life is always an expression of genetic predispositions and environmental influences combined.

Now I can say more precisely what I mean by talent in sport. It is an individual's genetic predisposition to develop phenotypes of relevance to performance in the sport in question. The distribution of talent in the natural lottery is a random process. Moreover, we know that talent has significant and systematic influence on athletic performance, and that different sports require different talents. Without a well-adapted nervous system and a high percentage of fast twitch muscle fibres to develop speed, a sprinter will have problems succeeding at a top level. As Sir Roger Bannister (1997) has said, '... the faculty of speed is inborn'. Performance in sports with more complex technical and tactical requirements depends to a lesser degree on advantageous predispositions to develop one specialized bio-motor ability. A football player, for instance, might lack speed, but with excellent endurance and a good understanding of the game she can still hope to become a top performer.

I shall return to the question of whether inequalities in talent ought to be eliminated or compensated for in the discussion of various interpretations of athletic performance below. Let us now look at the various environmental influences.

Environmental influences and the development of skills

Talent and the active exercise of relevant abilities through training provide the basis for the development of skills. Skills can be defined as the ability to bring about an end result with maximum certainty and minimum expenditure of time and energy (Schmidt 1991: 11). Skills do not develop in all 'normal' human beings as a result of genetic programming but rather depend upon specific environmental influences. Abilities provide the raw material for skill development. Skills are necessary to deal with the tasks and challenges of sport in an efficient way. In a simplified and reductionist version, the process goes something like this. Through sensation and cognition we perceive and interpret a specific task in a sport competition, and act based on previous experience, learning and memory. Using bio-motor abilities such as strength, flexibility and coordination, we perform motor actions of various kinds to carry out the tasks. In this sense, all kinds of performance are skill performances (Arnold 1986: 13–27; Schmidt 1991: 1ff.).

Skills are of general and specific kinds. Examples of what I shall call general motor skills are walking and running, and of general cognitive skills the mastery of language or the understanding of social norms and conventions. Specific skills are related to particular practices, such as sport, where they are incorporated in a framework of rules, or, to use my terminology, in the shared ethos of the sport in question. In sport, we usually distinguish between technical (motor) and tactical (cognitive) skills. A norm for technical skill in tennis might be 'look at the ball when you hit it', while a norm for tactical skill in football might be 'when the opposing team is superior, play defensively and concentrate on break-downs and quick counter attacks'.

Good sport technique can be defined as the execution of adequate and efficient movement patterns to perform defined tasks in particular sport situations (Martin *et al.* 1991: 45). A volleyball player with good technique controls the hits as defined in the rules (such as set, pass and dig) and tends to choose the optimal move in most situations that occur during games. Technique refers to the carrying out of movement patterns. Good tactical skill involves choosing the right plan of action from among many alternatives to optimize performance (Martin *et al.* 1991: 229). The volleyball team that in an attack feints high lay-ups on the sides and proceeds with a short lay-up down the middle, demonstrates skill in choosing an effective tactical solution.

In a way, the distinction between technical and tactical skills is artificial. In most sports, good technique and good tactics go together. The experienced table tennis player 'reads' the opponent's shot before it is made. The good boxer more or less intuitively anticipates the upper-cut and moves away just in time. We can say with Bompa (1994: 61) that 'tactics are a function of an athlete's technique'. Still, for our purposes we can simplify somewhat and say that tactics deal with (cognitive) choice among alternative solutions (often defined in terms of movement patterns) in the solving of sport-specific problems.

I choose to include among tactical skills sport-specific mental skills. Sport psychologists have developed a series of methods to enhance performance (Weinberg and Gould 1999: 221–350). For example, there are methods for somatic stress management (self-directed relaxation and biofeedback) and for cognitive stress management (imagery techniques, goal setting). Moreover, certain mental skills and the cultivation of certain ways of sensing and perceiving have specialized application in particular sport contexts. Stress management in a tennis match, in which there is a high number of 'time outs' between points and games, probably takes on a different character than stress management in a game of football. Without specialized mental skills, learned either through experience or through active intervention by experts, competitors will not be able to execute their technical skills in a successful way.

Athletic performance – a summary

I can now sum up. An athletic performance is a performance within the framework of a relevant ethos of a sport and is based upon:

- talent, that is, genetic pre-dispositions for the development of the relevant abilities and skills; and
- the actual realization of talent through development of the relevant abilities and learning of the relevant skills.

The critical question is whether this description can be justified from a moral point of view.

Athletic performance from a moral point of view

There are significant individual inequalities in genetic predispositions to develop relevant sport skills. I am speaking now of inequalities in talent that are the products of the natural lottery. Realization of talent through training and learning skills, on the other hand, is based on environmental influences. We are exposed to, and choose, different influences. Logically, as shown in Figure 4, athletic performance can be interpreted in four possible ways.

What is the right choice of interpretation of athletic performance from a moral point of view?

Interpretation	Inequalities in talent	Inequalities in environmental influences
1	Not relevant	Not relevant
2	Relevant	Not relevant
3	Not relevant	Relevant
4	Relevant	Relevant

Figure 4 Four interpretations of athletic performance

Interpretation 1: inequalities in talent and environmental influences are not relevant

This is an absolute egalitarian interpretation and requires complete equality of performance potential between competitors. To reach absolute egalitarianism, we would have to eliminate or compensate for inequalities in both talent and environmental influences. Is this possible? If so, what would competitions then look like?

Genetically, completely identical individuals (the possibility of cloning techniques not withstanding) are not a real possibility. Cell differentiation and specialization will always differ slightly – this is the case even with mono-zygotic twins. In the near future, however, we might come quite close. According to Bouchard *et al.* (1997: 369), control over genetic predispositions to develop certain basic abilities such as endurance and strength is only ten to fifteen years away. Somatic cell alteration or germ-line alteration in order to enhance athletic performance is possible even today.

When it comes to environmental influences, complete equality is not possible either. We are necessarily spatio-temporally unique and logically cannot relate to our environment in completely identical ways. Literally speaking, one person's perspective of the world will never be identical to another's. Still, through advances in behavioural science and technology, situations with almost full control over environmental influences on individuals will probably come quite close to realization. I am speaking here of advanced psychological and social manipulation, for instance through hypnosis and 'brainwashing'. In any case, the point is that the egalitarian interpretation considers identical athletes to be the ideal toward which we ought to strive, and contemplating its full realization is therefore a relevant thought experiment.

What would be the consequences for sport competitions of genetically identical competitors who have been exposed to identical environmental stimuli? Inequalities in performance, if any, will be chancy and coincidental. A gust of wind that enables the javelin to glide more smoothly through the air could decide the final ranking in javelin competitions. In football games between teams made up of genetically the same players who have been taught exactly the same technical and tactical skills, the decision could turn on a fortuitous kick of the ball that ends in a goal. Sport competitions would become games of chance and luck.

I have described the structural goal of sport competitions as a shared understanding among the parties engaged of how to measure, compare and rank competitors according to performance of athletic skills. Com-petitions are meritocratic practices. Pure games of chance cannot realize this goal. Therefore, the consequences of the egalitarian Interpretation 1, in which both talent and personal influence are held identical, would be that sport competitions could no longer take place. In sport, Interpretation 1 does not really make sense.

Interpretation 2: inequalities in talent are relevant, inequalities in influence are not relevant

In Interpretation 2, inequalities in talent are considered relevant whereas inequalities in environmental influences are eliminated or compensated for. This interpretation has a flavour of the traditional amateur ideology: what counts is 'natural grace' and the gift of talent, not the hard work of the instrumental training process of talent development.

Consequently, the outcome of competitions is left to the natural lottery to determine. Competitors who possess the 'right' talent also have the potential for the best athletic performance. The sprinter with the best-adapted nerve-muscle function, with the highest amount of fast twitch muscle fibres, and with the strongest predispositions to develop relevant mental abilities, will win the 100-metres. The swimmer with the strongest predispositions to develop her cardiovascular system and muscle endurance, and with the best body composition and shape, will be victorious in her sport. There would be no possibility of compensating for limited talent by training more than one's competitors.

In this interpretation, merit in the sense of being rewarded according to one's own willed efforts would be of no importance, for we imagine that everyone is exposed to identical environmental influence. When natural talent is the only decisive factor, competitions violates the regulative principle propounded in the discussion of equality, namely the principle of not treating people unequally based upon inequalities that they cannot influence and for which they cannot therefore be held responsible. All inequalities in performance would have the same basis as inequalities in body size, sex, and age discussed in the previous section. Moreover, the outcome of all future competitions would be decided by the natural lottery and the random pro-cesses of cell differentiation and specialization. As with Interpretation 1, Interpretation 2 turns sport into games of chance and so is similarly unreasonable.

Interpretation 3: inequalities in talent are not relevant, inequalities in influence are relevant

In Interpretation 3, competitors have identical talent but differ when it comes to environmental influences. All competitors have the genetic predispositions to perform identically. However, they have different personal backgrounds; they come from different economic and socio-cultural systems, from sport systems of different strength, and they have trained differently in terms of both quantity and quality. So inequalities in performance will be the direct result of inequalities in environmental influences.

If, as suggested by the equality norms, we eliminate or compensate for inequalities for which individuals cannot be held responsible, this interpretation would envisage an almost purely meritocratic scenario. Winners of 100-metre sprints and swimming competitions are simply those who have trained most effectively. Competitors are rewarded according to their own efforts only. Chance and luck are vitally eliminated. The structural goal of competitions could be realized accurately. Competitions would come close to the ideal scientific experiment. There would be almost perfect validity in measurements. If we accept the premise that meritocratic distribution of advantage is the primary aim in sport, Interpretation 3 seems to provide the optimal solution.

Still, intuitively this interpretation is problematic. Is it reasonable to accept genetic manipulation in order to realize complete equality of sporting talent? Are concerns for perfect meritocratic procedures of justice the only ones that matter here?

Later we shall see that in sport, chance and luck do not necessarily exert unjust influence. In the next section on unequal treatment I shall argue that chance and luck have a particular role to play in these practices. Here, however, I shall concentrate on the more general moral problems of Interpretation 3. In Chapter 2, I talked not just of the structural goal of competitions, but also of individuals' intentional goals and of moral goals. Intentional goals are expressions of individuals' subjective reasons for engaging in sport. The moral goals concern the meaning and value of sport in the broader framework of human life. I have argued from the premise that athletes are moral agents with the potential to make unforced, reasoned choices for which they can be held responsible. Without such a premise, we can talk neither of intentional nor of moral goals of sport. The idea of a pure meritocracy obtained through genetic manipulation, or the idea of manipulation of talent and/or environ-mental influences countenanced by Interpretations 1 and 2, seem to contradict this premise. Let me elaborate.

New insights into the human genome and how it interacts with environmental influences are, of course, of significant value. Munthe (2000) emphasizes correctly that innovations here should not be met with moral panic. For instance, rapidly evolving medical technology has great potential for increasing human health and welfare in general and the joy of sport in particular. Still, it is just as obvious that new technologies can be used destructively. Experience tells us how sport systems are willing to use almost any means to gain prestige and profit. Hoberman's (1992) detailed history of performance-enhancing substances and methods has the telling title *Mortal Engines – The Science of Performance and the Dehumanization of Sport*.

The problem that arises in Interpretations 1, 2, and 3, then, is that the athletes' status as moral agents is neglected. Athletes easily become guinea pigs of their own or their support system's misguided ambitions and acting as the means in service of powerful performance machineries. Building on the premise of athletes as moral agents, we have been concerned with not treating them unequally on the basis of inequalities for which they cannot reasonably be held responsible. In Interpretations 1, 2, and 3, there are no restrictions on what aspects of a person can be manipulated and controlled. Sprinters and swimmers can be genetically, mentally and socially 'designed' for peak performances by external forces and support systems. In such context, terms like 'voluntary choice' and 'responsibility for one's own actions' become empty phrases. The constitutive norm of the moral point of view developed here, meta-norm I, which prescribes choices that no one can reasonably reject as a basis for unforced, informed general agreement, becomes meaningless. So we can see that Interpretations 1, 2, and 3 of 'athletic performance' are morally problematic at the fundamental level of moral premises. This brings us to Interpretation 4.

Interpretation 4: both inequalities in talent and environmental influences are relevant

In Interpretation 4, we accept inequalities both in talent and in environmental influences. Our talents are the results of the natural lottery, and our possibilities to realize them are determined to a certain degree by our own efforts and to a certain degree by chance and luck. Performance is a result of both pure procedural and meritocratic justice.

Neither of these distribution processes is unjust as such. However, as we have seen in the discussion of equality, their consequences can be. I take it for granted here that unjust consequences are regulated by the equality norms developed above. If the equality norms are kept, there are always ways of compensating for unfortunate aspects of life by one's own efforts and there are always ways of developing and cultivating fortunate aspects even more. Athletes talented in terms of bio-motor abilities might lack mental discipline. Athletes moderately talented in terms of bio-motor abilities can compensate by strong mental qualities and learned skills. Lack of scientific and technological support can be compensated for by standardization procedures in the competitions, and by enthusiastic human support in training and preparation.

Within the framework of the equality norms, then, knowledge of and insights into the genetic and environmental factors underlying performance are not seen as means to control or manipulate individuals, but rather as possibilities to cultivate such variation and celebrate the diversity of persons as moral agents. In Chapter 1, I sympathized with the Aristotelian idea of human life as a life with a *telos*. This is a life in which our voluntary choices realize human flourishing and the fulfilment of our potential. This interpretation should not be understood in essentialist terms, as the idea that one particular way of life is better than all others, but more in line with Rawls' process-oriented 'Aristotelian principle':

> Other things equal, human beings enjoy the exercise of their realized capacities (their innate or trained abilities), and this enjoyment increases the more the capacity is realized, or the greater its complexity.
>
> Rawls (1971: 426)

The Aristotelian principle represents a valuing of, and respect for, individual differences.[9]

We now see that the question of choice between various interpretations of athletic performance comes down to a choice between basic understandings of what a human being is all about, and between fundamental moral outlooks. It is, in fact, a choice of ethical axioms. By contrasting with Interpretations 1, 2, and 3, the mixed Interpretation 4 opens the way for the flourishing of persons construed moral agents with the potential of reason and voluntary choice. My argument here, then, is that Interpretation 4 is the only interpretation that, in accordance with meta-norm I, cannot reasonably be rejected 'as a basis for unforced, informed general agreement'. Therefore, Interpretation 4 is the obvious choice given the moral point of view developed here.[10]

The duty not to inflict unnecessary harm

There is one more condition in the interpretation of 'athletic performance' that should be discussed. Sport competitions ought to be practised within a framework of what Rawls (1971: 108ff.) calls general 'natural duties' – norms considered valid for all human practices. One basic natural duty for individuals is to uphold justice as discussed in this part of this book. In addition, we need to complement this natural duty with another: not exposing others or oneself to unnecessary harm (the principle of *primum non nocere*). What are the consequences of this basic norm in sport?

In football, there are rules against tackles from behind and high kicks ('studs are shown') due to the risk of injuries. European handball has rules against jump shots with high knee lifts that can hurt opponents. To avoid face injuries in ice hockey, the stick has to be kept on the ice. Similarly, in all kinds of sport training and preparation, a primary concern is to avoid injuries and harm.

This may all sound obvious and simple but on second thoughts it emerges as a complex matter. Many sports involve risk of harm of various kinds. Some sports, such as parachuting and downhill skiing, involve the risk of death. Training regimes, at least at high levels of performance, search for a delicate balance between the catabolic and the anabolic processes of the body. Athletes who come out on the wrong side easily end up with injuries and problems of over-training. In comparison with competitive sport, light physical exercise represents a far less risky alternative. Does competitive sport as such represent a potential unnecessary harm that ought to be avoided?

Sport is not a biological necessity. We do not have to practice sport to survive. Sport arises primarily because we choose to engage in it in order to realize various intentional goals. Obviously, then, to most participants, the values of sport seem to outweigh its potential risks.

This does not mean that people's weighing of potential risks necessarily stands scrutiny from an objective, statistical point of view. For example, there are sports such as base-jumping in which the risk of serious injuries or even death seems unreasonably high. I cannot engage in a detailed assessment of what are acceptable and non-acceptable rules of harm here. But it can be said that in most sports, the risk of harm and injury is limited. Although the norm of not exposing oneself or others to unnecessary harm ought to promote a constant search for safer practice, some risk of injury and harm generally can be considered a necessary cost for intentional goals linked to sport to be realized at all.

There is another issue, that often arises in discussions of injuries and harm in sport. A number of sports involve severe body contact between competitors that may hurt, injure, and even kill. And there are sports in which the intentional infliction of harm is allowed and in some cases is rewarded. How can we deal with this from our moral point of view?

Good answers depend upon being able to make morally relevant distinctions, for instance as suggested by Parry (1998). I can sketch some of them here. Rugby, American football, and ice hockey involve severe body contact, but such contact is heavily regulated and is not really important to the techniques and tactics of the sports. The role played by intentionally inflicting bodily harm on competitors is marginal – so these sports are morally justifiable. Combat sports, on the other hand, such as professional boxing, full contact karate and kickboxing, have as their very essence the incapacitation of an opponent by intentionally punching or kicking him or her in the most effective way possible. Combat sports are therefore controversial. In the long-standing discussion of boxing, some argue on ethical considerations that it should be banned. The intentional inflicting of harm cannot be defended from a moral point of view, especially not from non-consequentialist perspectives that demand respect for persons as moral agents (Simon 1991: 54–64; Davies 1993–94). Others regard the call for such a ban as a prejudiced misunder-standing of the values of boxing and as a hegemonic condemning of the interests of the weaker parties, namely the boxers themselves (Burke 1998). The critical question would seem to be: are what some see as the virtues of boxing, such as courage, ability to endure pain and never to give in, depen-dent upon full contact punches? Or could the same values be realized with less risky conduct? Is the potential infliction of harm 'necessary' or 'unnecessary'?

A norm for the interpretation of athletic performance

Answers to these questions belong in a discussion of the application of an interpretation of athletic performance that cannot be pursued here. Let us sum up this discussion. From a moral point of view, the mixed Interpretation 4 is the right choice. The premise is that athletic performance is to be understood within the framework of the equality norms. Accordingly, we can say:

III.2.1.1 In sport, unequal treatment ought to be based upon inequalities in performance within the framework of the relevant ethos that are:

- based on talent, that is, genetic predispostions for the development of the relevant abilities and skills;
- based upon the actual realization of talent through the development of the relevant abilities and learning of the relevant skills; and
- in accordance with a basic norm of not exposing others and oneself to unnecessary harm.

Use of substances and methods on the doping list

I have just set out what I take to be a morally sound interpretation of 'athletic performance'. Such an interpretation should be able to offer guidance in actual moral dilemmas in sport. Along the way I have sketched applications of this interpretation with the help of examples. In order to test it more thoroughly, however, I shall now take a look at one of the most discussed moral dilemmas in sport today: the use of performance-enhancing substances and techniques known as 'doping'.

In IOC's Anti-Doping Code we find the following declarations:

1 Doping contravenes the fundamental principles of Olympianism and sports and medical ethics.
2 Doping is forbidden.
3 Recommending, proposing, authorizing, condoning or facilitating the use of any substance or method covered by the definition of doping or trafficking therein is also forbidden.

(IOC 2000a: 6)

Doping classes include stimulants (amphetamines, cocaine, etc.), narcotic analgesics (heroin, methadone), anabolic agents (anabolic-androgenic steroids, testosterone), diuretics, and peptide and glycoprotein hormones and analogues (among others human growth hormone) (Verroken 1996). Doping methods cover blood doping and pharmacological, chemical and physical manipulation. A third category consists of substances subject to certain restrictions: alcohol, marijuana, local anaesthetics, corticosteroids, and beta-blockers. The term 'certain restrictions' refers to the regulation of substances that are not necessarily performance-enhancing but may have long-term negative influences on the individual, such as addiction, and may hurt the image of sport in society. In what follows I shall be talking about 'performance-enhancing substances (or drugs) and methods'. The term 'doping' refers to a banned practice and the use of that term would indicate that I agree to the illegal and immoral status of such practices before this has been fully examined.

Drugs used in sport are either work-enhancing (ergogenic) or they stimulate growth (anabolic). When taken regularly they can have a performance-enhancing effect over time. Examples would be the discus thrower who through the use of anabolic steroids attempts to enhance lean muscle mass and explosive strength, or the cross-country skier who by the administration of erythropoietin (rEPO) increases her production of red blood cells and thus enhances oxygen transport and endurance. Other substances and techniques are taken prior to important competitions to enhance performance on a shorter-term basis. Examples would be the professional cyclist who undergoes blood transfusions with similar effects as the use of rEPO, or the shooter who takes beta-blockers to decrease heart rate and control nervousness during competition.

Performance-enhancing substances and techniques work in specific ways. Chemical substances interact with their biological targets and lead to changes in the biochemical systems of the body (Mottram 1996: 1). Some substances (agonists), such as anabolic steroids, mimic the action of endogenous bio-chemical substances, that is, substances that occur naturally in the body. Other substances, such as beta-blockers (antagonists), prevent biochemical agents produced by the body from interacting with their receptors but are not produced by the body itself. What these various substances and techniques have in common, however, is that they are primarily directed towards enhancing what we have called basic bio-motor abilities, such as strength, speed and endurance, and mental abilities such as perception and emotion.[11]

Should inequalities in performance due to performance-enhancing substances and techniques count as relevant or non-relevant inequalities in sport competitions? Should they be eliminated or compensated for, or should they be accepted? Most of the arguments in the debate deal with fairness, justice, athletes' rights, and/or the health risks associated with such use (Parry 1987; Simon 1991: 71–92; Houlihan 1999: 107–28; Butcher and Schneider 2000).

At first sight, it does not seem possible to support the ban on certain performance-enhancing substances and techniques by appeal to justice. Quite the opposite: critics often refer to justice in terms of an equality norm. Because the ban is hard to enforce, the current situation has the consequence that cleverness and cheating are rewarded. Not all users are caught, while substances such as the human chorionic gonadotrophin (hCG), a human growth hormone, and rEPO are hard to trace. Therefore, some athletes gain advantage based on rule violations. To enhance justice, some critics claim that the ban on drugs should be lifted. All competitors ought to be given equal access to this form of environmental influence. In fact, the issue is sometimes seen as a question of athletes' rights. The ban is considered a case of unjustified paternalism, in which mature individuals are prevented from making their own prudential choices, a virtue that competitive sport is supposed to cultivate (Brown 1984, 1990). Others, among them Burke and Roberts (1997) and Tamburrini (2000: 34–61), have developed this argument further. They contend that doping rules are based on prejudices and the repressive *mos majorum* of a conservative sport society. In an ideal liberal sport system, athletes would be given the liberty of self-creation and be free to distinguish themselves via their own choices, as long as these choices do not impose harm on others.

On closer inspection, however, these views can be challenged. First, the fact that not all rule violaters are caught, or that there are banned substances that are hard to trace, should not surprise anyone. Critics of the ban seem to demand perfect procedural justice. But here, as in most other human practices, perfect procedural justice is an impossible ideal. Of course, key sport governing bodies like the IOC should critically examine how to improve their enforcement of the ban. If it is really true that, in general, moral athletes suffer disadvantages, there is indeed a problem. But imperfect realization of rules in practice is no decisive argument against these rules, and can just as well be used to justify far stricter and better rule enforcement.

The other counter-argument claims that of a liberal drug policy would solve problems to do with non-relevant inequalities, and finally free athletes to choose prudently or to engage in some kind of creative self-development. However, this seems to romanticize the current logic of the high-performance sport system. Such experiences as the systematic use of performance-enhancing drugs in East Germany, the American cyclists who had undergone blood transfusions before the Los Angeles Games of 1984, synthetic hormone use among Chinese swimmers in the mid 1990s, or the systematic use of rEPO in professional cycling, are not encouraging. Under the coercive force of the external expert system, athletes become involved in practices over which they exert little control (Murray 1983; Breivik 1987; Simon 1991: 77–80). Moreover, liberal drug policies would probably increase already significant inequalities between athletes from strong sport systems and those from weaker systems. Efficient drug use requires medical expertise. Heinilä's (1982) nightmare of the totalization of high-performance sport could come closer to reality. Competitions could become, even more than today, tests between strong bio-medical and technological support systems, within which athletes and teams would serve merely as a means in the struggle for success.[12]

There is, of course, another and quite contrary way of seeing this latter point. We could argue that, following similar equality norms to those developed above, inequalities in system strength could be eliminated or compensated for. Sport bodies could regulate the application of bio-medical knowledge in such a way that it becomes accessible to all. If all athletes are given equal access to, make equal use of, and use of performance-enhancing drugs, then any advantages due to drugs are 'competed away' and the most naturally gifted athlete will again be the most successful (Black and Pape 1998: 85). As indicated above, my reply to this argument is based on experience: the possibility of equal access is a romantic illusion. Further, even if the possibility were real, what would be gained by such a development? Here, the health argument becomes relevant.

In my interpretation of athletic performance I have made a place for the norm of avoiding the infliction of unnecessary harm. Most doping substances and techniques involve health risks. Extensive rEPO use can lead to an extreme increase in red blood cells and to increased blood viscosity and systolic blood pressure, the consequences of which can be heart failure, thrombosis and stroke (Armstrong and Reilly 1996). The use of anabolic steroids over time can lead to abnormal bone and soft-tissue growth, diabetes, hepatic tumors, sex and personality disorders, and so on (George 1996). Given their potential harm to health, substances and techniques on the doping list can at least on first sight be disqualified as acceptable elements of 'athletic performance'.

But, as we have seen from the examples above, the health argument is problematic: there is a need for nuances. The influence of competitive sport on health should indeed be discussed as a whole. In tough training periods, risks of strain injuries are high. The intense activity of competition readily leads to acute injuries. In risk sports, deaths occur. Why should certain drugs and techniques that involve health risks be banned when so many other forms of health risk are allowed?

In line with norm III.2.1.1, we must try to differentiate between relevant health risks that in some way or the other add value to, and are integrated parts of, sport, and non-relevant health risks that do not seem to add value to these practices and represent 'unnecessary' costs. In rigorous training periods athletes develop their talent; the goal is performance enhancement without injuries. If the equality norms are followed, improvement is based primarily on the athlete's own efforts, which are part of the relevant inequality that we want to evaluate. When it comes to the intensity of the competitive situation, and to risk sports such as parachute jumping, mountain climbing and downhill skiing, we can argue in a similar way. A relevant part of the performance is to be able to calculate and master risk and to tackle such stress situations. In these examples, certain risks are not 'unnecessary': they are in one way or another relevant to the sport in question.

Most of the users of performance-enhancing substances and techniques know that negative side-effects may occur. However, due to the belief that it is necessary to succeed, and to the coercive power of widespread use, they chose these means anyway. My argument against such use is that the risks add little or nothing to the activity itself.

Here the distinction between abilities and skills becomes relevant. I assume that the substances and methods under discussion influence primarily bio-motor abilities. Their aim is agonistic or antagonistic effects on the biochemistry of the body. If we adopt the proposal that all competitors be given equal access to the same substances and techniques, relative inequalities in technical and tactical skills may well remain the same, and so little is gained. A football game between teams of drug users is not necessarily experienced as better or more exciting than a football game between 'clean' competitors. A 100-metre sprint with field containing no drug-users can be just as even and exciting as a field of doped runners. Even if drug use leads to individual differences in athletic per-formance, these differences would be of a non-relevant kind. Among equally talented competitors, the winner will be the athlete with the bio-chemical constitution best suited to drug use (Simon 1991: 84ff.). Obviously, this contradicts Interpretation 4 of athletic performance, because it undermines the idea of sport as an arena for moral agents, and transfers responsibility for performance from the athlete to the support system.

My argument is that in a situation in which all competitors use drugs, something is lost. We would reach what Breivik (1987) describes as 'a negative equilibrium', in which all parties are worse off. A destructive logic of narrow self-interest undermines the common good. Choice of drugs exposes others and the drug-using athlete to unnecessary harm.

The view that the use of potentially harmful performance-enhancing drugs and techniques on the doping list is unnecessary and therefore a non-relevant risk can be linked to ideas about the values and 'essence' of sport, and the idea that doping is on 'unnatural' and 'artificial' performance enhancement. A decade ago, such ideas constituted the basic justification for doping rules and regulations. Since 1986, the term 'artificial' has been deleted from the IOC rules because it caused a lot of problems in terms of operationalization. This is understandable. Terms such as 'natural' and 'artificial' are unfortunate, because they are closely linked to particular socio-cultural views and interests. Discrimination against women in sport demonstrates how such ideas can be used in exploitative and repressive ways. Moreover, ideas about what is natural and what is artificial are constantly changing. For example, when systematic weight training was introduced in the 1950s, it was considered by many to be 'artificial' performance enhancement. Today most would consider such a view as a (humorous) anachronism.

However, even if ideas of the natural and the artificial are vague, the very fact that such terms are used is cautionary. They seem to reflect what I have called first-order moral beliefs, in which we firmly believe and have confidence. To most of us, it is reasonable to claim that the use of drugs to enhance sport performances is different from their therapeutic or clinical use in traditional medicine. I assume, in accord with most people's moral beliefs, that it makes sense to say that the use of rEPO to boost the production of red blood cells in a healthy body in which the red blood cell level is already high has a certain artificiality to it. I assume that it coheres with prevailing first-order moral beliefs, too, to accept medical use of rEPO as a way of getting an anaemic body back in 'natural' shape.

In discussing over performance-enhancing drugs, first-order moral beliefs need to be made articulate and critically scrutinized. There is a need for some kind of interpretation of what 'the name of the game' actually is – of what sport competitions ought to be all about. We cannot discuss drug use in a meaningful way without being able to distinguish sport as a social practice from, say, the practice of medicine. My purpose here is to develop an interpretation of the goals of competitive sport in terms of a theory of fair play. One part of this is an interpretation of athletic performance as expressed in norm III.2.1.1, as a combination of talent and the athlete's own efforts within a framework of non-harm. The use of performance-enhancing drugs is inconsistent with this view. Such use is more related to Interpretation 2 of athletic performance, according to which talent can be manipulated. Given the choice between two practices where the main difference is that one practice implies unnecessary health risks and represents a larger threat to the potential of athletes as moral agents than the other, the choice should be clear. As is the situation today, we ought to support the ban on the substances and techniques on the doping list.[13]

UNEQUAL TREATMENT AND ACTUAL INEQUALITIES IN SPORT COMPETITIONS

So far I have established norms for matters that ought to be held equal in sport competitions, and suggested an understanding of the relevant inequality, athletic performance, according to which competitors ought to be measured, compared and ranked. However, the third and final part of the formal justice norm (III) has not yet been specified.

> III.3 Unequal treatment ought to stand in reasonable accordance with the actual inequality between cases.

What does 'reasonable' mean here? The requirement of reasonableness must be understood within the framework of the moral point of view developed earlier. The relation between actual inequality and unequal treatment is reasonable if it satisfies meta-norm I, that is, if it cannot be reasonably rejected as a basis for unforced, informed general agreement. That does not necessarily mean that the relationship completely satisfies ideal norms for just distribution. On the contrary, as we have seen in the discussion of equality, perfect procedures are hard to realize in practice. The point is that our distributive procedures should come as close to the ideal as is practically possible.

Unequal treatment in sport can take various forms. A good performance in a 5000-metre race results in an improved chance of being the first to cross the finishing line. Through a successful move in basketball, a player creates a better position for the scoring of points and improves the chance for her team to win. Moreover, unequal treatment does not only take the form of rewarding good performances. Norm III.3 indicates that there ought to be a reasonable accordance between unsuccessful performance and loss of advantage. Slow running in a marathon decreases the chances of a good position at the finishing line. A basketball player who loses the ball turns the advantage of ball possession over to the other team. In some sports, disadvantages due to unsuccessful performances are formally defined in the rules. Simon (1991: 48ff.) cites the examples of 'the unplayable lie' rule in golf. If, for instance, the ball lands in deep sand or water, it has to be replayed according to the player's choice, from the original location, from a location two clubs away from either side of the original location, or from a new location behind its current location.

Typically, unequal treatment in sport takes the form of unequal distribution of advantage. So we can say:

> III.3.1 Unequal treatment in the distribution of advantage among competitors ought to stand in a reasonable accordance with the actual inequality in athletic performance.

There is another main category of unequal treatment that must be considered here. The fairness norm 1 prescribes adherence to a shared, just sport ethos. In Chapter 1, I said that an ethos of a sport is a set of norms shared among its participants for the interpretation of its sport-specific goal. In an ethos, then, certain actions are proscribed and penalties defined. Violations of these rules cause non-relevant inequalities that ought to be eliminated or compensated for. We can specify norm III.3 further:

> III.3.2 Inequalities due to rule violations ought to be eliminated or compensated for and there ought to be a reasonable accordance between degree of violation and the penalties imposed.

Let us now take a closer look at norms III.3.1 and III.3.2 respectively.

Competitive advantage – a taxonomy

Measurements, comparisons and rankings of athletic performance are carried out via the distribution of advantage. In order to establish more concrete criteria for the reasonableness of these procedures, I shall continue to use the analogy of competitions as scientific experiments. Advantage can be understood as an operationalization of the dependent variable 'athletic performance'. If norm III.3.1 for a reasonable accordance is to be met, the operationalized entity 'advantage' ought to express all essential elements found in athletic performance. In the terminology of scientific methodology, it should be possible to make valid inferences from the manifest level of measurement (in terms of distribution of advantage) to the latent level (in terms of athletic performance) (Galtung 1967: 29).

We can differentiate between nominal, ordinal, interval, and absolute levels of measurements of a variable (Galtung 1967: 73ff.). At the nominal level we operate with mutually exclusive categories. Only differences and similarities are indicated. An example of athletic performance measured at the nominal level is a chariot race in the ancient Olympic Games, which identified a winner and considered the rest as non-winners, or losers. At the ordinal level, we have in addition a rank ordering. We rank competitors as first, second, third, fourth, and so on but say nothing of relative differences between them. The interval level not only ranks performances but also operates with entities that make it possible to measure the exact intervals between them. In 100-metre races we operate with fine-grained and exact intervals between runners, down to hundredths of seconds. Finally, we have the level of absolute scales. Here there are equal ratios between the units of measurements, and an absolute zero point. An example would be measuring of a person's age. The absolute zero point is the moment of birth. A person who is twenty years of age is twice as old as a ten-year old and half the age of a person of forty. Absolute scales are not really found in sport. Although there is a zero-point of 0.00 seconds in a running race, this represents no logical possibility. For example, we cannot claim without qualifications that a sprinter who runs the 100 metres in 9.00 has a 10 per cent higher level of performance than a 10.00 sprinter. And, the one-tenth of a second improvement from 9.00 to 8.90 is considered far more difficult than the one from 11.00 to 10.90. In most sports, athletic performance is measured at the ordinal and interval level.

What characterizes the process of distributing advantages in sport? We can differentiate between advantage based on exact physical-mathematical measurements, and what can be called sport-specific advantage. Further we can differentiate between advantage gained formally and informally in the process of competing, and a final formal ranking at the end of a competition (see Figure 5).

The 1500-metres runner is awarded advantage based on measurement of performance in exact physical-mathematical units of time. The discus thrower and the long jumper are awarded advantage in exact units of space, and the weight lifter in exact units of mass. Such awards are formally described in the rules and are the basis both for preliminary evaluations and formal distribution of advantage during, and at the end of, competitions. 'Javelin thrower X is in the lead after three throws with a distance of 67.15 metres'; 'javelin thrower Y won with a throw of 72.50 metres.'

Advantages can be gained in informal ways, too. Gaining an informal advantage implies achieving a position in the process of competing in which the possibilities for formal advantages improve. Informal advantages are not defined in the rules and they are measured and compared pretty much on ordinal and nominal levels during competitions. To save energy, the tactically skilled 1500-metres runner follows the leading runner in the inside lane: 'X is in the lead, ahead of Y'. At a certain point in time, informal advantage can be converted to a formal one: 'X won by two-tenths of a second because she crossed the finishing line two-tenths of a second ahead of Y'. In sports with exact physical-mathematical measurements of performance, we operate at the ordinal, nominal, and interval levels.

The other main category of advantage units here consists of units that are specific to certain sports. In tennis, formal advantages are awarded in terms of games and sets. Basketball players and pistol shooters compete for points, while football and handball teams are awarded goals. In contrast to physical-mathematical measurements, sport-specific advantages are defined in the rules of a sport in a way that provides meaning only within the context of that particular sport. Definitions of sport-specific advantages are classic examples of constitutive rules.

The awarding of sport-specific advantage occurs formally during competitions. We can at a given point of time in a tennis match say that one player leads by 1–0 in sets, 5–2 in games and 15–0 in points, or during a football match that one team is leading by two goals. Informal advantages are found in sports with sport-specific advantages as well. The tennis player who serves hard towards her opponent's weak backhand and then approaches the net for a volley, increases her chances of winning the point. A football player who dribbles around an opponent and moves into a good position for a shot, increases her chances of scoring a goal.

The awarding of sport-specific advantage does not normally imply any visible advantage in terms of improved external conditions or positions. After finishing a point in tennis the players return to their initial positions. After scoring a goal in football the teams line up again at halfway. The norm here is equal opportunity to perform. At the end of a competition, sport-specific advantages are accumulated and determine the final ranking. The measurements are carried out at the nominal and ordinal levels. A tennis player wins by three sets to two, a football team is deemed victorious because they scored four goals while their opponents only scored two.

Advantage category	Awarding procedure	Level of measurement
Advantage measured in physical-mathematical units of time, space and mass	Informal and formal	Nominal and ordinal Interval
Sport-specific advantage	Informal and formal	Nominal and ordinal

Figure 5 Advantage in sport competitions – a taxonomy

The question now is whether the requirements of norm III.3.1, which prescribe a reasonable accordance between the awarding of advantage and athletic performance, can actually be met.

Advantage, luck and merit

In competitions in which performance is measured in physical-mathematical units there seems to be close correspondence between performance and advantage awarded. The fastest runner over 100 metres wins the 100 metres, and the weight lifter who lifts the highest number of kilograms is victorious in his competition. As measurement and comparison methodologies are exact, we operate with a high degree of validity. The relation between athletic performance and distribution of advantage seems to be reasonable – norm III.3.1 is followed closely.

But on close inspection, the relation is not as clear as it might seem. Quantification of performance must be based on valid scales of evaluation. One problem with modern high-tech measurement methods is that they may distinguish too finely. In a tight 100-metre race that is won by one hundredth of a second, uncontrollable factors seem to play a role. No sprinter can fully control such small margins. Clear perceptions of marginal inequalities like hundredths of a second are neuro-physiologically impossible. The question is whether such margins ought to be counted in sport events at all.

If we want to evaluate only inequalities in time taken over the 100 metres, this is unproblematic. But if we want to measure inequalities based on the interpretation of athletic performance set out above, problems arise. According to norm III.2.1, athletic performance is the product of talent, or chance in the natural lottery, and cultivation of talent through the athlete's own efforts, for which the athlete can be held responsible. Advantages in sport ought to be distributed primarily on an individual, meritocratic basis. The paradox is that, due to what is often considered progress in terms of justice afforded by finer calibration of measurement technology, non-meritocratic elements now exert a stronger influence on outcomes.

A 100-metre race is a direct competition in which participants compete simultaneously. Outdoor indirect competitions such as traditional cross-country skiing, alpine skiing, or the high and long jump and throwing events in athletics, are even more vulnerable to the influence of non-meritocratic elements. In the discussion of equality we saw how evaluations of performance in outdoor sports could become imprecise due to weather changes. To differentiate between two competitors in a cross-country skiing race by one-tenth of a second, or between long jumpers by one centimetre, seems to be treating competitors unequally in an arbitrary manner. For example, during the 1980 Lake Placid Winter Games, new electronic timers gave Thomas Wassberg of Sweden a one-hundredth of a second lead (equivalent to approximately 55 millimetres, or 2 inches, in distance) over Juha Mieto of

Finland in the 15-kilometre cross-country skiing race. Wassberg considered sharing the gold medal with Mieto as he thought their performances were more or less identical. Officials later agreed that no race would be measured that closely again. Today, one-tenth of a second is the official timing standard of the sport. But if a race takes place during significantly unstable conditions, it is still possible that the skier ranked number two, three or four could really have been the one who under equal conditions would have performed the best.

Should the limits for fine calibration of measurement technologies be drawn within the area of control of competitors? What, more precisely, characterizes the non-meritocratic elements that influence our measurements here?

It is common knowledge that to win tight sport competitions with small margins, skills are not enough. Everyone needs good luck! Rescher (1995: 19ff.) distinguishes a pure chance process, which by definition cannot be predicted and controlled (like that of the genetic lottery), from various kinds of luck that seem unpredictable and out of the control of the affected persons due to ignorance of some kind. Luck seems to come about 'by accident' – it cannot be controlled there and then. While racing towards the finishing line, an alpine skier may lose balance and be about to fall. However, due to good luck, a bump in the course pushes him back onto his feet again. In her last attempt, a javelin thrower may stumble and fall for the first time in her career and ruin her chance of winning. Bad luck! To use de Wachter's (1985: 55) definition, these are examples of '... an incongruence between result produced and the intended action produced from the skill and the effort of the player'. The question now is whether the possible influence of luck, good and bad, can and should be minimized?

In contradistinction to pure chance events such as 'the natural lottery', bad luck can be compensated for by skill or increased by the lack of it. Good skiers and javelin throwers are focussed and do not easily lose balance. And even if once in a while they are about to fall, they have the skills to compensate for it with quick adjustments of body position. In good performances, luck is often marginal. As the golfer Lee Trevino said: 'The more I practice, the luckier I get!' Where luck follows skill, there is no serious threat to norm III.3.1 for the meritocratic distribution of advantage.

Sports with sport-specific advantage, however, represent a further challenge. Here, the influence of luck sometimes works against merit. A football player may attempt to pass to a team-mate in a better position, but miss-kicks and instead finds the net and scores. To everyone's surprise, a technically bad shot on the tennis court can drop down on the right side of the net. These athletes experience good luck without merit. Their opponents, however, may experience bad luck in spite of performing well. The better-playing football team might lose once in a while due to the opposing team being gifted an easy goal. A technically well-executed return on a mediocre serve in tennis might end up one centimetre too long and result in the loss of a point. It is usually in situations like these that we hear remarks about 'unfair outcomes', and the loser as 'the moral winner'.

A certain influence of luck seems unavoidable in sport as in other areas of life. Full control over all our actions and their consequences seems impossible, but it is not necessarily an ideal to be wished for either. In sport, luck usually follows skill and the meritocratic distribution of advantage is not really challenged. However, in the case of sport-specific advantage, luck can lead to advantage in spite of the lack of skill. How are we to deal with this from a moral point of view?

There are several possible interpretations of the role of luck in sport. Here I shall discuss what I consider to be three representative positions.[14]

The cynic

The first is that of the sport cynic. Characteristically, the sport cynic reasons as follows: 'The point in sprint races is to cross the finishing line first. Whoever does this, is always the better sprinter.' Likewise, 'The point in football is to score more goals than the opponents. Whoever does that is always the better team.' The sport cynic's view is built on the premise that, in all sports, there is complete correspondence between performance of skills and advantage gained. Our evaluations are completely reliable and valid. Athletic performance is not a theoretical variable. It is operationalized directly through the rule-defined procedures for rewarding performance in the sports in question. Athletic performance simply is advantage gained. Sport competitions are by definition cases in which an ideal norm for meritocratic distribution is realized through perfect procedures.

The cynic's standpoint is unreasonable. As was said above, a certain influence from non-meritocratic elements is unavoidable in sport as in other spheres of life. Non-meritocratic factors cause inequalities that are impossible to eliminate. We can merely compensate for good and bad luck up to a certain point. Moreover, especially in games like football and tennis, the cynic's position seems to be mistaken. The idea that in football the best team is always the one that wins leaves us with little scope for critical reflection. For example, in endorsing statements such as 'the score tells it all', the position ignores the idea of the lost but well-played game. Because the sport cynic rejects sport ideals, there is little basis for critical reflection on good play in spite of a loss, on how winning performances can be improved, on changes and developments of games, and so on. This clearly contradicts the way sport is understood and practised in real life.

Paradoxically, the cynical position seems to be naive. The cynic can be compared to a researcher who, with a blind faith in his own observations, rejects any critical, systematic examination of the reliability and validity of the research. Like such a researcher, the cynic reduces the complexity and diversity of the sport under discussion. The cynic is a sport reductionist. We need to look at a more feasible alternative.

The rationalist

Even if we disagree with the cynic, we can still seek to improve the accordance between actual performance and advantage gained in some sports. The second position on the role of luck is that of the scientifically inspired sport enthusiast who argues that, to increase the validity of our 'experiments', we should differentiate in the distribution of advantage to a greater extent. We can call this the position of the rationalist. Sprint races should be measured in time units that have been proven scientifically to be within the range of control of individual athletes. Football could follow the example of basketball. Goals from penalties could be given one point, those scored from within the penalty area two points, and those from outside the penalty area three points. In tennis, points could be through a much more precise operationalization of the quality of play, evaluated for instance by a board of referees. On a longer-term basis, more advanced operationalizations of performance could increase the accuracy of performance measurements. Through greater differentiation, the level of measurement could be raised from the ordinal to the interval level. For the rationalist, the ultimate solution would be exact physical-mathematical measurements of performance in all sports. Then the requirement for reasonableness given in norm III.3.1 would be satisfied to an even greater extent. Even if our procedures are still imperfect, we come closer to the ideal: pure meritocratic distribution of advantage.

The rationalist argues consistently. Unlike the cynic, the rationalist accepts the influence of luck, but shares the cynic's dislike for it. The influence of luck ought to be minimized. Their view seems to be in line with much of what has already been said about justice. The structural goal of sport competitions is to measure, compare and rank competitors according to athletic performance. The primary norm of distribution is meritocratic in kind. By analogy with scientific experiment, 'athletic performance' has been regarded as the theoretical variable and advantage its operationalization, and high definitional validity has been called for.

Still, the implications of the rationalist's view raise fundamental challenges to sport as we know, experience, and practise it, in particular to sports with sport-specific advantage. Is it really the case that all sports should search for physical-mathematical evaluations of performance? Should the ideal governing all sports be the scientific experiment?

The player

As we have seen in the discussion of athletic performance in the previous chapter, the experiment analogy and one-sided reasoning based on justice norm III have their limitations. Here we are working within the framework of a mixed ethical theory, where consequentialist ideas about the satisfaction of preferences and the experiential, 'lived' aspects of a practice count as morally relevant. There is more to sport than just schemes of distribution of advantage. Again, we should not confuse the structural goal of these practices, to evaluate and rank players according to performance, with intentional goals among participants. In what we may call the player's position, subjective reasons for engagement, in particular a search for experiential qualities and 'lived' dimensions, are of key importance. From this perspective, sport-specific advantages have a role to play. In Chapters 4 and 5, I shall discuss more closely what I see as the phenomenological structure of the good sport experience. In the present context I shall mention just two relevant points.

First, the fact that luck is more or less a product of ignorance and lack of skill, and not a pure chance event, increases the complexity and challenge of athletic performances. How finely tuned can sprinters become in terms of perceiving marginal differences in performance during a race? How clever can a football team become in handling mentally, technically and tactically a lucky goal to the opposing team? Is it possible for tennis players to develop the skill to specialize in net-cord shots with sufficient topspin to fall on the right side of the net? A certain influence of luck renders sport an arena for the pursuit of excellence in which there will always be room for improvement. To a larger extent than in a sport mono-culture based narrowly on the ideal of the scientific experiment, sport becomes an arena for the cultivation of a diversity of human talent and ability. This view is in line with the implicit values of the moral interpretation of 'athletic performance' set out above.

Second, a degree of influence of luck seems to increase the exciting uncertainty of outcome in competitions. Finely tuned calibration of performance measurements, and 'inaccurate' sport-specific advantages, produces an openness and uncertainty of outcome that seems to add excitement to sport. It is a fact that the final of the 100 metres at the Olympic Games can be won by one-hundredth of a second, and that in football the team that plays best may lose once in a while. As the saying goes among football fans: 'The ball is round'.

The role of luck in sport

Consideration of the player's position suggests there is a particular local scheme of justice in competitions that is related to the specific goals of sport (Loland 1999). Although the allegory has rendered good service in our discussion of justice, sport is not a scientific experiment aiming at valid or scientifically 'true' knowledge, nor is it like a court of law that strives towards perfect meritocratic (or rather retributive) justice. As I shall argue below, its particular value is to be found in a delicate mix between meritocratic justice, chance and luck. The possibility for the influence of luck should not, as in the rationalist scheme of thought, be minimized, but rather optimized. The primary distributive norm is meritocratic, while chance and luck can enhance the openness of competitions and the complexity of performance.

What more specifically does this mean? How much influence should properly be allowed to non-meritocratic elements such as chance and luck? Norm III.3.1 prescribes a reasonable accordance between actual inequality in performance and advantage gained. If most 100-metre races are won by one-hundredth of a second, and by different runners every time, or if most football matches are decided on lucky goals, and what is commonly considered the better playing teams lose just as often as they win. Luck seems to turn into chance, which again seems to be playing a significant and a systematic role. The very idea of sport as a meritocratic practice loses meaning. Luck plays different roles in different sports. Usually, sports with sport-specific advantages allow luck a more significant role than do sports with exact physical-mathematical measurements of performance. However, as in our treatment of chance in the equality discussion, we can say that luck ought never to exert significant and systematic influence on performance.

Game advantage based on aesthetic criteria

Before summing up the discussion of norm III.3.1 for a reasonable accordance between performance and advantage, there is a particular sub-class of sport-specific advantages that ought to be mentioned. In some sports, distribution of advantage is based on aesthetic evaluations.

Best (1978: 99ff.) distinguishes aesthetic sports from purposive sports. In purposive sports, such as athletics, tennis and football, the aim is to win more points and score more goals than one's opponents within the framework of the relevant ethos. The manner in which this is done has no formal significance. In aesthetic sports, such as figure skating, gymnastics and ski jumping, successful performance depends in part upon the manner in which the sport-specific goals are pursued. It is not enough to be efficient; to be successful, the various movement patterns must satisfy certain stylistic criteria. What then can be said about a reasonable accordance between skills performed and advantage gained in aesthetic sports?

First of all: what does an aesthetic criterion look like? What do we actually evaluate? In Lowe's (1977: 68ff.) interpretation of the aesthetics of sport, we find terms such as harmony, rhythm, flow, intensity, precision, power and strategy.[15] In most aesthetic sports, phrases such as 'the overall impression' or 'the artistic expression' of the performance are frequently used. Expert performers move with ease and grace, and at the same time forcefully and decisively. Well-played team sports demonstrate human interaction at perhaps its most harmonious. No doubt aesthetic qualities play an important role in our fascination with these practices.

However, from the perspective of justice, there are problems with using aesthetic criteria in the evaluation of performance. Aesthetic criteria point to qualities that are hard to operationalize. As indicated by the terms used ('overall impression', 'artistic expression'), we are dealing with holistic qualities that are difficult to quantify. Whereas in figure skating, for instance, the evaluation of technical execution is made according to relatively objective standards, criteria for artistic impression are far less clear. With artistic impression, the total evaluation is considered more than the sum of its parts. Evaluations rest on more or less intuitive and subjective interpretations and assessments, to a greater extent than on explicit analytic procedures.

Of course, subjectivity is not wrong *per se*. A judge in gymnastics or ski jumping may be subjective but still follow her honest convictions about the standards of excellence of her sport. The point is that in most aesthetic sports, there are several judges involved and the final score is based upon an average of their evaluations. If all judges follow their own convictions, and if the group of judges is representative of views in the sport community as a whole, the resultant evaluations of performances are based on sound premises.

Still, perhaps the most serious justice problem here is that, as distinct from a 100-metre sprint in which performance is measured in exact units of time, or a football game with a clear definition of what counts as a goal, aesthetic evaluation criteria are vulnerable to manipulation and cheating. Refereeing scandals to do with secret agreements among judges have ruined many competitions. One of the more recent examples occurred during the World Championships in figure skating in Helsinki in March 1999, where TV cameras captured a Russian and a Ukrainian judge communicating extensively during evaluations via gestures and signs. They collaborated to improve the rankings of competitors from their own countries. Although these judges were penalized and the routines for judging were critically re-evaluated, vague aesthetic criteria for the distribution of advantage, combined with high pay-off in case of success, will probably give rise to similar incidents in aesthetic sports in the future.

Another problem caused by the openness and ambiguity of aesthetic evaluation is that its standards are often the expressions of views among the prevailing and (to a certain extent) conservative 'sport establishment'. This establishment tends to be a step behind the evolution of the 'unwritten' but commonly accepted standards of excellence in the sport. A good example is ski jumping. In recent years, new movement patterns that are more rational from the aero-dynamic point of view, such as the so-called V-style, were accepted among athletes, coaches and spectators long before they were given credit by judges or recognized in the rules of evaluation.

Finally, when subjected to scrutiny, the very distinction between aesthetic and purposive sports seems less than absolute. Aesthetic elements are important in most sports (Kupfer 1995). From a critical point of view, the aesthetic qualities of Michael 'Air' Jordan's jump shots in basketball or of a wonderful 'double play' on the baseball field seem to be just as prominent as those of champion Katarina Witt's movements on the ice in figure skating.

Although grace and competitive success do not always go together (Cordner 1984), aesthetic evaluation of performance could be a criterion for distributing advantage in all sports. Or, rather, if we are to take seriously the critical arguments presented above, aesthetic elements in sport should indeed be cherished and cultivated, but should not be used as a basis for evaluating performance at all.

There is a need for further systematic and critical analysis of aesthetic values in sport, notably of how these can eventually provide a reasonable basis for the awarding of advantage. Any evaluation criteria should be based on inter-subjectivity, and how they are applied should be open to critical examination. As aesthetic evaluation is practised today, the requirements of norm III.3.1 for reasonable accordance between performance and advantage are not always met. Perhaps aesthetic evaluations should be replaced by analytic 'objective' criteria, such as technical execution in figure skating and length of jump in ski jumping, or by sport-specific advantage systems within which cheating and manipulation are more difficult? Has the time come to abandon aesthetic judgements and base evaluations and rankings of competitors on objective criteria alone?

A norm for reasonable awarding of advantage

I have discussed two bases for distributing advantage in sport: evaluation of performance in exact physical-mathematical units, and operationalization in terms of sport-specific advantage. I have found that in spite of being affected by non-meritocratic elements such as luck, both of them can satisfy norm III.3.1 by virtue of a reasonable accordance between unequal treatment and actual inequality. Luck is unavoidable and has therefore to be accepted. Moreover, I have argued that a certain influence of luck increases experiential values and adds to the openness of competitions, to the complexity of performance, and hence to the cultivation of diversity in human talent and ability. Still, we need to hold on to the idea of competitions as primarily meritocratic practices. Luck ought never to exert a significant and systematic influence on performance.

In addition I have looked at a sub-class of sport-specific advantages: advantage based on aesthetic evaluations of performance. Aesthetic experiences are no doubt important elements of our fascination with sport. But we can still be critical of using them as criteria for distribution of advantage, because they are non-operationalizable and because they render competitions vulnerable to cheating and to unfair outcomes.

A closer specification of norm III.3.1 can now be articulated as follows:

> III.3.1.1 Luck ought not to exert significant and systematic influence on the measuring, comparison and ranking of competitors according to

athletic performance, and possibilities for subjective and partial evaluation ought to be eliminated to the greatest possible extent.

Rule violations and penalties

What, then, can be said of the accordance between inequalities arising from rule violations and the penalties imposed? Based on norm III.3 for a reasonable accordance between unequal treatment and actual inequality, I formulated norm III.3.2:

> III.3.2 Inequalities due to rule violations ought to be eliminated or compensated for and there ought to be a reasonable accordance between degree of violation and penalties imposed.

Rule violations are of several kinds. The long jumper who steps over the board has her jump measured longer than it really is. By illegally hitting a competitor on the arm, a basketball player 'steals' the ball and scores two points. I have argued that without adhering to a shared, just ethos, evaluations of performance among competitors become invalid. Advantages resulting from rule violations that are no part of such an ethos must be considered non-relevant inequalities that ought to be eliminated or compensated for. The argument is similar to that in the discussion of equality. This time, however, we are dealing not with external conditions, equipment or support systems, but with competitors' actions themselves.

We need to bear in mind that competitors may violate rules in different ways. The long jumper who steps over the board may violate a rule without really intending to. His aim is to jump from close to the far edge of the board as possible, in order to maximize the length of the part of the jump that is to be measured. The basketball player may hit another player illegally with the intention of getting the ball, in spite of thereby violating the rules. Obviously, from a moral point of view, we evaluate the two violations differently. The basic distinction is between unintentional and intentional violations (Fraleigh 1984: 71–9).[16]

Unintentional rule violations

In Chapter 2, I discussed intentionality and interpreted the term pragmatically in saying that we act intentionally when we make an unforced choice between alternative courses of action. What, then, can be said of unintentional rule violations? Unintentional violations can be defined negatively as consequences of actions that come about due to circumstances over which we have little or no control. They are the results of, for instance, bad luck, lack of skill, or lack of knowledge. An inexperienced boxer may hit his opponent below the belt while aiming at the abdomen. A handball player may accidentally kick the ball in her attempt to pick it up from the floor.

In sports, unintentional rule violations are hard to avoid. Few (if any) competitions are held without them. Still, if there are no responses to them and their consequences, non-relevant inequalities would arise between competitors. These would render the evaluation of performance unreliable and invalid. Advantages based on unintentional rule violations are unfair. What ought we to do about them?

The answer is a procedure to restore the initial fair situation. In practice this can be done in different ways. The long jumper who unintentionally steps over the board has her advantage eliminated by deletion of the result. The jump is declared foul. Similarly, the sprinter with a false start is called back, to rejoin with the other sprinters at the starting line, while football players who unintentionally run into each other line up again and the ball is dropped between them, to restore the initial situation.

In most competitions, however, we cannot completely eliminate non-relevant inequalities caused by rule violations; we can only compensate for them. The long jumper gets a reduction of advantage because one of her six jumps is eliminated. Similarly, a sprinter with the false start has only one more chance before he is disqualified. In addition, a false start may disturb, and sometimes ruin, the concentration of other competitors. Even if in football the initial situation is restored to a large degree by the ball-drop, it will never be identical with the situation when the violation occurred.

There are no perfect procedures here. A degree of inequality is unavoidable. We devise procedures that restore the initial situation as far as possible. In other words:

> III.3.2.1 Advantage gained through unintentional rule violations ought to be eliminated or compensated for so that the initial position is restored to the greatest possible extent.

What can now be said of intentional rule violations?

Intentional rule violations

Perhaps the most common intentional rule violation is cheating. Cheating has received considerable attention in the philosophical literature on sport (Pearson 1973; McIntosh 1979: 182ff.; Leaman 1981; Fraleigh 1984: 71–82; Simon 1991: 37ff.). Simply defined, cheating is an attempt to gain an advantage by violating the shared interpretation of the basic rules (the ethos) of the parties engaged without being caught and held responsible for it. The goal of the cheater is that the advantage gained is not eliminated nor compensated for. Examples of cheating would be the badminton player who, in a self-refereed match, intentionally makes false calls on his opponent's good shots, or the basketball player who impedes an opponent by surreptitiously holding on to her shirt.

A special category of cheating found primarily in ball games, is so-called play-acting (what is known as 'diving'). A football player fakes a foul by falling over and acting as if in pain. The result is a free kick or a penalty to his team. In addition, the player from the other team who is incorrectly held responsible for the foul may be cautioned or sometimes sent off the field. Play-acting is indeed cheating, but it can have a further dimension. The aim of the cheater may be not only to get away with an unfair advantage, but also to construct a situation in which an innocent player is formally penalized. What are reasonable responses to such cheating?

As with unintentional violations, we should seek to restore the initial situation to the greatest possible extent. But restoration is not enough. Cheating involves attempts to gain advantage through 'hidden' rule violations. It represents a direct contradiction of fairness norm 1. The cheat uses other competitors as a means to secure exclusive advantage for the cheat. The whole point is that the advantage is not available to others. The very foundation of the fairness ideal, mutual respect between persons and respect for the shared ethos according to which all compete, is violated. If cheating implies, as in the case of play-acting, a construction of situations in which innocent competitors are penalized, the wrongdoing becomes the more grave.

In addition to trying to restore the initial situation, therefore, cheats ought to be penalized. In the case of severe violations, or if the cheating continues, cheats should be disqualified. In practice this norm is adhered to in most sports. In handball and football yellow or red cards are given, in basketball a player is expelled after committing five fouls, and in track and field a sprinter is disqualified after a second false start. In some sports, the procedures for imposing just penalties are quite sophisticated. The 'advantage paragraph' in football is a good example. Suppose player X fouls opponent Y on Y's way to the goal. Y stumbles but is nevertheless able to make an excellent pass. If a free kick were awarded, X's team would be able to organize their defence and Y's advantage would be reduced. But it is necessary that X be penalized for an intentional rule violation. In such a case, a good referee lets the attack be completed, then warns or penalizes the rule breaker at the next break in play.

A second kind of intentional rule violation in addition to cheating that has become quite common is the 'tactical violation', what Fraleigh (1982) calls 'the good foul' and elsewhere is referred as 'the professional foul'. The offender breaks the rules intentionally but openly this time, and accepts a penalty in the form of an immediate reduction of advantage, on the calculation that the rule violation will give an advantage in the long term. For example, an ice hockey player brutally fouls what he considers the key player on the opposing team in order to eliminate him from the game. The rule-breaker accepts expulsion for two minutes or sometimes for the match, on the understanding that the violation will serve his team's interests. Another example is the football player who pulls down an opponent who is in a scoring position, judging that a penalty kick will give the other team a lesser chance for a goal than the situation in which the foul is committed.

What can be said of such 'tactical' rule violations? As with cheating, tactical violations should be viewed as violations against fairness norm 1 and so should result in a caution, or in severe cases, in disqualification. More specifically, what are needed here are penalties that fit the 'crime'. If such penalties can be devised, the term 'tactical violation' will no longer have any meaning. There will be nothing to gain by breaking the rules openly and taking the penalty that follows from it. That tactical violations are possible indicates that there exists an unreasonable relation between the non-relevant inequalities that arise through a rule violation and the response devised a penalty. Therefore, rules and the various kinds of ethos of sport should be under constant and critical revision, and adjusted when necessary.

An example of such adjustment comes from FIFA, the international governing body of football. In the late 1980s and the early 1990s, the number of 'tactical fouls' increased. FIFA was concerned with the public image of the game. The 1990 World Cup in Italy became a turning point. Players and coaches considered tactical fouls threatened key elements in football, such as good technical and tactical play and the scoring of goals. FIFA decided to enforce the existing rules more strictly, especially in the case of rough and potentially harmful tackles. In addition, it implemented a new rule, Law XII on Fouls and Misconduct, that prescribed sending off players who, by unlawful means, deny attacking players obvious goal-scoring opportunities.[17] Here we see how the rules and the ethos of a sport were scrutinized and adjusted to secure what was considered the important values: safety of players, fairness and justice, realization of the commonly accepted standards of excellence; but also entertainment values, commercial interests, and so forth.

The FIFA example points to one aspect of intentional rule violation that has not yet been discussed. Rough tackles may cause injury to other competitors. The ice hockey player who goes in for a rough tackle on the other team's key player may deliberately injure for instrumental reasons. To take a key player 'out' could result in victory in a game that otherwise would have been lost. Or the action could be an end in itself. It might be revenge of some kind, while some players may even get pleasure from hurting others. Intentionally injuring other competitors violates the natural duty not to expose others or oneself to unnecessary harm. This norm is one of the cornerstones of my interpretation of athletic performance and is tightly linked to the view I take of the need to respect competitors as moral agents. Player actions such as rough tackles ought to lead to a warning in mild cases and, in more serious cases, disqualification from the competition, from a series of competitions, or ultimately from sport in general.

A norm for unequal treatment linked to rule violations

Norm III.3.2.2 can be formulated concerning intentional rule violations:

> III.3.2.2 Advantage gained through intentional rule violations ought to be eliminated or compensated for so that the initial situation is restored to the greatest possible extent; and the rule breaker ought to receive an additional penalty that reduces advantage and, for serious or repeated violations, leads to expulsion.

Unequal treatment in meta-competitions

I have formulated norms that prescribe a reasonable accordance between unequal treatment and inequalities in performance within single competitions. But unequal treatment can have further consequences. A young skier's performance in decisive cross-country skiing races can result in his being selected for a representative team that might provide him with better coaching and support for the next season. Beach volleyball players can earn large amounts of money from the tightest possible victory of two points in the final set, whereas the losing finalists make only half the amount. There seems to be no reasonable relationship between athletic performance and the external advantages and disadvantages that may follow.

Still, norms III.3.1 and III.3.2 for reasonable unequal treatment through the awarding of advantage or the imposing of penalties, cannot be applied outside sport without further discussion. I have developed a scheme of justice linked to the particular ends and goals of competitions themselves. Norms for the distribution of money external to the competitions, or of goods and burdens in society at large, belong to other schemes of justice and are beyond the scope of my present concern.

However, one exception can be made. Individual competitions often do not stand by themselves but are part of what may be called meta-competitions. I am now speaking of knockout competitions or cups, and series. Final ranking in the individual competition decides the distribution of advantage in the meta-competition. In the Norwegian football cup, the winner ends up as the national champion. The series of international Grand Prix meetings in track and field has, among other things, the aim of deciding the world's best track and field athlete in each event. As in individual competitions, the goal of meta-competitions is to measure, compare and rank competitors based on athletic performance. Therefore, the norms for a reasonable accordance between performance and advantages and disadvantages (III.3.1 and III.3.2 and their specifications) may be of relevance. Is there a reasonable accordance between actual inequality and unequal treatment in meta-competitions?

Knockout competitions

At the outset of a knockout competition, a number of competitors are engaged. The schedule of individual competitions is drawn up by a lottery. The winners of each individual competition go forward to meet each other in a new round of competitions, while the losers are excluded – they are 'out'. In the end, or what is called 'the final', only two competitors are left. The winner of the final is the winner of the knockout competition as a whole.

Advantage here is given simply in the form of further advancement. Is there a reasonable accordance between performance and advantage? One individual competition can decide it all. And, as we have seen above, in an individual competition merit does not always determine the outcome. Definitional validity is not always high. Chance plays a role in the drawing of competitors in the early rounds. Luck, good and bad, arises in the competition itself. Once in a while, chance and luck have a decisive impact. A football team can proceed all the way to the final due in part to luck in drawing weaker opponents. The 'unseeded' tennis player can, on her lucky day, beat the overall best player and win the tournament.

In individual competitions I have accepted (indeed valued) elements of chance and luck as long as they do not exert significant and systematic influence on performance. In a knockout competition, chance and luck not only determine the outcome of single competitions once in a while but may have as a consequence that the best team is excluded from the meta-competition as a whole. Can this be justified? Is it reasonable?

Again: I accept non-meritocratic elements such as chance and luck because they can increase excitement and uncertainty of outcome and the complexity of performance. Knockout competitions are very dramatic forms of meta-competition. To lose means exclusion – one is 'out'. This normally leads to hard and exciting competitions, in which there is great uncertainty of outcome up to the last minute and every technical and tactical move can be decisive. As long as all parties engaged share this understanding, knockout competitions can be said to be fair.

However, the norm III.3.1 for reasonable accordance between performance and advantage still applies. We should constantly and critically re-evaluate the reasonableness of the distribution of advantage. We must demand the same requirements for reasonableness here as in individual competitions. If the bottom team in a series wins the national football cup every second year, or if unseeded players win tennis tournaments as often as the seeded ones, non-meritocratic elements seem to be exerting significant and systematic influence on performance and the procedures for awarding advantage ought to be adjusted.

Series

In a series, procedures for unequal treatment are more complicated. An example would be the series in ball games such as basketball, volleyball, football, and handball. Every season every team plays each other twice (home and away) and points are awarded based on losses, draws and wins. In most football series, three points are given for a win, one point for a tie, and no points for a loss. In tennis and alpine skiing, competitors are awarded ranking points according, among other things, to the time interval between them and the winning skier. We are now moving away from the distribution of advantage in the competitions themselves and establish a new advantage system based on final rankings from individual competitions. Is there a reasonable accordance between athletic performance and the distribution of advantage here?

In series, the influence of chance and luck is reduced simply by virtue of the accumulation of performances over time. It is commonly acknowledged that the overall best performing athlete or team will win in the end. In this way, validity can be increased. We measure to a greater degree what we really want to measure.[18]

It has to be said, though, that once in a while chance and luck can be the decisive factors in the outcome of series as well. Imagine two volleyball teams that track each other through the season and have the same number of points when one game remains. They then play each other. This is 'the final of the series'. The game is tight and even, and one team wins by a more or less randomly scored point in the final set.

Nevertheless, due to the accumulation of points over the whole season, the impact of luck is less than in the knockout competition. Even if luck decides the ranking of the two best teams in a close final, they qualified for it through strong play and a meritocratically based ranking over a whole season's play. In the final ranking between them, luck only adds excitement and complexity and is not of negative value.

Knockout competitions and series combined

It appears that both knockout competitions and series can meet the requirements for a reasonable accordance between performance and advantage. Still, both forms of meta-competition have weaknesses. Knockout competitions might allow chance and luck to play too large a role, whereas series once in a while lack intensity and drama. In certain situations, individual competitions may in fact become insignificant. Sometimes a competitor or a team leads by such a large margin that they will end on top in the final ranking independently of the result of the last game. Often, therefore, in larger tournaments, the series and the knockout system are combined. First, teams are seeded into groups in which they play each other in so-called mini-series. The teams that end up with most points in their mini-series proceed to the 'play-off'. Now the knockout competition takes over. Teams have to win to proceed and just two teams end up in the final.

More advanced combinations of the knockout and series-systems can be found as well. A good example is the current organization of beach volleyball tournaments. In the 2000 Sydney Olympic Games, the event included twenty-four teams of each sex. The teams were seeded according to expected performance potential, and the number one team first played team number twenty-four, and so on. The twelve losing teams in the first round played two more rounds in a 'losers' bracket', and the four survivors rejoined the original twelve winners for a sixteen-team, single-elimination tournament. Even if a team lost its first match, there was still a possibility of proceeding to the final. In this way, the influence of chance and luck in individual competitions is reduced while at the same time keeping up the drama and intensity of each individual event. In discussions of meta-competitions, this mode of organization may perhaps be said to include 'the best of both worlds'.

Rule violations in meta-competitions

So far I have discussed distribution of advantage. What can be said of the relation between non-relevant inequalities based on rule violations and unequal treatment via penalties in meta-competitions? What is a reasonable treatment for the handball team that bribes its competitors in a knockout competition and gains the advantage of proceeding through a tournament, or the youth football team that participates in a series with two players who are too old and therefore ineligible? Is there, as prescribed by norm III.3.2 and its specifications, a reasonable accordance between unfair advantage and penalties imposed?

Tentatively, we can say that, as with rule violations in individual competitions, non-relevant inequalities ought to be eliminated or compensated for by reduction of advantage. If rule violations are intentional, as with attempted bribery, expulsion from the tournament or the series is a reasonable penalty. If rule violations are more or less unintentional (there can be reasons for players or trainers not knowing the eligibility rules in detail), eliminating the advantage gained, for instance, by a certain deduction of points, might be the best penalty.

A norm for unequal treatment in meta-competitions

The discussion above serves to emphasize an important point. In meta-competitions we apply the same norms for unequal treatment as in single competitions. Meta-competitions are realized through individual competitions. Individual competitions are their building blocks. Therefore, in meta-competitions, the structural goal of individual competitions, the intentional goals of competitors, and possible moral goals of sport, ought to be granted action-guiding force. Meta-competitions are only a means for realizing these goals. Knockout competitions can increase excitement in individual competitions, while series can place individual competitions in a larger context, reduce the influence of chance and luck, and increase the accuracy of the measuring, comparing and ranking of competitors. Therefore, meta-competitions ought never to become goals in themselves, but be treated as secondary to the goals of their constitutive elements: individual competitions.

Practical experience bears out this point. It can be a problem, particularly in high-performance sport, that good results in meta-competitions are sometimes given higher priority than the structural goal and intentional goals of individual competitions. Football teams may take the field intending to play for a particular result, on which basis both teams will proceed. In a famous football match during the 1982 World Championships, West Germany beat Austria 1–0. The goal came in the first half, and both teams knew they would proceed (at the expense of Algeria) with that result. The second half became a parody in which neither team even tried to score. The match violated both the structural goal of competitions and the intentional goals of other parties concerned. FIFA now schedules matches so that the 'planning' of results becomes impossible. Another example can be found in tennis. In the Davis Cup in 1988, the Swedish team pulled out of the last match against West Germany because it had lost the first three games and would lose the meta-competition regardless of the outcome in that match. The individual competition lost 'significance'. This led to a public uproar and was one of the main reasons the team captain eventually had to resign.

Obviously, there seems to be a more or less tacit understanding among sports people and the public that single competitions are of primary importance. In order to avoid any concern that success in meta-competitions will be given priority over the values of single competitions, we should continually critically evaluate unequal treatment in meta-competitions, in accordance with the following norm:

> III.3.3 In meta-competitions, unequal treatment ought to increase the possibility for realizing the structural goal, the intentional goals among parties engaged, and the moral goal of single competitions.

SUMMARY

I set out at the beginning to articulate norms for 'morally right' conduct in sport competitions, understanding 'morally right' as having primarily to do with fairness and justice. I combined these two terms in formulating fairness norm 1.

I understood fairness norm 1 as an obligation that arises when we engage voluntarily in sport competitions. The norm prescribes conformity to the shared ethos among the participants in the sport in which they are engaged.

III Relevantly equal cases ought to be treated equally, cases that are relevantly unequal can be treated unequally, and unequal treatment ought to stand in a reasonable accordance to the actual inequality between cases

Equality

III.1 Relevantly equal cases ought to be treated equally

III.1.1 All competitors ought to be given equal opportunity to perform through eliminating or compensating for non-relevant inequalities

III.1.1.1 Uncontrollable inequalities in external conditions ought to be distributed by the drawing of competitors' positions

III.1.1.2 Controllable inequalities in external conditions ought to be eliminated whereas partly controllable inequalities in external conditions ought to be compensated for by mixed procedures that to the largest possible extent realize equal opportunity to perform

III.1.1.3 Competitors ought to be differentiated in classes only in cases where inequalities in person-dependent matters that they cannot influence in any significant way and for which they cannot be held responsible have systematic and significant influence on athletic performance

III.1.1.3.1 Where inequalities in body size, sex and age exert significant and systematic influence on athletic performance, such inequalities ought to be eliminated or compensated for by establishing reasonably standardized weight, height, sex, and age classes

III.1.1.4 Inequalities in access to resources that are not open to voluntary choice, and that exert significant and systematic influence on athletic performance, ought to be eliminated or compensated for by regulation of the competitive situation and/or by relevant standardization procedures

Inequality

III.2 Cases that are relevantly unequal can be treated unequally

III.2.1 In sport, unequal treatment ought to be based upon inequalities in athletic performance

III.2.1.1 In sport, unequal treatment ought to be based upon inequalities in performance within the framework of the relevant ethos that are:
• based upon talent, that is genetic pre-dispositions for the development of the relevant abilities and skills;
• based upon the actual realization of talent through the development of the relevant abilities and the learning of the relevant skills;
• in accordance with basic norm of not exposing others and oneself to unnecessary harm

Unequal treatment

III.3 Unequal treatment ought to stand in a reasonable accordance with the actual inequality between cases

III.3.1 Unequal treatment in the distribution of advantage among competitors ought to stand in a reasonable accordance with the actual inequality in athletic performance

III.3.1.1 Luck ought not to exert significant and systematic influence on the measuring, comparison, and ranking of competitors according to athletic performance, and possibilities for subjective and partial evaluation ought to be eliminated to the greatest possible extent

III.3.2 Inequalities due to rule violations ought to be eliminated or compensated for and there ought to be a reasonable accordance between the degree of violation and the penalties imposed

III.3.2.1 Advantage gained through unintentional rule violations ought to be eliminated or compensated for so that the initial position is restored to the greatest possible extent

III.3.2.2 Advantage gained through intentional rule violations ought to be eliminated or compensated for so that the initial situation is restored to the greatest possible extent; and the rule breaker ought to receive an additional penalty that reduces advantage and, for serious and repeated violations, leads to expulsion

III.3.3 In meta-competitions, unequal treatment ought to increase the possibility for realizing the structural goal, intentional goals among parties concerned, and the moral goal of single competitors

Figure 6 Justice in sport competitions

But this norm is valid only if the shared ethos can be said to be just. By elaborating requirements for justice I specified norm 1. In the process I have continually weighed my conclusions against first-order moral beliefs and common practice. Given this procedure, I believe the norms formulated are in line with meta-norm I and that no one can reasonably reject as a basis for unforced, informed general agreement.

The norms for justice are many and detailed. To clarify them and their relation to one another, see Figure 6 opposite.

We can now complete the formulation of fairness norm 1 by specifying the general norms for justice in competitions:

1 Parties voluntarily engaged in sport competitions ought to act in accordance with the shared ethos of the competitions, if this ethos is just, that is, if:

- the competitors are given equal opportunity to perform by eliminating or compensating for significant inequalities that the competitors cannot influence in any significant way and for which they cannot be held responsible;
- athletic performance is interpreted as based on talent and individual effort, and performances adhere to a basic norm of not exposing others or oneself to unnecessary harm;
- unequal treatment in the distribution of advantage is in reasonable accordance with actual inequality in athletic performance, and unequal treatment in terms of eliminating or compensating for advantage gained through rule violations is in reasonable accordance with the actual inequality that has arisen due to the violation.

In summing up, some important points should be emphasized. As in other social practices, in sport too we normally end up with imperfect procedures of justice. But the fact that one or a set of norms or actions is unjust does not mean the practice as a whole is unjust. We might think that the offside rule in football is vaguely formulated and impossible to implement in a just way, but we can still accept football games as basically just. We might think that a 3000-metres runner pushed another runner unwarrantedly at the first turn, but still find their ranking at the finishing line fair. The obligation of fairness applies in all situations in competitions. The general norm for upholding justice means that persons engaged in sport ought critically to explore how the shared ethos can better satisfy demands for justice. Sportspeople should exercise their sense of justice, and if they see possibilities to enhance justice, they ought to argue in favour of more just alternatives.

Lastly, if sport competitions as a whole do not satisfy demands for justice, the obligation to abide by fairness norm 1 does not arise. If competitors find an ethos gravely unjust, they should not take part at all in the practice regulated by it. If in the process of competing, participants find that the way competition is being run is fundamentally unjust, they should withdraw. A badminton player, who is constantly subjected to cheating upon by an opponent who calls good shots out, should inform her opponent of the wrongness of her actions before that player leaves the court. An ice hockey team that encounters consistent unfair, violent play should inform the violating team of its wrongdoing and stop playing. This is what Fraleigh (1984: 143, 152) refers to with various versions of 'the guide of prudent withdrawal'.[19]

Chapter 4

Good sport competitions

Play

SPORT: PLAY, WORK OR WAR?[1]

In Chapter 3 I looked at what can be adjusted morally right in sport competitions, concentrating on ideas of fairness and justice. However, this is not enough for a comprehensive theory of fair play in sport. When I took up the question of the role of chance and luck, and considered how to choose between different interpretations of athletic performance, I complemented these ideas with others about what constitutes a good competition, not merely a fair one. I shall now look more closely at these matters. How can we formulate action-guiding norms intended to give rise to good competitions?

There are many views of what are the proper or the 'real' norms and values of sport. The powerful amateurist ideology, with norms of a disinterested and non-instrumental attitude at its core, developed historically in the culture of social elites. At first sight, the amateur ethos may seem to be a morally elegant and sophisticated philosophy of life. I am talking here of the ideal of the English gentleman and of 'the joy found in effort', to borrow the formulation used in the statement of the fundamental principles of the Olympic Movement (IOC 2000b). However, the social and political realities associated with this ideology were harsh. Reading between the lines of the amateur ethos we find a degree of contempt for the customs and attitudes of the lower socio-economic classes. In practice, amateur rules and regulations led to discrimination and the exclusion of people from sport, based on their social status.

A less ideologically repressive view of the values of a non-instrumental attitude is found in what we may call the 'play' tradition. A wide range of historians, psychologists and philosophers, among them Plato (1995), Schiller (1988), Huizinga (1950), Sartre (1995), and Csikszentmihaly (1975), offer a variety of arguments in favour of play. In play we are most truly human; play lies at the heart of culture; moments of play provide experiences of 'deep flow'; play offers existential self-realization. Meier echoes this tradition when he declares:

> ... I wish to proclaim, to extol, to champion, and to celebrate the cause of

frivolity, uselessness, unproductivity, inconsequentiality, nonachievment, gratuitousness, irrelevance, and irreverence. In short, I wish to offer an apology for, and an appreciation of, play.

(Meier 1980: 24)

More specifically, philosophical texts on sport, such as those of Suits (1978), Meier (1988), Hyland (1990), and Morgan (1994), centre in various ways on ideas of the distinctive playful, gratuitous logic of sport, or claims that sport is at its best when practised from 'the stance of play' (Hyland 1990: 125ff.), with a certain playful or non-instrumental attitude.

The view that play is a morally superior human endeavour, and that sport is at its best when it realizes such play, has its appeal and no doubt is relevant to the philosophy of sport. At the same time, such a view can be criticized for idealizing reality. There are other competing and to a certain extent opposed views that need to be mentioned here. Radical critics, among them Hortleder (1978), Rigauer (1969), Brohm (1978), Beamish (1982), and Gruneau (1999), understand sport as a mirror of the repressive norms and values of capitalist society. In these views, sport is a kind of work. Competition nourishes individualism and egoism, and results in alienating practices. As the title of Brohm's (1978) book puts it, sport is a 'prison of measured time'. Tännsjö's (1998) critique is even stronger: competitive sport tends to cultivate the unhealthy admiration of the strong and contempt for weakness that are key characteristics of a 'fascistoid' attitude. To these critics, the play tradition serves as a false ideology, in a Marxist sense of that term. The rhetoric of freedom and human values draws attention away from the true degenerative forces of sport systems.

To a certain extent, critical views find support among sport practitioners. Some competitors, support systems and spectators talk of competitions as more or less a kind of war. As the legendary football coach Bill Shankley of Liverpool FC said on the day he retired: 'Some people say football is a matter of life and death, but it is much more important than that.' Coakley (1998: 98) describes an interpretation of sport according to 'the power and performance model': the aggressive use of power and strength among athletes to dominate. Opponents are seen as antagonists and enemies, and athletes' bodies are considered mere means to maximize performance and win.

It is difficult to reject categorically one or another of these views from the outset of an argument about good sport. Like other social practices, sport is ambiguous and can be interpreted and practised in various ways. Is it possible to proceed from such diversity and make progress in devising a normative argument about good competitions? In Book VI of the *Nichomachean Ethics*, Aristotle (1976) distinguishes between various intellectual virtues and links prudence or practical rationality to the political sciences and ethics. A convincing argument based on practical rationality should start from commonly accepted premises and proceed from there to more specific conclusions. If we suppose that, *a priori*, all views of sport are of equal value, and then in a critical and systematic way proceed to weigh them against each other, our argument becomes more inclusive. We have the possibility of addressing the interests of most of the parties engaged and of exploring to what extent it is possible to reach some common ground as defined by meta-norm I – to formulate norms that cannot be reasonably rejected as a basis for unforced, informed general agreement.

GOOD COMPETITIONS AS THE REALIZATION OF INTENTIONAL GOALS

Let us start by looking at common-sense understandings of the characteristics of good competitions. Consider the 1999 final of the French Open tennis tournament between the American Andre Agassi, at that time thirteenth in the world ranking, and the Russian Andrei Medvedev, ranked hundredth and the lowest-ranked player ever to reach the final of this tournament. Medvedev began brilliantly and won the first two sets easily, 6–1 and 6–2. Agassi then managed to turn the match around and take the last three sets 6–4, 6–3 and 6–4. The event was later described by commentators and the public as the match that 'had everything'. Both players played according to a shared, just ethos, both performed close to the highest standards of excellence of tennis, and both were happy with the result. Medvedev unexpectedly reached the final and played very well. As he said: 'I cannot say I did anything wrong, he (Agassi) just played unbelievably ... I left my heart and soul on the court. I had nothing left' (CNN/SI 1999: 1). Agassi was outplayed in the first two sets but came back and finally won the match: 'What I've managed to accomplish is astonishing .... This was the greatest thing I could ever do' (CNN/SI 1999: 2).

Now imagine, another tennis match between the star women's player Venus Williams and an amateur player. Let us assume that both players abide by fairness norm 1 – they play in accordance with a shared, just ethos. The structural goal of competitions is achieved – the players are measured, compared and ranked according to athletic performance. In spite of this, none or very few of us would characterize the competition as 'good'. Williams's service would be almost unreturnable for the amateur who, in addition, could do little at the base line or at the net. Neither of the players would really be challenged on their skills. Neither of them would be able to play at her best. The outcome is a foregone conclusion. Neither the players nor any other parties engaged would probably find the game of good quality.

What, from a systematic and critical point of view, characterizes good competitions? In working out norms for fair play, I based my argument on the premise that we take part in sport on a voluntary basis. We are not forced to engage in the practice; we have the choice between participation and non-participation. I further assumed that such a choice is an expression of intentional goals. Some competitors are motivated by experiential qualities of the activity itself, such as the experience of joy, fun, mastery, challenge, and excitement. Others have goals that can be realized outside the activity, such as improving health, building up social networks and friendship, or achieving prestige and profit. Most competitors combine a variety of intentional goals in more or less complex goal structures. Irrespective of the origins and content of intentional goals, however, it seems reasonable to assume that a competitor would consider a competition to be good if it realized the full range of his or her intentional goals to the greatest possible extent.

Can we draw normative conclusions from this? The intuitive idea of fairness set out in Chapter 3 holds that if we are voluntarily engaged in a practice that requires the cooperation of others, we benefit from such cooperation and should therefore contribute to it by doing our share of cooperating. In my terminology, we can say that if we are given the opportunity to realize our intentional goals linked to a practice by the cooperation of others, it is reasonable that we give others a similar fair chance to realize their intentional goals through our cooperation. The guiding idea is that, in principle, our own intentional goals cannot be given priority over and above other persons' intentional goals. We can now formulate a preliminary norm 2 for good competitions:

> 2 Parties voluntarily engaged in sport competitions ought to act in such a way that all parties concerned have their intentional goals linked to the competitions realized to the greatest possible extent.

Norm 2 prescribes choice of actions according to their consequences. Although norm 2 is based on the idea of fairness, its main prescription is consequentialist in kind. We need to examine the relevance of norm 2 in more detail. In Chapter 2, we discussed the potential and limitations of consequentialist reasoning and formulated general backing norm II based on preference-utilitarianism:

> II Maximize average preference-satisfaction among all parties concerned.

Can norm II be of help in the specification of norm 2 and, if so, how?

UTILITARIANISM APPLIED

Norm II is not unproblematic. In Chapter 2 I discussed the problem of accepting all kinds of preferences in a utilitarian calculus, even those most of us would consider confused or evil. I also discussed the problem that utilitarianism operates with persons as 'sites of preference-satisfaction' and seems to lack an adequate conception of persons as moral agents. Similarly, the utilitarian approach seems to build on a reductionist understanding of social life, in that it cannot clearly distinguish between general norms and obliga-tions, and has little room for individual rights and duties.

Modern utilitarian theories, such as Hare's (1963, 1981) 'universal prescriptivism', from which norm II is derived, are capable of withstanding some of this criticism. Hare's (1981) distinction between two levels of moral thinking reserves a place for non-consequentialist reasoning in daily life. However, in dilemmas of choice, Hare recommends recourse to the critical level and the adoption of a strict utilitarian approach.

I contended that consequentialist reasoning is an intuitively appealing and important part of an ethical argument, but that it ought to be complemented by non-consequentialist considerations, in what Frankena (1967) calls a mixed theory. Fairness norm 1 was devised based on a non-consequentialist norm of justice. In the specification of norm 2, a utilitarian approach seems relevant. If conclusions based on consequentialist reasoning are consistent with our idea of fairness, this should strengthen their justification. If utilitarian conclusions contradict fairness norm 1, we ought to reconsider the utilitarian approach, and perhaps the more extensive framework in terms of our moral point of view as well. The aim is to reach a consistent articulation of fair play that is in reflective equilibrium between general norms and first-order moral beliefs and which, in line with meta-norm I, no one can reasonably reject as a basis for informed, unforced general agreement.

Still, even if we accept the utilitarian view of good competitions whereby we try to maximize expected average preference-satisfaction among all parties concerned, there are significant difficulties in measuring and comparing exactly what kinds of competitions that can realize this ideal. In a given situation, each party concerned usually has a range of preferences of varying strength. In many situations we are not even able to describe our own preference structures with accuracy. And even if we could describe them, we face an even greater challenge at the next step, where our own preferences are to be compared with another person's, or those of ten others, or in complex ethical dilemmas, with hundreds, thousands, or millions of other affected parties. Moreover, who are to count as affected parties? Are we dealing with human beings only, or with all sentient beings that are able to feel pleasure and pain?

There are also problems linked to the time frame of utilitarian calculations, too. Are we talking of preference satisfaction now, in the immediate future, within the next five years, or *sub specie aeternis*? Many of our preferences change over time. Ought we to calculate them as they are now, or as they presumably will be in the near or distant future? Even if the time frame and the relevant parties affected by the dilemma under discussion are strongly limited, utilitarians seem to take too much for granted when it comes to the prediction of future events in terms of consequences. Individuals and societies do not seem to develop and change according to strict chains of cause and effect. Our preferences are influenced and altered according to the socio-psychological and socio-cultural contexts in which we live, to our own reflection over our preferences, and the consequences of our choices and actions.

Bentham's dream of mathematically precise calculations of felt pleasure and pain is nothing more than utopian. Indeed, utilitarians today have generally abandoned it as just that. But this does not mean that an attempt to estimate average preference satisfaction loses all meaning. First, there is no need to make exaggerated claims about the accuracy of estimations of 'the good'. As norm II indicates, modern utility theory talks of expected, not actual, utility. Moreover, developments in the post-war era of decision and game theory demonstrate the possibility of reducing complexity in dilemmas of choice and of constructing hypothetical scenarios in which agents are considered as carriers of one or a few predominant preferences with well-defined strengths. In spite of the reductionism involved, utilitarian approaches can provide analytic insights into dilemma situations that can be of significant help.

Therefore, I shall seek to specify norm 2 for good competitions based on the utilitarian backing norm II. First, I shall give an overview of the parties concerned and their main preferences. Alternative norms in competitions will then be weighed and compared in terms of utility.

PREFERENCES AMONG PARTIES CONCERNED

What preferences linked to their engagement in sport do people have? As we know, there is a bewildering variety here. Still, analytically speaking, preferences linked to sport can be placed in two main categories: internal and external preferences.

Internal preferences

Internal preferences are preferences that are satisfied in the very activity of competing. Preference satisfaction takes the form of experiential values of different kinds that are realized in the sport activity itself. Football players experience excitement in challenging for the ball; gymnasts are motivated by the experience of mastery in performing advanced techniques on the different apparatus; the alpine skier enjoys the rhythm and speed of a well-designed giant slalom course. More generally, competitors seem to value the excitement and challenge linked to the uncertainty of outcome in close competitions.

Internal preferences are best described in phenomenological terms. I am talking here of 'the tacit dimension' of sport – experiences of bodily movements and social interactions that are hard to describe. Moreover, logically, the realization of such experiential values depends on the realization of the sport within which they arise. It is hard to experience excitement in a game of football where the shared ethos is constantly broken. An alpine skier cannot fully enjoy a well-designed course if she neglects the gates of a difficult part of it. We are dealing here with preferences for the internal goods of sport in a MacIntyrean sense of the word: goods that can only be realized inside the very practice of a shared, just ethos of the sport in question.

External preferences

Competitors with external preferences view their athletic engagement as means to the realization of goals outside the competitive activity. Some people engage in competitions to attain social prestige and acclaim; others seek friends and to build up social networks; high-performance athletes compete, at least to a certain extent, for fame and fortune. Again, we find a great variety of preference content. Perhaps more than internal preferences, external ones are shaped and developed by the socio-cultural contexts of which sport is a part.

Historically, competitions and sport have been regarded as instrumental to realizing external values ever since ancient Sparta, where physical training was seen as an important part of the rearing of young boys and girls for military purposes. The roots of modern mass sport are to be found in part in the philanthropic movement on the European continent at the turn of the eighteenth century, with Guts Muths and Friedrich Ludwig Jahn ('Turnvater Jahn') as the dominant figures. Influenced by the pedagogical ideas of Rousseau, among others, sport and gymnastics were to serve socio-hygienic and socio-political purposes. A strong and well-conditioned body was the basis for sound development and a good and healthy life. Gymnastics in particular was considered a useful means in a nationalistic and patriotic upbringing (Mandell 1984: 158ff.).

The direct origin of competitive sport as we know it is found in England, 'the land of sport', in the second half of the eighteenth century (Holt 1989). Sport changed with the material, social and economic development of society. The rapidly emerging industrialized, capitalist world, provided one normative framework, with a focus on teamwork, productivity, performance and results. Rules were standardized and sport competitions were established using speci-fications of general application, according to which records and progress could be measured in objective ways (Guttmann 1978). Another normative framework was provided by the British public school system, in which sport developed as a pedagogical tool for the socialization of potential leaders of the British Empire. Finally, through the rise of the Olympic Movement in the twentieth century, sport gradually became a global testing ground for the strength of nations and ideological systems (Hill 1992; Guttmann 1992). Today, parts of the high-performance sport system are integrated into an international entertainment industry with profit as a major, driving force. Political ideology seems at least in part to have been absorbed by economics.

Typically, then, external preferences can be realized outside of sport competitions only, and they have no necessary connection with internal preferences and the experiential values of sport.

Preference content among all parties concerned

I have drawn an analytic distinction between two categories of preferences that are relevant to sport. According to norm II, we should choose those options that can be expected to maximize average preference satisfaction among all parties concerned. Who are the parties concerned in sport and what are their preferences?

Parties concerned

Among the primary parties concerned, of course, are the competitors themselves, who are affected by the immediate consequences of what happens in the practice. In competitive sport at club and regional levels of performance, competitors are pretty much the only ones concerned.[2]

At higher levels of performance, the number grows significantly. First, in addition to competitors, we often find officials. Their primary role is to uphold justice and to contribute in accordance with what is officially considered the just ethos of the sport.

Second, as we have seen in the discussion of equality in Chapter 3, sport at national and international levels often includes extensive support systems of human, scientific, technological, and economic resources. The people involved in support systems do not compete directly but are significantly affected by the outcomes of competitions. If a professional football team has a bad losing streak, the coach will normally be fired. If the team wins the series, the coach has a very good basis for negotiating a new contract.

A third group of affected parties comprises the spectators. Here, preferences are extremely heterogeneous both in content and in strength. This group will be discussed in greater detail below.

Finally, in a comprehensive utilitarian analysis, the circle of parties concerned ought to be expanded. We must acknowledge the global impact of our actions and practices. The vast material, economic and human resources spent on sport could have been spent otherwise. If we stretch the argument, we could say that if a particular sport event had not been realized, the world would have been a different (perhaps significantly different, to someone at some time) place to live. The first Olympic Games in Athens in 1896 were the start of a tradition that has played a decisive role in the development of sport and its role in society in the twentieth century. A World Cup qualifying football match in 1969 between El Salvador and Honduras is said to have been the spark that ignited the so-called football war between the two countries. The war lasted five days, six thousand people were killed and fifty thousand were made homeless (Espy 1979). Today, a game of tennis with a friend could have been dropped in favour of a few hours of extra work for a salary that could have gone to charity and perhaps saved a child from starvation in a Third World country.

One of the useful features of utilitarian reasoning is that it stimulates global thinking. This coheres, so to speak, with the important ecological ideal of thinking globally and acting locally. However, a large-scale examination of whether the resources spent on competitive sport can be morally justified is beyond the scope of my task here. I seek to examine the necessary but not sufficient conditions for sport to have moral value and for sport competitions to be just and good, not questions such as whether sport can be morally justified in a global perspective. I exclude from this analysis, therefore, all parties who are indirectly concerned and who do not have any direct preferences in relation to sporting events. The weighing of preference-satisfaction in the calculations to follow will concern only the following directly affected parties:

- competitors (and officials)
- support systems
- spectators.

Let us discuss these parties one by one. I shall describe the logic of their role in the sport system, and with support from empirical material where possible, suggest what might be assumed to be their main preferences.

Preference content among competitors

What are the preferences of competitors? From what has been said above we can see that they are of both internal and external kinds.

At lower levels of performance I assume that most competitors act on internal preferences, that is, on preferences for experiential values realized in the competitions themselves. Most people take part for the joy of it, for fun and pleasure, for experiences of challenge and mastery, and for social values such as cooperation and the feeling of community (Weinberg and Gould 1999: 115ff.).

This does not, of course, exclude the possibility that competitors have external preferences. We may join the local football club to make friends, we may engage in orienteering to learn to handle a map and a compass. Still, at the local level of performance, it seems reasonable to assume that the realization of external preferences depends to a large extent on competitions being run according to a just, shared ethos. If we break the ethos of football, friendship is unlikely to be the outcome of our engagement. If we do not take the techniques and tactics of orienteering seriously, we will not learn to handle the map and compass.

At higher levels of performance, external preferences seem to play a more significant role. Studies of the social logic of high-performance sport portray a harsh reality (Heikkala 1993). What counts here is progress and success. Heinilä (1982) talks of the over-evaluation of success and the weakened position of the individual athlete in relation to the system. Win or perish! In such a context, the dominant rationality becomes that of 'economic man' – competitors are pragmatic and view sport merely as a means towards external goals (Breivik 1987).

It has to be said, though, that the experiences of sport among elite athletes point towards the significance of internal preferences, too. The Danish handball star Anja Andersen does not play handball just for the money. She claims, and she acts as if, she loves the sport. Michael 'Air' Jordan would probably never have reached his levels of performance in basketball if he had not loved the game. Dreyfus and Dreyfus (1986: 30–36) portray the expert's execution of skills in various fields as one of creativity and complete devotion. A survey among Norwegian elite athletes demonstrates that inner motivation, or what I call internal preferences, play a predominant role (Gilberg and Breivik 1998).

The only conclusion we can draw at this stage is that some competitors have predominant internal preferences and that others have predominant external preferences. Probably, preference orientations vary from situation to situation, too. The question of what kind of preferences ought to be the action-guiding ones can be answered only by a systematic weighing of their consequences for all parties concerned. This will be done in what follows.

A note on officials

Whereas at amateur levels the competitors themselves are usually responsible for officiating, high-performance sport allocates this to specialized officials. Their role, among other things, is to discipline competitors with extreme 'win at any cost' preferences to ensure that competitions are realized according to what is considered a just ethos of the sport in question.

Officials are hardly ever well paid for their job. Moreover, to perform well they need relatively advanced theoretical and practical insights into their sport. The very logic of their role, and the general lack of possibilities for material and economic rewards, would suggest that their main preferences are internal. Weinberg and Richardson (1990) claim that officials are primarily motivated by being able to continue their engagement in the sports that they love after their athletic careers have ended. An American study of high-school basketball officials points to a similar conclusion (Purdy and Snyder 1985). Officials enjoy their sporting environment and want to be part of it for as long as possible. In addition, they value the challenge of officiating and the feeling of being able to contribute to their favourite sports. No doubt, just as with competitors, we would also find external preferences, such as a quest for social networks and friends, and for fame and prestige. But, again as with amateur competitors, these external goals are realizable only if officials perform successfully. We may assume that their predominant preference is that competitions should be fair, just, and good. It is internal in kind.

Preference content in support systems

Competitors' support systems consist of coaches, managers, sport physicians, equipment specialists and technologists, and researchers and scientists of various kinds. This is a heterogeneous group. However, in terms of preferences some generalizations can be made.

Most coaches are engaged due to their competence in, and feeling for, their sport. They are knowledgeable about its technical and tactical finesse, its physical and psychological demands, and so on. Moreover, coaches play a more or less active part in the very process of competing and may directly or indirectly influence the outcome of competitions. What are their predominant preferences?

At lower levels of performance we find self-appointed coaches and leaders who are engaged on a voluntary basis. As with athletes at the same level, there are few possibilities for prestige and profit. In fact, most coaches spend their own money and time on their engagement. We may assume that, at this level, internal preferences are dominant.

At higher levels of performance, preferences are often different. The role of the professional coach is characterized by ambivalence and what appear to be contradictory expectations (Cratty 1983; Jones *et al.* 1988: 3–42). Coaches are expected to be successful, and at the same time to represent moral values such as justice and fairness. They are supposed to maximize the performance potential of each individual athlete and team, and at the same time care for each individual's well being in the larger scheme of things.

Good coaches are able to deal with these ambivalences. The gymnastics coach with no sense for the internal values of the sport, or the alpine coach who sees her athletes only as a means to reach external goals, will probably never get very far. Internal preferences are significant. Still, Heinilä's (1982) thesis of 'the iron law of success' in high-performance sport holds among coaches as well. Their employers, such as clubs and national federations, demand success, profit and/or prestige. Sponsors and advertisers demand success and a positive public image. The public and the media want success and good entertainment. So there are strong external preferences among coaches, too.

Other people in the support system, such as the bio-medical staff, technicians, researchers, administrators, and sponsors, obviously take an interest in and are motivated by the experiential values of sport. But perhaps to an even greater degree than coaches they are dominated by external preferences, because competition outcomes determine their future. Most of them are engaged due to external expertise (and not for 'the love of the game' as often as with coaches), and their professional survival depends totally on success, that is, on getting 'their' competitors to the top of the final ranking. The history of drug use and manipulation of performance demonstrate that there seem to be few scruples when it comes to what support systems are willing to do to reach their goals (Hoberman 1992).

Although coaches and members of support systems have strong internal preferences for fair and good competitions, the very existence of such systems depends upon 'their' athletes performing successfully and thus attracting public attention. We may assume, therefore, that their predominant preferences are external in kind.

Preference content among spectators

Spectators make up a large preference group. One of the largest stadiums of the world, the Brazilian football stadium Maracana, holds 140,000 spectators. On average, the ten largest sport facilities in the world can hold just above 100,000 people.[3] Competitive sport is among the most popular products in the international commercial entertainment market. The Olympic Games and the Football World Cup are televised to approximately one billion people (Spà *et al.* 1995). What are the predominant preferences among spectators?

The view of spectators as passive consumers or casual observers should be rejected. Spectators are active constructors of meanings (Whannel 1998). Their socio-cultural background, gender and age, and the characteristics of the sport to which they are attracted, are all significant factors in understanding their preferences. At the risk of somewhat reducing this diversity, I shall suggest three preference structures associated with what I consider to be three representative spectator groups.

Group I: the connoisseurs

The traditional ideal is that of the knowledgeable and morally conscious spectator. This ideal stems primarily from middle and upper class spectators of sport in Victorian Britain at the end of the nineteenth century. Here there seems to be a more or less shared ethos of spectatorship. Guttmann (1986) quotes Walter Camp of Yale, who wrote in 1889:

> It is not courtesy upon a ballfield to cheer an error of the opponents. If it is on your grounds, it is the worst kind of boorishness. Moreover, if there are remarkable plays made by your rivals you yourselves should cheer.
>
> (Guttmann 1986: 88)

The key values are knowledge of the game, impartiality, and (masculine) and social class-related dignity. An updated version of the ideal impartial spectator is expressed in Lasch's (1979: 103–108) notion of 'the knowledgeable spectator'.

The connoisseurs are deeply and seriously engaged in their favourite sport in many ways; in its history, its technical and tactical complexity, its standards of excellence, and its role as a societal ideal. Their main preference is for competitions to reach their structural goal in fair, just, good, and exciting ways. Sport is an expression of significant moral values. As Skillen (1998) points out, at its best sport is a paradigmatic expression of the strength and beauty of the human spirit.

Are such group I spectators historical anachronisms? Do they have a role to play in today's highly commercialized entertainment sport? Lasch is critical of what he sees as the trivialization and corruption of sport: 'Television has enlarged the audience for sport while lowering the level of its understanding' (Lasch 1979: 106). Players, promoters and spectators alike deny the seriousness of sport and turn it into sensationalist and sometimes aggressive, chauvinist and sexist entertainment. Similarly, Morgan (1994) argues against what he sees as the current degeneration of sport and in favour of a deliberative and value-sensitive sporting community.

The predominant preference among the connoisseurs is to experience the relevant standards of excellence (technical, tactical and morally) of the sport in question. The preference is internal in kind.

Group II: the supporters

Other spectator groups see sport to a large extent as an arena for identification and identity construction. Competitions invite partisanship and choice of favourites, and encourage alignments of 'us' against 'them'. Since ancient times, important spectator virtues have been partiality, loyalty and solidarity linked to favourite athletes and teams (Guttmann 1986).

In modern pluralistic and secularized societies, these possibilities have perhaps become more relevant than ever. But the support of favourites has various intensities. To most of us, identification with a competitor or a team is not of a deep and fundamental kind. American track and field fans cheered for Marion Jones during the 1999 World Athletics Championships and were disappointed when she pulled a muscle during the 200 metres. Still, the next day most of them had probably no strong feelings about the event. At an international football match, supporters stand by their team passionately during the game but a few hours afterwards return to their ordinary lives without having been significantly changed by the result. Jarvie and Walker (1994) rightly talk of '90-minute patriots'.

To others, sport is a matter of intense engagement and indeed of identification in fundamental existential terms. Beisser (1967) writes of such sports fans as 'members of the tribe'. We are moving now from what could be called situational identification to identity construction. Studies of supporter cultures as arenas for such constructions have proliferated significantly in the last few decades (Armstrong and Guilianotti 1997, 1999). Archetti (1999), for instance, has shown how in Argentina, rural polo, urban football and the tango constitute three pillars in the construction of national masculinity. In extreme situations, the outcomes of competitions can become matters of life and death.

A paradigmatic (and amusing) version of the preferences of group II spectators can be found in author Nick Hornby's description of the good football game. Hornby (1992: 235–7) lists a series of characteristics, among them as many goals as possible, some bad officiating decisions ('indignation is a crucial ingredient of the perfect football experience ...), a rainy day and a wet pitch ('. . . you can't beat the sight of players sliding ten of fifteen yards for a tackle or in an attempt to get a touch to a cross'), bad misses such as missed penalties from the opposing team, red cards to players from the opposing team, and a bit of aggression ('. . . there is nothing like a punch-up to enliven an otherwise dull game').

However, the degree of roughness desired by Hornby is not necessarily of a serious kind. Too many unfair refereeing decisions can ruin a match and too much aggression can turn matches into chaos. Most supporter cultures have relatively clear images of what norms and values need to be upheld in order for competitions to be meaningful. In some sports, supporters have become a significant political force in the development of the sport and the teams they support. In the fall of 1998, the Murdoch-controlled TV-channel BSkyB offered more than £600 million for the football team Manchester United. The team's independent supporters' club reacted sharply, for they feared the influence of investors with no 'love for the game'. Indeed, supporter protest was one of the main reasons why the deal was never realized.[4]

Sport binds supporters together in communities of agreement, loyalty and solidarity. If their sport degenerates, their communities will too. The predominant preference of group II spectators is to experience intensity, drama, and to identify with their favourites via some degree of conflict between 'them' and 'us'. They confirm and construct identity linked to their sport by finding affirmation in times of success, and by giving moral support in times of trouble. The realization of these preferences depends at least to a certain extent on competitions being run in a fair and morally good way. So the preferences of group II spectators are primarily internal in kind.

Group III: the fans

The third group of spectators consists of people who are less knowledgeable about sport than the connoisseur and less devoted than group II supporters, but who follow sport casually, primarily on TV. This is a large group. More than a billion people are said to follow events such as the Summer Olympic Games or the Football World Cup via the mass media. Why do people watch sport on TV? What are their preferences?

Factor analysis of empirical data on spectator satisfaction indicates some common features. As with most entertainment products, TV sport gives spectators an opportunity to 'let loose', get 'psyched up', 'let off steam', and to 'fill in' or 'kill time'. At the same time, Wenner and Gantz (1998) emphasize the diversity of spectator experiences. Different sports have their particular entertainment qualities, men and women experience sport differently, and experiences vary according to age, socio-economic class, and ethnicity. Bryant *et al.* (1999) note an additional aspect: player aggressiveness enhances spectators' enjoyment of the event especially for males.[5]

There are structural characteristics of sport as TV entertainment that may help explain their immense popularity. In common with the spectators in group II, but with less intensity, TV audiences enjoy following their favourite teams and athletes, and the experience of 'basking in reflected glory' when their favourites succeed. The possibility of experiencing tension and excitement is enhanced because sport competitions offer simple plots that even inexperienced spectators can understand. Will the high jumper make it over the bar? Will the attack result in a goal? Who will win in the end? Finally, the excitement and tension of a good competition is somehow 'the real thing'. As Whannel says:

> Sport events offer a liminal moment between uncertainty and certainty; unlike fictional narrative, they are not predetermined by authorship, nor can they be predicted by cultural code or even by specialized knowledge. They offer a rare opportunity to experience genuine uncertainty.
>
> (Whannel 1998: 229)

The fan group III is difficult to locate with respect to the internal–external preference distinction. Fans want exciting and close competitions, and appreciate and admire fairness and justice. At the same time, preference satisfaction seems to increase if conflict and aggression are involved. The fans can enjoy competitions between extremely instrumentally oriented athletes as well as between players with a love for the game. So in terms of the internal/external distinction, there are really no clear preferences here. The fan group represents total relativism.

Preference strength

I have now tried to map preference content among all parties concerned in sport competitions. To carry out a utilitarian calculation of average preference satisfaction in a given situation, however, this is not enough. Such calculations need to take into account the intensity or strength of preferences as well. For instance, imagine a competition between X and Y, where X and Y are the only parties concerned and X has a burning desire to win whereas Y does not really care about the result. A strict utilitarian would have to argue that X ought to win even at the cost of ethos violations, because this solution can be expected to maximize average preference-satisfaction among the two. If, on the other hand, Y's preference for a fair and good game is the stronger one, Y ought to win.

In a utilitarian argument, calculation of preference strength is necessary but difficult. Each individual is unique and no two preferences are identical, whether we talk of content or of strength. As with preference content, preference strength can be calculated only to a degree of approximation.

At first sight it seems reasonable to assume that preferences among competitors, officials and support systems are stronger than preferences among spectators. After all, these seem to be the parties that have to bear the direct consequences of whatever happens in competitions. On closer inspection, however, we realize that this is not always the case. Whereas a fan may forget a loss by her favourite team within an hour, a loyal supporter may commit suicide. Variation in the strength of spectator preferences is probably large but incalculable.

At this stage, therefore, I shall make no attempt to compare preference strength between individuals or groups of individuals. Instead I shall concentrate on within-group calculations for competitors, officials, support systems, and spectators, respectively. If, in the end, predominant preferences of all parties concerned point towards the same solution, between-group comparisons of preference strength are not in fact needed. However, if the outcome of the calculation is uncertain or unclear, I must go back to the beginning and try to establish fine-grained and more detailed distinctions, and perhaps include between-group comparisons of preference strength as well.

Preferences of all parties concerned – an overview

Figure 7 (opposite) provides an overview of my conclusions about the preferences of the parties concerned in sport competitions.

AN ARGUMENT AT THE CRITICAL LEVEL OF MORAL THOUGHT

Oscar Wilde is said to have declared that 'a cynic is someone who knows the price of everything and the value of nothing'. In the following section I shall try to estimate the 'price' of some alternative norms, in terms of expected average preference satisfaction. But unlike Wilde's cynic, I shall not fail to reflect upon the values implicit in the conclusion reached. Rather, I shall critically examine whether these values can be said to be in line with my moral point of view and satisfy meta-norm I, which requires us to choose norms that no one can reasonably reject as a basis for unforced, informed general agreement.

Let us now return to Hare's description of the critical level of moral thinking. The task is to evaluate alternative solutions to the question of good competitions in which, as prescribed by norm 2, intentional goals among all

Party concerned	Predominant preferences
Competitors	Internal preferences: to realize experiential values in the process of competing External preferences: to reach external goals – competitions are means only
Support system	External preferences: to reach external goals – competitions are means only
Spectators and the mass media	Internal preferences: to realize experiential values within the competitions External preferences: to reach external goals – competitions are means only

Figure 7 Preference content among parties concerned in sport competitions

parties concerned are realized to the greatest possible extent. This shall be done with the utilitarian norm II as the criterion for choice.

External and internal winning preferences

I have described a variety of internal and external preferences linked to sport. But these preferences are not unique. We find process-oriented internal preferences in other leisure activities, such as bridge, music or amateur acting. Similarly with external preferences: people go for walks to improve health, join philatelist clubs to meet friends, and enter the movie business to become rich and famous. In discussion at the critical level of moral thought, we therefore need to define dilemmas of choice in more specific terms.

The structural goal of sport competitions is to measure, compare and rank competitors according to athletic performance. Getting to the top of the formal ranking is defined as 'winning'. Hence competitions are often called 'win-or-lose games'. A competition is not normally regarded as over until a final ranking of all competitors is complete. If in baseball, the score is tied after the ninth inning, the teams play additional innings one at a time until one team gains a lead. Ice hockey and football matches can be brought to an end by playing extra time under the 'sudden death' principle: the first team to score wins. Obviously, both external and internal preferences must somehow relate to the structural goal of competitions and to interpretations of 'winning'.

The minimum interpretation is linked to external preferences. Usually, external goals such as fame and fortune depend upon competitors being ranked at or near the top of the final ranking. Ethos conformity, or the idea of winning in a manner deemed fair, is considered secondary, and must be forsaken when other means appear to be more effective. The external interpretation of winning is 'to win by being ranked first in the final ranking (even at the cost of ethos violations)!', or simply:

- Win!

The more elaborate interpretation of winning discussed in Chapter 1 is linked to internal preferences. The constitutive rules of a sport define its specific goals and the means with which to reach them. In tennis, advantage is gained by placing the ball within the other player's court half but out of her reach. In handball and ice hockey, a team scores a goal by getting the ball or the puck over the goal line, in accordance with the ethos of the game. The winning team is the team that has performed the best according to the commonly accepted standards of excellence of the sport in question. Here, winning is not related solely to an outcome in terms of a ranking, but to the way we compete during the competitions. To win presupposes fairness, that is, competing according to a shared, just ethos. The internal winning preference can be expressed as 'play (according to a shared, just ethos) to win!' or more simply as

- Play to win!

A utilitarian analysis

These two kinds of winning preference can now be matched against each other in three alternative competitions A1, A2, and A3:

- A1: both competitors have external winning preferences. I shall call this the instrumentalists' competition;
- A2: one competitor has external winning preferences, and the other has internal ones. This is called a mixed competition;
- A3: both competitors have internal winning preferences. Here, competing according to a shared, just ethos becomes a goal in itself. This can be called the players' competition.

Which alternative gives us the best competitions? Which alternative can be expected to maximize average preference satisfaction among all parties concerned?

In the utilitarian analysis that follows, I shall use the framework of decision theory. Decision theory is designed as a tool for rational choice in situations of uncertainty. It has developed into something of a science in itself, between the domains of philosophy, probability theory, mathematics, and logic. Through more or less formal models of rationality, classic puzzles to do with the relations between morality, rationality, and self-interest can be illuminated, and to a certain extent, solved (Hammond *et al.* 1993; Follesdal *et al.* 1996: 276ff.).

A decision-theoretical argument includes information about what aims and values we search to realize, the alternative courses of action and strategies open to us, their possible consequences, and the probabilities of the realization of these consequences. It also includes attempts to estimate the values for alternative courses of action.

We are seeking norms for competitions that, if followed, can be expected to maximize average preference satisfaction among all parties concerned. I have already assumed that groups of concerned parties can be characterized by one predominant action-guiding preference, and I have tried to articulate such preferences for what I see as the relevant groups. The task now is to weigh the content of these preferences against each other. But first, there is a need for some specifications and a few methodological notes.

As mentioned above, at this stage of the argument we do not need to take differences in preference strength into consideration. I assume that within each group of parties concerned preference strength is equal. However, there is another variable that may have significant influence on preference satisfaction but has not yet been mentioned: athletic performance potential. The structural goal of competitions is to measure, compare and rank participants according to performance. Uneven competitions somehow render this goal meaningless – the ranking is given in advance. As with preference strength, I shall consider possible differences in performance potential to be non-relevant variables and 'sources of error' in the weighing of preference content. So let us assume we are dealing with competitors at an equal potential performance level. We shall examine both these assumptions more critically below.

In other words, the competitors in our hypothetical competitions are:

- carriers of one stable winning preference, upon which they act;
- relatively equal in preference strength; and
- relatively equal in athletic performance potential.[6]

A decision-theoretical argument outlines the consequences (C) of mutually exclusive but as far as possible collectively exhaustive alternatives (A). In each alternative I shall try to estimate maximum average preference satisfaction for all parties concerned. For example, in competitions with two parties we can say that if both reach full preference satisfaction, average preference satisfaction is 100 per cent. If only one of the two competitors is fully satisfied, average preference satisfaction is 100 per cent divided by two, that is, 50 per cent. And, when one competitor is fully satisfied (100 per cent) and the other is partially satisfied (50 per cent), average preference satisfaction becomes 100 per cent plus 50 per cent divided by two, that is, 75 per cent.

In most cases, decision-theoretical arguments deal with situations of uncertainty where some of the consequences and their probabilities are not known. These uncertainties can be treated systematically. I shall try to estimate the probability for the realization of the various consequences of the three alternative competitors A1, A2 and A3. The degree of probability will be expressed as a probability value (p).

Probabilities can be expressed by numbers between zero and one, or by percentages. We talk of objective probabilities, which express the limit of the relative frequency of an occurrence, and of subjective probabilities, which express degrees of beliefs. I can operate with objective probabilities based on the logic of the situation only in the instrumentalists' competition A1 only. In the mixed competition A2 and the players' competition A3, as we shall see, the probabilities are subjective estimates based on degrees of belief.

When we flip a coin we are operating with a pure chance event. The probability of each of the two possible outcomes is equal. But when we apply for a job, together with a thousand others, figuring out the exact probability of getting the job becomes impossible. Nevertheless, we can still try to estimate it. First, we can express the likelihood for an event to occur in ordinary language terms, such as 'unlikely', 'barely likely', 'fairly likely', or 'almost sure'. Second, in order to increase the accuracy, we can then carefully quantify some key variables by gathering relevant information and facts and try to zero in from the extremes to arrive at our estimate (Hammond *et al.* 1999).

In the argument below, I shall express probability values (p) as numbers from zero to one. If an outcome in terms of a certain level of average preference satisfaction can be expected with certainty, the probability is 1 : 1. This means that p: 1. If there is equal probability for a certain level of average preference satisfaction to occur or not to occur, the outcome is completely uncertain. The probability can be expressed as 1 : 2, that is, p: 0.5. If there is good reason to believe that a certain level of average preference satisfaction will occur ('fairly likely'), we calculate the average value between complete certainty (p: 1) and complete uncertainty (p: 0.5). In that case, p: 0.75. Finally, if there is relatively high certainty that a certain level of average preference satisfaction will not occur ('barely likely'), we calculate the average value between uncertainty (p: 0.5) and complete certainty of not occurring (p: 0). Then p: 0.25.

When we can estimate expected maximum average preference satisfaction in terms of percentages, and estimate the probabilities of such satisfaction between zero and one, it is then possible to quantify values (v) linked to the different alternatives. For instance, the value (v) of the instrumentalists' competition A1 will be the sum of each consequence C of A1 multiplied with their respective probabilities: $(CA1_1 \times pA1_1) + (CA1_2 \times pA1_2) \ldots + (CA1_n \times pA1_n)$. The final step of the analysis consists in ranking A1, A2 and A3 according to their values.

Before proceeding, I should add that attempts at fine-grained quantification of average preference satisfaction ought not to be taken too far. We are dealing here with 'soft' values that are hard to compare. At the same time, to be able to rank the alternatives in the present context I do not need more than an ordinal scale, to distinguish more or less acceptable from a utilitarian point of view. Such an ordinal ordering will be enough to choose. Let us begin by looking at A1.

A1: The instrumentalists' competition

We can imagine a sport competition in which both competitors R and S have strong external preferences to be ranked number one in the final ranking, that is, to win. For R and S the competition becomes a means in a struggle over external goals. Even though R and S might enjoy competing, basic rules of the sport have no value in themselves and can be broken if necessary. There is no such thing as a shared ethos here, only a pragmatic consensus on rule interpretation – as long as this consensus serves the self-interest of the competitors. If intentional rule violations such as cheating and 'professional fouls' provide a strategic advantage, they are considered acceptable.

The instrumentalists' competition is similar to a constant-sum game. Awarding advantage to one competitor leads to a similar loss of advantage by the other. Only one of the parties achieves preference satisfaction. If R wins, R will experience 100 per cent preference satisfaction and S no preference satisfaction at all, and vice versa if S wins. Because we have assumed that the competitors are of equal performance potential and preference strength, we can estimate the probability of winning for each competitor to be (p1): 0.5. Consequences, probabilities and values are shown in Matrix 1.

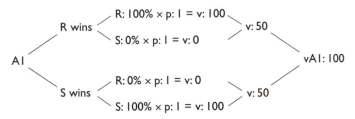

Matrix 1: A1 – external versus external preferences

Whoever is declared the winner in terms of being ranked first in the final ranking, maximum average preference satisfaction will never go above 50 per cent. In the instrumentalists' competition, only one competitor can be satisfied. The sum of the products of consequences and their probabilities for A1, or the value (vA1), will always be 100.

A2: The mixed competition

Let us imagine another competition between S with external winning preferences and T with internal winning preferences. S attempts to win by being ranked first in the final ranking, while T attempts to play (according to a shared, just ethos) to win.

As before, to S intentional rule violations are acceptable if they increase the possibility of being ranked number one. Both the competition and the presence of T are merely means towards external goals.

T wants 'to play to win' in order to realize experiential values in the activity itself. T competes according to what T believes to be a shared, just ethos of the practice. For T, intentional rule violations are not an option. S is considered not as an obstacle towards an external pay-off but as a partner in striving for mutual excellence and a good competition. As long as T realizes the experience of 'playing to win', T will be satisfied regardless of the final ranking.

Because we have assumed that the competitors are at an equal level of performance, S's strategy will succeed. Everything else being equal, the cheater has a wider range of means to reach his goals. For S, we can calculate with full certainty, p: 1, full preference satisfaction (100 per cent).

What about T? Let us take as an example a game of tennis between S and T. S employs all the available tactical and technical skills according to the shared, just ethos. In addition, S cheats, for instance by calling good balls out. To T, then, it becomes difficult 'to play to win', that is, to do her best according to what T considers the shared, just ethos of the game. S's conduct sabotages this possibility. T might not discover S's cheating and be reasonably content with the competition. But that would be the exception rather than the rule. I assume that T's chance of full preference satisfaction (100 per cent) is relatively small; p: 0.25. Again, consequences, probabilities and values are illustrated in Matrix 2. The value (vA2) of this mixed competition is 62.5.

A2 —— S wins
$$S: 100\% \times p: 1 = v: 100$$
$$T: 100\% \times p: 0.25 = v: 25$$
vA2: 62.5

Matrix 2: A2 – external versus internal preferences

A3: The players' competition

Finally, we imagine a competition between competitors with internal winning preferences. T holds the preference 'play to win' and meets a participant U with the same kind of preference.

Both T and U are seeking experiential values in the activity and relate to a shared, just ethos, which is the condition for such values to arise. Intentional rule violations do not occur. Possible unfair advantages resulting from unintentional rule violations are eliminated or compensated for by just procedures.

Unlike the previous examples, this competition has the character of a 'win–win situation'. Both T's and U's preferences can be satisfied within the activity itself. Independently of who is ranked first in the final ranking, both competitors can realize their predominant preference. I have assumed they are evenly matched in terms of preference strength and performance potential. This increases the chance that they will compete at their very best. We have a relatively high probability of full preference satisfaction (p), which can be estimated at 0.75.

The players' competition seems to offer a relatively high degree of preference-satisfaction to both competitors, and the value (vA3) becomes 150 (see Matrix 3).

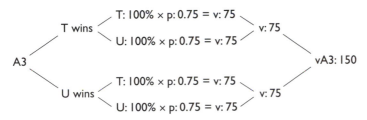

Matrix 3: A3 – internal versus internal preferences

A preliminary conclusion

The point of departure for this analysis was norm 2, which prescribes the realization of intentional goals among all parties engaged to the greatest possible extent. With the help of the more technical backing norm II, I have tried to estimate expected average preference satisfaction in three different competitions between competitors with predominant internal and external winning preferences. The values of the three alternatives were these:

- in A1, the instrumentalists' competition, $vA1 = 100$;
- in A2, the mixed competition, $vA2 = 62.5$;
- in A3, the players' competition, $vA3 = 150$.

So A3 is the most valuable alternative. As a preliminary specification of norm 2 we can now say:

> Competitors voluntarily engaged in sport competitions ought to play (according to a shared, just ethos) to win.[7]

Officials and support systems

So far, competitions A1, A2, and A3 have concerned competitors only. Norm 2 requires choices of actions that can be expected to realize the intentional goals of all parties concerned to the greatest possible extent. I now have to extend the analysis by looking at preference satisfaction among officials, support systems and spectators.

Among officials in general, and in support systems in amateur sport at lower levels of performance, I have assumed that we find primarily internal preferences. Most of the parties concerned are engaged due to experiential values realized in the practice itself. Or at least it is the case that the realization of possible external goals, such as friendship and a sense of community, depends to a greater or lesser extent on the running of competitions constituted by a shared, just ethos. Here, then, the preliminary specification of norm 2 seems to hold.

In high-performance sport, on the other hand, support systems seem to a large degree to act on external preferences. In addition, billions of spectators may be engaged. How can such parties be included in our argument?

If all people engaged in support systems have predominantly external preferences, this neither supports nor weakens the conclusion. Similar to the A1-scenario of the instrumentalists' competition, where competitors with external preferences meet, only one of the two support systems can be satisfied. Average preference satisfaction will be 50 per cent no matter what the outcome. In competitions A1 and A3, with two possible outcomes, the sum value for support systems $(vA1_{su})$ and $(vA3_{su})$ respectively will be 100. In the mixed competition, with only one outcome, the sum value $(vA2_{su})$ will be 50. The preferences of the support systems, then, do not challenge the preliminary specification of norm 2.

Spectators

The spectator group is more complex. In the previous section I argued that spectators of groups I and II are engaged primarily due to internal preferences. Most of their preferences depend upon competitions being run according to a shared, just ethos. They seek experiences of the standards of excellence of the sport in question (group I, the connoisseurs), or for identification, confirmation and construction of identity (group II, the supporters). Group III, the fans, are relativists. As long as competitions realize entertainment values, such as intensity, drama, and excitement, they obtain reasonably high degrees of preference satisfaction. Given this background, let us now look at the competitions one by one.

For competitors with predominantly external preferences (as in competition A1), the ethos is followed only if ethos conformity seems rational in relation to the pursuit of external goals. These competitions can be intense, dramatic and exciting. They resemble the idea of sport as a kind of war. Indeed, we can expect high levels of average preference satisfaction in the three spectator groups. At the same time, instrumentalists' competitions can turn out low when it comes to performance according to the standards of excellence of the sport that are highly valued by spectator group I: the connoisseurs. A basketball team that has already won the series might lack motivation to play well in their last game. Two football teams that are desperate to end on top of the final ranking might play defensively and unadventurously. Still, we should estimate the probability for 100 per cent average preference satisfaction among spectators as relatively high p: 0.75. If we sum the spectator value for the two outcomes of A1, we get $vA1_{sp} = 150$.

From the spectators' perspective, mixed competitions like A2, involving competitors with predominant external and internal winning preferences, will be unstable. They can be of high entertainment value. To the ice hockey connoisseur of spectator group I it must have been a pleasure to watch the technically elegant and fair-playing Russians of the 1980s beat the less skilful and aggressive (and to a certain extent violent) Canadians. The virtues of fair-playing tennis stars like Stefan Edberg must have shone particularly bright in matches against tennis's *enfant terrible*, John McEnroe. In competition A2, however, there is only one possible outcome. If competitors have an equal level of skill, the unfair player will win. Justice will not be done. Connoisseur spectators of group I will be disappointed. Even spectators of group II and III, who seek identification, identity construction and entertainment values, tend to have an ambiguous attitude towards mixed competitions. To the supporters, the favourite athlete or team may win but there has been no real match and the victory does not generate real pride. To the fans, it would often be better if both competitors cheated to cause conflict and perhaps arouse intense aggression. However, we may just as readily end up with non-entertaining competitions as with entertaining ones. Preference satisfaction, when it comes to A2, is unpredictable. So we should estimate p = 0.5. Then $vA2_{sp}$ will be 100 per cent multiplied by 0.5, that is, 50.

Players' competitions such as A3, where competitors share a just ethos and in addition are engaged due to internal preferences, will normally appear as intense, exciting and even. If competitors are evenly matched, they can raise each other to perform close to the standards of excellence in their sport. Competitions of this kind can more often than not express technical, tactical and moral ideals. Here, all three groups of spectators can reach a high degree of preference satisfaction. What A3 possibly lacks in conflict and violence, it may gain in quality of play. The outcome seems similar to that of A1. The probabilities of high preference satisfaction among spectators are high, p: 0.75. When we add spectator values for the two possible outcomes of A3, we get 2×100 per cent $\times 0.75$, so $vA3_{sp} = 150$.

A1: external versus external preferences

$$vA1_c = 100$$
$$vA1_{su} = 100$$
$$vA1_{sp} = 150$$

vA1: 350

A2: external versus internal preferences

$$vA2_c = 62.5$$
$$vA2_{su} = 50$$
$$vA2_{sp} = 50$$

vA2: 162.5

A3: internal versus internal preferences

$$vA3_c = 150$$
$$vA3_{su} = 100$$
$$vA3_{sp} = 150$$

vA3: 400

Matrix 4: An overview of the concluding utilitarian calculus

A concluding utilitarian calculus

The time has now come to conclude the calculus. I have estimated values for competitions A1, A2 and A3 among all parties concerned and can compare the outcomes.

To provide an overview of the analysis, the different alternatives can be placed in a decision-theoretical model, or what is sometimes called a decision tree. This is a graphical representation of the decisive elements of a decision, displaying the relationships among alternatives and probable consequences. I have given an overview of the argument in matrices 1–3, so here I concentrate for sum values of alternatives A1, A2 and A3 (see matrix 4).

For the instrumentalists' competition A1, external versus external preferences, the sum value vA1 = 350. The sum value of the mixed competition A2 external versus internal preferences, is vA2 = 162.5. Finally, for the players' competition A3, internal against internal preferences, the sum value is vA3 = 400.

It is important to stress again that the values above are estimations at the ordinal level of measurement. This means that the numbers do not indicate the exact intervals between the various alternatives, only a tentative ranking of them.

The preliminary specification of norm 2 formulated on p. 133, that competitors ought to act upon internal winning preferences, has been supported. The best alternative from a utilitarian point of view is the players' competition A3, in which competitors act according to the internal winning preference 'play (according to a shared, just ethos) to win'. If competitors act according to this preference, we can expect maximization of average preference satisfaction among all parties concerned. Moreover, we can expect maximization of the number of good sport competitions in general.

The preliminary specification of norm 2 was valid for competitors only. Its domain of validity can now be expanded to all parties concerned. The final formulation goes as follows:

> 2.1 Parties voluntarily engaged in sport competitions ought to act in such a way that a norm for competitors' playing (according to a shared, just ethos) to win is realized to the greatest possible extent.

Norm 2.1 has a series of practical consequences. Officials have the responsibility not only to ensure fairness and justice but also to do their best to see that all the competitions are experienced as good competitions. Good officials are aware of this obligation. They do not unnecessarily interfere in the flow of play, they contribute to a good atmosphere during sport events, and so on.

Similarly, members of the many support systems in high-performance sport ought to regard just and good competitions as their highest priority. If my assumption that this group has strong external preferences is correct, this is where norm 2.1 will probably have the most dramatic consequences. It seems to contradict the social logic of their situation, in which success is the very condition of their continuing existence.

Among the spectator groups, the immediate impression might be that norm 2.1 supports group I spectators: the connoisseurs. But this is not necessarily so. I have argued that supporter cultures of group II spectators acknowledge more or less intuitively that adherence to shared and just kinds of ethos are necessary for sport to provide possibilities of identification and identity construction. Moreover, it is not unreasonable to assume that fans find just as strong entertainment values in well-played and fair but still intense, dramatic and close competitions as in more aggressive and violent ones. Norm 2.1 does not necessarily contradict their views.

Further discussion of the implications of norm 2.1 is beyond my scope here. I have formulated another possible fair-play norm and shall now proceed by critically examining some of the assumptions made initially to reduce the complexity of the utilitarian calculus.

Variation in preference strength and athletic performance potential

First, I assumed that we are dealing with competitors of equal preference strength, and I avoided intra-group comparisons of preference strength with other parties concerned (support systems and spectators). Can these assumptions be justified?

The calculus has shown that the competitor and spectator groups lean in the same direction in support of norm 2.1, 'playing to win'. The support systems with assumed predominant external preferences reach 50% average preference satisfaction no matter who wins, and so do not influence the calculus in any direction. Because two of the three groups support norm 2.1 and the third group is neutral, there is no need for inter-group comparisons.

This does not necessarily mean these assumptions are morally justified. In real-life competitions, preference strength and performance potential of course show great variety. Let me elaborate.

Variation in preference strength

Variations in preference strength can have consequences for the degree of preference satisfaction among the parties concerned. Imagine a game of squash between X and Y. X has played only for a few years but is highly motivated and eager to progress. He trains regularly and tries to find the right balance between technical and tactical training, and matching. When playing for points, X is internally motivated – he is always doing his very best and tries to balance risk and offensive play to maximize the number of points he scores. X plays (according to a shared, just ethos) to win. Y on the other hand is an experienced player. He does not spend time on skill development but plays primarily for points. He needs a skilful and inspiring opponent for him to play well and with intensity. Y plays (according to a shared, just ethos) to win, too. The difference between X and Y is not one of preference content but one of preference strength. The point here is that this might lead to reductions in average preference satisfaction. X plays with high intensity no matter who is his opponent. Y does not have the same preference strength and his attitude is more relaxed. In games of this kind, X tends to feel frustration due to what X considers Y's lack of engagement, whereas Y might feel uncomfortable because he is not able to match X's novice enthusiasm.

In unorganized sport we often see a tacit norm of even matching of preference strength at work. After competitions of the kind just described between X and Y, competitors usually try to restore motivational symmetry by looking for other competitors with similar preference strength to their own. We intuitively seek competitors to whom we feel in accord. Kretchmar's (1975) idea of 'testing families' is to the point here: we ought to seek competitors of similar preference content and strength to our own. At higher levels of performance, this norm tends to be an implicit part of the organizational set up. The basic organizing principle is performance. No one with only medium-strength preferences will make much progress. Equality of preference strength is effectively secured through the logic of the system.

What, then, can be said of preference satisfaction among other concerned parties? In high-performance sport, I again assume that support systems are dominated by external preferences. There will, with certainty, be 50 per cent preference satisfaction here, independently of competitor preferences. In general we can say that spectator groups prefer competitors of equal preference strength. As with inequalities in performance potential, the reason is simply that competitors with inequalities in preference strength usually produce competitions with lower quality of play and less uncertainty of outcome.

I can now formulate an additional specification of norm 2:

> 2.2 Parties voluntarily engaged in sport competitions ought to act in such a way that a matching of competitors of similar preference strength is realized to the greatest possible extent.

Athletic performance potential

The structural goal of competitions is to measure, compare and rank competitors according to athletic performance. To reach reliable and valid evaluations, all competitors have to compete according to a shared, just ethos of the sport in question. All competitors have to be evaluated on equal terms. Moreover, as we have seen from the arguments set out above, such evaluations become most valuable when all competitors 'play to win'.

Another of my assumptions was that competitions tend to be realized at their best between competitors of equal performance potential. As illustrated by the Agassi–Medvedev example, evenly matched competitors usually challenge each other and help each other to perform at their best. The Williams–amateur example illustrates the claim the other way round: with unevenly matched competitors, there will usually be reduced experiences of mastery and challenge. Pursuing the structural goal of competitions with radically uneven performers seems meaningless – questions of measuring, comparing and ranking of competitors can be answered in advance.

The idea of evenly matched competitors is to a large extent borne out in practice. In informal competitive play, children usually seek to match teams well. They try to select even teams and will make adjustments by switching players if necessary. Most competitors seek partners at a similar level of athletic performance. Again, Kretchmar's idea of 'testing families' is relevant. Few if any want to compete with significantly superior or inferior partners.

In organized sport the pattern seems even clearer. Here we compete as individuals or in teams and matches are organized in series, leagues, knockout competitions and tournaments according to performance potential. In most ball games, teams are classified according to results from the previous season. In sports with individual competitors, there are comparable procedures: for instance, players may be classified according to ranking points.

What are the consequences of evenly matched competitors when it comes to performance potential among other parties concerned? A support system with dominant external preferences is satisfied only if 'their' competitor is successful. Here we shall most certainly end up with similar preference satisfaction as before, independent of whether there is even matching or not.

What are the spectators' views? We have seen that in the three spectator groups, but perhaps especially in group II (supporters) and group III (fans), good competitions ought to have intensity and tension. There has to be an exciting openness to the question 'who is going to win?' If the competitors are even in athletic performance potential and do their best to win, uncertainty of outcome arises. So in general we can say that spectators prefer even matching.

Perhaps the clearest expression of the quest for evenly matched competitors is found in commercial sport systems such as the American leagues in basketball, football and ice hockey. Each year college players who are ready for contracts (drafting) are ranked. Roughly speaking, the idea is that teams with the weakest record choose first and normally draft the highest-ranked college players. The obvious reason is that there should be no clear candidates to win the series title, and no team ought to be considered easy to beat. For owners and managers, this arrangement is probably based purely on profit considerations. Open outcomes enhance entertainment values and draw more spectators. Still, for once, commercial interests seem to accord with cost–benefit analyses from a utilitarian point of view.

I can now provide a third specification of norm 2:

> 2.3 Parties voluntarily engaged in sport competitions ought to act in such a way that a matching of competitors of similar performance potential is realized to the greatest possible extent.

Two objections

I have argued in favour of norms 2.1, 2.2, and 2.3 as ideals for competitors. Although further discussion of their practical implementation is beyond the scope of the present context, there is need to address two possible objections directly linked to the above findings.

First, as we can see from the overview of the utilitarian calculus sketched in Matrix 4, the instrumentalists' competition A1 represents the second-best outcome, and the mixed competition A2 the worst. In other words, it is better if two competitors with external preferences meet than two competitors with different preference contents. What distinguishes the best outcomes (A1 and A3) from the worst (A2) is that we are dealing with preferences with equal content. Norm 2.1 that prescribes internal winning preferences as the action-guiding ones represents an ideal. A possibly more realistic and less idealistic formulation would be:

> Parties voluntarily engaged in sport competitions ought to act in such a way that a matching of competitors of similar preference content is realized to the greatest possible extent.

This alternative formulation is based on the idea of minimizing the number of bad competitions. Although it may be more realistic, especially in high-performance sport where external preferences are many and strong, it represents a somewhat defensive moral strategy. Should we settle here for what from a moral point of view is the second-best alternative, because we live in an imperfect world? Perhaps strongly idealistic norms can change our attitudes and practices more than norms based upon some kind of *fait accompli*? The task is to formulate norms that can be expected to maximize average preference satisfaction for all parties concerned. To be true to this maximization scheme, we should choose the players' competition A3 as the ideal.

A second objection concerns norm 2.2, which prescribes competitors of even performance potential. As competitors, do we not go for easy wins once in while? Does not a football team that has suffered a series of losses need a 6–0 victory to increase self-confidence? And do not support systems and supporters enjoy the occasional feeling of complete superiority?

The answer is probably yes. At this stage, however, I am not aiming at psychological or sociological descriptions of actual preferences but at normative conclusions about what preferences ought to be action-guiding in order to maximize average preference satisfaction among all. From a utilitarian point of view, weak opponents are no good. One-sided victories may stimulate the ego in the short-term, but they reduce the satisfaction of the losing party and often of other parties concerned. Moreover, it is reasonable to assume that for most competitors, narrow wins over worthy opponents give stronger preference-satisfaction than one-sided victories. The wish for an easy win once in a while or the search for weak opponents, therefore, seems to be more an expression of weakness of character among competitors than of competitive ideals.

Of course, as Dixon (1992) argues, there is nothing necessarily unsporting or immoral about one-sided contests. All competitors may compete in a fair manner and do their best. The point, however, is that, from a utilitarian point of view, uneven competitions can be expected to produce less preference satisfaction among the parties concerned than even competitions. One-sided contests simply do not make good competitions.

Norm 2 for good sport competitions

I began with a tentative formulation of norm 2. Aided by the general utilitarian norm II I have been able to confirm and specify it via norms 2.1, 2.2, and 2.3. I can now state norm 2 in its complete form:

> 2 Parties voluntarily engaged in sport competitions ought to act so that all parties concerned have their intentional goals linked to the competition realized to the greatest possible extent by:
>
> - realizing a norm for competitors playing (according to a shared, just ethos) to win to the greatest possible extent;

- realizing a matching of competitors of similar preference strength and of similar performance potential to the greatest possible extent.

GOOD COMPETITIONS AS PLAYFUL COMPETITIONS

The strategy of my argument for good competitions has been to start with as few ideal premises as possible. At the outset I followed the utilitarian principle of accepting all kinds of view as being of potentially equal worth independent of content. Among these were views which considered sport to be a playful autotelic activity, critical views which considered modern sport as merely an expression of degenerate capitalist societies, and views in which sport appears as more or less a kind of war. Do the conclusions reached above contradict or support any of these views?

In the utilitarian analysis, the paradigmatic case of the good competition is the players' competition, in which the action-guiding preferences are internal in kind. There seem to be obvious links here to the view of sport as play. What, more precisely, are these links? To answer systematically I shall compare norm 2 with the characteristics of play.

Huizinga's *Homo Ludens* is the paradigmatic work. In the first section of his book, Huizinga (1955: 18–21) outlines the characteristics of play.[8] A first characteristic is freedom. According to Huizinga, there is no need here for in-depth analyses of the metaphysics of human freedom. Play is not a result of physical necessity. Neither is there any moral duty to play. Play is leisure. Play constitutes a realm of freedom outside the demands of ordinary life. Huizinga's idea of free play is therefore quite simple, and similar to the idea of practical freedom presented in Chapter 2. When play is chosen without external force of any kind in favour of non-play, this is done on a free, or voluntary, basis. Similar to this conception of play, the condition for norm 2 to arise at all is voluntary engagement. As with Huizinga, the criterion of voluntariness is simply that players have exercised unforced choice between engaging or not engaging.

Why do we voluntarily engage in play activities? Huizinga's answer is that we play for the sake of playing itself. Unlike work, play does not have instrumental value. We do not play to achieve some state of affairs outside of play, such as riches or prestige. Similarly, the focus of norm 2 on internal preferences expresses a similar concern with values realized in the activity of competing. If practised according to norm 2 and with the unforced acceptance of 'unnecessary obstacles' in order to achieve sport-specific goals, we manifest what Suits (1973: 49) calls a 'lusory attitude': '. . . the knowing acceptance of constitutive rules just so the activity made possible by such acceptance can occur'. In this way, norm 2 represents an understanding of good competitions as autotelic activities.

But even if play is voluntary rather than compulsory, and is of little value in an instrumental sense of the term, it can still absorb its participants 'intensely and utterly'. Even if children know they are only pretending, they may be completely captivated by their role-play. For a moment, children 'become' the roles they are playing. Chess players concentrating on their next move are fully and totally immersed in the world of their game. And, as in play, competitions practised according to norm 2 require the intense engagement of their participants. The obligation 'to play to win' leaves no room for half-heartedness. And the rewards of effort are legion. Good competitions offer strong experiential values to participants.

To play means voluntarily to engage in an activity with its own rules, norms, meanings, and values. According to Huizinga, the formal distinctions between play and ordinary life are usually sharp and well-defined in time and space by a set of rules. Play starts when the players agree to keep such rules, and play ends when certain rule-defined states of affairs have been obtained. The top of the tree has been reached; the balance-walk has come to the end of the fence; the ball lands in the basket. Play 'plays itself to an end'.

Norm 2 is designed to secure a common framework for competitions. The premise needed for shared, experiential values to arise among sport competitors is a certain order in the activity. We have seen how consistent instrumentalists who see competitions as means only towards external goals, reduce the value of such competitions. 'Play to win' means playing according to a shared, just ethos that defines clearly the spatio-temporal limits of the sport in question.

The well-defined frameworks and orderliness of play are particularly important in realizing what is deemed an optimal role for chance and luck, and so an exciting uncertainty of outcome. Huizinga describes tension as a basic quality in all kinds of play, ranging from solitary skill games like puzzles, jigsaws and mosaic making, to gambling and athletics. Players want to reach a goal, to succeed, but it is precisely the tension and uncertainty of outcome that makes the play valuable. Norm 2 also underlines the significance of tension and uncertainty of outcome, notably where it prescribes even competitors in respect of preference strength and performance potential.

The idea of play theorists is that the experiential values of play have depth and, indeed, fundamental existential dimensions. In play's make-believe, in its repudiation of reality and everyday life, Huizinga underlines the kinship of play with other non-instrumental activities: cults and rituals, music and art. As he puts it, play

> ... adorns life, amplifies it and is to that extent a necessity both for the individual – as a life function – and for society by reason of the meaning it contains, its significance, its expressive value, its spiritual and social associations, in short, as a culture function.
>
> (Huizinga 1955: 19)

Sport practised according to norm 2 can be justified with reference to more fundamental values as well. First of all, the norm has been formulated within a utilitarian framework based on the impartial view of everyone's happiness as being with equal worth, and with the maximization of happiness among all parties concerned as a final goal. Moreover, with Huizinga, I contend that in the very choice of autotelic activities we can find fundamental messages of human freedom, potential and possibility. I shall return to and elaborate this point in the discussion of the moral goal of sport competitions in Chapter 5.

We ought to be careful, of course, in citing Huizinga in support of a normative theory of the potential values of competitive sport. He was critical of the sport of his own time, and complaining about 'the fatal shift towards over-seriousness' and the rationalization and technical emphasis of training and performance. He saw in sport a contamination and a reduction of play to profane commercial entertainment.

Indeed, much of Huizinga's critique of sport can be deployed with even more force today. My argument, however, is not that sport is play. As we have seen from the examples given above, sport is ambiguous; it can also be a Hobbesian struggle of all against all – a kind of war. Neither have I attempted to solve conceptual problems by making claims about the similarities and differences between play, games, and sport.[9] In line with Meier (1988), my point is simply that sport practised according to norm 2 is practised with a playful attitude that, from my point of view, realizes sport at its best. That is why I choose to call norm 2 a norm for play.

SUMMARY

Chapter 4 began by asking what characterizes good sport competitions, and how norms for good competitions can be articulated and justified. Based on considerations of fairness I formulated a tentative norm 2 that prescribes the realization of the intentional goals of all parties concerned in sport competitions to the greatest possible extent. Norm 2 was elaborated by undertaking a utilitarian analysis, with norm II, which prescribes expected maximization of average preference satisfaction among all parties concerned, serving as the backing norm.

There are several preferences of relevance here. Some see sport as essentially play. The values of sport are those that arise in the course of practising it. Others see sport as a reflection of degenerate, capitalist societies, or as means to external goals such as: prestige, fame and fortune. As my point of departure I held all kinds of view to be potentially of equal validity. Having operationalized the preferences of all parties concerned and weighed them against each other in a detailed decision-theoretical argument, I concluded with the following specification of norm 2:

2 Parties voluntarily engaged in sport competitions ought to act so that all parties concerned have their intentional goals linked to the competition realized to the greatest possible extent by:

- realizing a norm for competitors playing (according to a shared, just ethos) to win to the greatest possible extent;
- realizing a matching of competitors of similar preference strength and of similar performance potential to the greatest possible extent.

Norm 2 serves to realize experiential values in competitions. Inspired by Huizinga's description of play as voluntary, autotelic activities, I argued that norm 2 prescribes a playful attitude towards sport. Therefore, norm 2 can be called a norm for play.

Chapter 5

Fair play in sport competitions
A moral norm system

My aim here has been to suggest moral norms to guide actions in sport competitions. I have pursued this aim by suggesting a particular interpretation of the ideal of fair play. As a point of departure I referred to a traditional understanding of the ideal. 'Formal' fair play is commonly understood as a set of norms for rule conformity and justice. 'Informal' fair play prescribes competing with effort and devotion and with respect for other persons engaged. In order to examine in a critical and systematic way whether, and eventually how, these ideals can be justified, I developed a moral point of view that included a consequentialist norm II inspired by utilitarian reasoning, and a non-consequentialist norm III for justice. Fairness norm 1 was articulated against the background of norm III for justice and gives 'formal' fair play a more detailed interpretation and justification. The play norm 2 was articulated with the help of the consequentialist norm II and is designed to maximize 'the good' in competitions. Norm 2 can be seen as a re-articulation and justification of 'informal' fair play.

In this way, I have worked within the framework of a mixed ethical theory with potential conflict between its main norms. So my moral point of view also included the meta-norm I, which served as a testing ground for cases of conflict and for the reasonableness of my conclusions. Following a con-tractualist line of reasoning, I have sought norms that 'no one can reject as a basis for unforced, informed general agreement'.

Methodologically, I have been looking for a reflective equilibrium where systematically developed norms and first-order moral beliefs cohere and mutually support each other. To reach such equilibrium has involved a process of constantly weighing different considerations. Sometimes, such as in Chapter 3 where I discussed classification of competitors, I found that there were cases in which moral beliefs and current practice violate the norm for equal opportunity to perform. More specific norms were formulated in order to provide a guide to better practice. In other cases, such as when I discussed the idea of the even matching of competitors, theoretically deduced norms and first-order beliefs cohered and supported each other. The norms I have formulated, then, can be regarded as a systematic articulation of fair play in

Fairness

1 Parties voluntarily engaged in sport competitions ought to act in accordance with the shared ethos of the competitions if this ethos is just, ie., if:

- the competitors are given equal opportunity to perform by eliminating or compensating for significant inequalities that the competitors cannot influence in any significant way and for which they cannot be held responsible;

- athletic performance is interpreted as based on talent and individual effort, and performances adhere to a basic norm of not exposing others or oneself to unnecessary harm;

- unequal treatment in the distribution of advantage is in reasonable accordance with actual inequality in athletic performance;

- unequal treatment in terms of eliminating or compensating for advantage gained through rule violations is in reasonable accordance with the actual inequality that has arisen due to the violation.

Play

2 Parties voluntarily engaged in sport competitions ought to act so that all parties concerned have their intentional goals linked to the competition realized to the greatest possible extent by:

- realizing a norm for competitors' playing (according to a shared, just ethos) to win to the greatest possible extent;

- realizing a matching of competitors of similar preference strength, and of similar performance potential to the greatest possible extent.

Figure 8 Fair play: a moral norm system

sport (see Figure 8 opposite). I now consider the fairness norm 1 and the play norm 2 to be morally justified.

Still, questions remain as to the relationships between them. Can fairness norm 1 and play norm 2 together constitute a moral system for sport competitions, or are they single norms with no strict connection between them or even no clearly related meanings?

FAIR PLAY AS A MORAL NORM SYSTEM

In Chapter 2, I said that a norm system has to satisfy requirements of clarity, simplicity, completeness, and internal consistency. Let us look at 1 and 2 in relation to each requirement in turn.

Are the norms for fairness 1 and play 2 clear? My answer would be 'yes'. First and foremost their domain of validity is clearly defined. Their qualifiers indicate that they have the character of obligations – they are valid for all parties voluntarily engaged in sport competitions. Moreover, I have tried to articulate the norms as clearly as possible and use terms that are quite easy to understand. To the extent that I have used special terminology, or where traditional terms are given non-traditional meanings, this is explained in order to avoid ambiguity. For instance, in Chapter 3, important concepts such as 'fairness', 'justice', and 'non-relevant' and 'relevant' equalities and inequalities were all discussed in detail. Similarly, in Chapter 4, key expressions such as 'intentional goals' and 'internal' and 'external winning preferences' and 'preference strength' were examined and clarified.

Are the norms for fairness and play simple? This is questionable, especially when it comes to norms for just competitions. We are operating here with nineteen norms of different levels of generality. Still, there are reasons for accepting a certain complexity. The norms must be specific, in order to express the characteristics of a local scheme of justice in sport. Moreover, only through specifications can we test the reasonableness in practical circumstances of the way the norms are formulated. Play norm 2, on the other hand, does not require the same degree of specification. As long as the terms used are given precise definitions, we can assume that the play norm satisfies the requirement for simplicity.

We see that the demand for simplicity must yield to a certain extent to the demand for completeness. Do the norms for fairness and play satisfy this demand? Do they cover in a satisfactory way all of their putative domain of validity? Do they have action-guiding force in actual and possible moral dilemmas in competitive sport?

Fairness norm 1 requires conformity to a shared, just ethos. Play norm 2 prescribes the maximization of intentional goal-realization among all parties engaged. Norm 1 prescribes what is fair and just in competitions. Norm 2 prescribes how competitors should act in order to bring about good competitions. The sphere of morality can be defined as the sphere of the right and the good. As we have seen in Chapter 2, there are many ethical theories and various views regarding the proper criteria of the moral. As regards theory, my approach has been selective. It represents one among several possible approaches. Still, I argue that norms 1 and 2 cover the domain of practical morality in that, from the perspective chosen, they are able to guide action in all kinds of questions of the morally right and good in sport.

The next question is whether the norms for fairness and play satisfy the requirement of internal consistency. A necessary condition for this is that a norm and its negation must not be found within the same norm system.

The conditions for the obligation fairness set out in norm 1 to be incumbent on us is that we are voluntarily engaged, and that the competitions we participate in are just and satisfy a general norm for avoiding exposing others and ourselves to unnecessary harm. The obligation of fairness and its conditions are in accord. I described how their obligation arises as a result of voluntary engagement, and discussed how the obligation is valid only within a just framework. My claim, then, is that fairness norm 1 is internally consistent.

The same can be said of play norm 2. This prescribes the satisfaction of intentional goals among all parties concerned to the greatest possible extent. By conducting a utilitarian analysis, I showed that we come closest to this ideal if all parties engaged act according to what I called internal winning preferences, that is, if they play according to a shared, just ethos to win. In addition, I argued in favour of norms for equality of preference content and strength. These norms all bear in the direction of realizing intentional goals among competitors to the greatest possible extent. The norms linked to play norm 2 are interconnected and internally consistent.

What, then, can be said of the relationship between the fairness norm 1 and the play norm 2? Norm 1 deals with fairness and justice. The framework is contractualist non-consequentialist ethical theory. Nonetheless, consequentialism plays an important part in the argument. The acceptance, in the discussion of game advantage, of a certain element of chance and luck, and the choice of interpretation of athletic performance, are justified among other things by references to the realization of intentional goals among competitors.

Play norm 2 is based on analyses of intentional goals or preferences among all parties engaged, and it is specified with the help of the utilitarian backing norm II. Norm 2 has a strong consequentialist flavour. However, it is formulated within a contractualist framework as an obligation that arises when we voluntarily engage in rule-governed practices. Moreover, the outcome of the consequentialist argument is a norm for playing according to a shared, just ethos, or for playing fairly to win.

Interestingly, norms 1 and 2 share elements of both consequentialist and non-consequentialist reasoning. I am not working just within the framework of a general mixed ethical theory here; rather I have outlined a mixed ethical theory specific to sport. The fair play-norms 1 and 2 overlap both in justification and in practical consequences, and thus they can meet demands for internal consistency.

The fairness norm 1 and the play norm 2 satisfy requirements for clarity, simplicity, completeness, and internal consistency. And, as I have argued throughout the discussion, these norms seem to cohere with our first-order moral beliefs and stand as a systematic expression of our sense of fair play in sport. In other words, I consider norms 1 and 2 to constitute the moral norm system for fair play. This is a norm system that, as prescribed by meta-norm I, no one can reasonably reject as a basis for informed, unforced general agreement.

THE MORAL GOAL OF SPORT COMPETITIONS

The moral norm system Fair Play prescribes how we ought to act in order to promote the morally right and the good in sport. If we are challenged on our moral views, we normally justify them by referring to more general norms, such as those of fair play, and finally to what we hold to be the most important or ultimate values and goals in life. In the preliminary account of morality sport in Chapter 1, I concluded the discussion by asking about the moral goal of sport and sport's possible role viewed in the broader perspective of human flourishing. What can be said of this now?

In the opening lines of the *Nichomachean Ethics*, Aristotle (1976) talks of 'the good' as 'that at which all things aim', or their *telos*. The *telos* of human beings is said to be *eudaimonia*, 'human flourishing' (Cooper 1975: 89ff.). For Aristotle, human flourishing involves living a life in accordance with reason. Now reason can be exercised in both theoretical and practical ways. In the more comprehensive, inclusive interpretation of Rawls' (1971: 426) 'Aristotelian Principle', human beings flourish when they '... enjoy the exercise of their realized capacities (their innate or trained abilities)'. Moreover, this enjoyment is considered to increase the more we realize our capacities and the more complex they become. Can sport be an arena for human flourishing in this sense?

Let us return to the norms for fairness and play. The argument now is that they are not only consistent in the weak sense of not contradicting each other, but that there are strong connections in meaning between them. In fact, they express what I understand as a core value and the moral goal of sport.

Fairness norm 1 defines a constitutive framework for competitions to take place at all. In adhering to norm 1, all parties follow a shared, just ethos of their sport. All parties are given an equal opportunity to perform. Norm 1 facilitates the realization of the structural goal to measure, compare and rank competitors according to athletic performance. In this way, norm 1 represents predictability. We know that the main challenge in tennis is to return the ball within the boundaries of our opponent's court but out of his reach, and we know that a downhill skiing race requires all skiers to ski as fast as possible through the gates that define the course. With requirements for ethos conformity and justice, fairness norm 1 realizes the game element that Caillois (1988: 9) calls *agon*: participants are given equal opportunity to perform and are ranked based on individual or team merit.[1]

However, norm 1 does not answer the further question of why we seek to realize this goal. What is the point of evaluating competitors according to athletic performance? Why do we voluntarily agree to compete at all?

In Chapter 1, I discussed Suits' (1973) idea of a particular 'lusory attitude' linked to game playing, and what Morgan (1994) calls the 'gratuitous logic' of sport. Both authors point to the paradoxical nature of these practices. In games and sport, we voluntarily accept 'unnecessary obstacles' to reaching a certain state of affairs as defined in the rules. I have found support for these ideas. From the consequentialist perspective of play norm 2, the 'lusory attitude' originates in the experiential values of sport themselves. With its prescriptions of 'playing to win', and of seeking evenly matched competitors, norm 2 represents a quest for a certain experiential tension. More precisely, when we do our best in competitions with equally able competitors, there will be an exciting unpredictability at all levels. Are the technical and tactical choices successful? Who is in the lead at present? Who will win at the final whistle? Moreover, in the discussion of game advantages and of interpretations of athletic performance, I argued we should accept a certain influence of chance and luck in competitions. Again, the justification of such non-meritocratic elements is based primarily on consequentialist reasoning. Non-meritocratic elements may add experiential values to sport. In this way, norm 2 secures the play element that Caillois (1988: 9–10) calls *alea* (Latin: 'play', 'dice'). In my interpretation, *alea* refers to both chance and luck, and to the exciting experience of unpredictability in close competitions.

In good sport competitions, there is a delicate balance between the apparently contradictory elements of *agon* and *alea*. If there is too much weight on *agon*, we easily end up with a reductionist understanding of sport as more or less scientific experiments in which non-meritocratic elements are considered sources of error that ought to be eliminated. With a one-sided emphasis on *alea*, competitions can end up as non-meritocratic games of chance. Because the structural goal of sport is basically meritocratic, I have argued that chance and luck ought never to exert significant and systematic influence on performance.

In order to reach an optimal tension between *agon* and *alea*, competitions need to be run according to requirements of fair play. Then the ideal tension between fairness and play, between predictability and unpredictability, and between merit, luck, and chance, can arise. Fairness norm 1 secures a predictable framework within which the play norm 2 is designed to realize experiential values and unpredictability. The distribution of advantage is primarily meritocratic, but once in a while chance and luck are decisive in the outcome.

An optimal tension gives rise to a certain experiential structure, which after Fraleigh I call 'the sweet tension of uncertainty of outcome'.[2] I am speaking now of the 'lived' experience of fair and good competition, an experience I consider one of sport's key values. Reference to 'the sweet tension of uncertainty of outcome' is meant not as an essentialist claim about the core value of sport, but as a tentative description of a common, phenomenological structure of the good sport experience, to which particular understandings of particular sports and particular competitions can relate.

Even if we accept experiences characterized by 'the sweet tension of uncertainty of outcome' as a key value in sport, questions arise as to its moral status. Can apparently superficial experiential values have any moral significance at all? How can references to experiences of excitement and tension serve as key elements of a theory of 'fair play'? What does all this have to do with the moral goal of competitions, conceived in the more comprehensive framework of human flourishing?

Again, we can return to the theories of play discussed in Chapter 4. There is a long tradition of scholars, from Plato to Huizinga, who argue that deep and complete engagement in autotelic activities has important existential dimensions, and that sport has fundamental cultural value (Grupe 1987). Strong and immediate experiences present us with existential questions about who are we, to whom we belong, and what can we achieve. Rawls (1971: 525ff.) talks of the social significance of a good game as a social union. Social unions are practices that are valued for themselves, in which the participants strive together within a shared ethos towards shared goals. In social unions, everyone contributes to, and takes pleasure in, the realization of one another's potential to a higher degree than would have been possible by individual efforts or within more strategic, instrumental schemes of interaction. William James described the strong and valuable experience of autotelic activities:

> Wherever a process of life communicates an eagerness to those who live it, the life becomes genuinely significant. Sometimes the eagerness is more knit up with motor abilities, sometimes with perceptions, sometimes with imagination, sometimes with reflective thought. But, whenever it is found, there is the zest, the tingle, the excitement of reality: and there is 'importance' in the only real and positive sense in which importance ever anywhere can be.
>
> (James 1958: 152)

Given this background, I argue that shared experiences among all parties engaged with the phenomenological structure of 'a sweet tension of uncertainty of outcome' are connected to moral values and can serve as a moral goal in sport. Hence, if practised in accordance with my norms for fair play, sport possesses special potential to provide an arena for human flourishing and so find a place as one among many possible practices constitutive of a good life.

Notes

1 Sport competitions: rules, goals and social logic

1   A similar definition of sport as a social phenomenon is found in Coakley (1998: 19).
    For philosophical discussions of the meaning of, and relations between, terms
    such as 'play', 'games', and 'sports', see for instance Huizinga (1950), Loy (1968),
    Suits (1973, 1978), McBride (1975), Guttmann (1978), Kretchmar (1975), Loy,
    McPherson and Kenyon (1978), Sutton-Smith and Roberts (1980), Tangen (1985,
    1997), Caillois (1988), Meier (1988), and Chick and Loy (1996).
2   These distinctions are inspired by Suits (1973). In Suits' terminology, 'prelusory
    goals' are set out ' … before, or independently, of any game of which it may be,
    or come to be, a part' (p. 48), while ideas of winning he calls the 'lusory goals' of
    games.
3   Heinilä's survey is presented in McIntosh 1979, Chapter 9.
4   See note 2.
5   Webster's *New World Dictionary*, 1984: 220.

2 A moral point of view

1   A more usual distinction is drawn between teleological and deontological ethical
    theories. In teleological theories (from the Greek *telos*, 'goal') an action is seen as
    right if it promotes a set of goals deemed good (Rawls 1971: 24). Such theories
    include consideration of consequences where these are relevant but emphasize in
    addition other aspects of actions. Consequentialism in general, and utilitarianism
    in particular, are typical teleological theories. A deontological theory, on the
    other hand (from the Greek *to deon*, 'duty'), is a non-consequentialist theory,
    according to which the good is not defined independently of the right, and/or
    where the right is not understood simply as the maximization of the good (Rawls
    1971: 30). I have chosen a different terminology, because it better demonstrates
    the tensions between, and the complementary functions of, my two perspectives.
2   However, this solution is not free of problematic consequences either. For example,
    as Parfit (1984: 381ff.) has shown, if we go for the maximization of average
    preference-satisfaction of all parties concerned, we may end up with 'repugnant'
    conclusions. Parfit's example is that, in order to enhance average preference
    satisfaction, it would be best if two-thirds of the current world population (those
    who are starving and suffering) simply disappeared. Still, the problematic aspects
    of the average preference-satisfaction criteria do not necessarily affect my more
    restricted argument to do with sport competitions. I assume that people are

engaged in sport in an unforced, voluntary manner. They can choose between engagement or not. If their preferences are not satisfied, or if average preference satisfaction is low, they can withdraw. Therefore, to avoid 'the tyranny of the masses', I have opted for the criterion of average preference satisfaction.

3 Scanlon (1985) initially introduces a definition of moral wrongness: acts are considered wrong if they '. . . would be disallowed by any system of rules for the general regulation of behavior which no one could reasonably reject as a basis for informed, unforced general agreement' (Scanlon 1985: 223). Later in his essay, however, he suggests a similar criterion for how we ought to choose and act, and this is the prime inspiration for our meta-norm (p. 240).

4 The requirements of a rational system of norms are based on Beauchamp and Childress (1983: 12–14), Darwall (1983: 203–39), von Wright (1983: 130ff.), Næss (1977), Tranøy (1986: 144–64), Aarnio (1987: 195ff.), and Eckhoff and Sundby (1988).

5 I seek here what Rawls would call a narrow equilibrium. To establish a wide equilibrium, we should also consider alternative moral points of view, alternative theories of fair play, and more general philosophical arguments to decide between the different normative theories. I have done this to a certain extent in my choice and description of basic premises but nonetheless shall concentrate on a particular perspective in my theory of fair play. Coherentist schemes of justifications in general, and Rawls' (1971) model of reflective equilibrium in particular, have been much debated (Jamieson 1993). Among other things, Rawls has been criticized for intuitionism and relativism: for drawing normative conclusions from descriptive premises. See, for instance, Hare (1975: 81–107), Hudson (1983: 387–9), and Kukhatas and Pettit (1990: 69–71).

6 The meta-ethical discussion between realist and anti-realist positions is complex and cannot be dealt with in a satisfactory way here. For a good introduction, see Beauchamp (1991: 111ff.). My aim here is simply to articulate the premises of my own work. As it happens, my position in the realist and anti-realist debate is not crucial to my argument. My theory of fair play can be read, understood, and criticized as a normative theory of sport independent of meta-ethical position.

3 Right sport competitions: fairness

1 In what follows, specific fair play norms will be referred to using arabic figures 1 and 2 to distinguish them from general backing norms of our moral point of view referred to using Roman figures I, II, and III.

2 The examples are based on Perelman 1980: 1–23.

3 In Rae's terminology (1981: 65 ff.), we can say that in sport we are dealing not with prospect-regarding equal opportunities, such as those in a lottery in which all participants have an equal chance to win, but rather with means-regarding equal opportunities. Everyone ought to be given equal access to the same set of means to win.

4 There is need for an additional comment, though. The consequences of inequalities in external conditions are not always dramatic, and there are ways for competitors to cope with them. Through good performances, competitors can improve their position in the next competition. Improvement in results for a young skier will improve her position on the ranking lists. Further, starting positions can be improved within a particular competition. A slalom race consists of two courses. In the second course, skiers start in an order based on performances in the first. The saying among sports people that 'there will always be another chance' is in this sense indeed true.

5 A further consideration weighing against more extensive classification systems is that from the spectator's perspective, the fascination with sports such as basketball, volleyball and the shot putt will decrease. These sports cultivate extreme body types in terms of size. We might suspect that classes for small competitors would become less spectacular and less fascinating. In boxing, in which competitors are classified according to weight, the heavyweight bouts are considered 'the greatest'. It is arguable, however, that classification according to body size necessarily leads to reduction of interest among spectators. Boxing enthusiasts will assert that the fastest and technically the best boxing is often found in the lighter weight classes. Similarly, we could think of developing in basketball or volleyball another playing style for competitors in light weight-classes. If that were done, we might expect that public interest in the sport would increase due to the increasing number of good players and teams.

6 This discussion might give the impression that the strengths of the different 'systems' completely determine the results in sport. This would be an exaggeration. Individual competitors and teams can still succeed against all odds. Kenya has the best long-distance running team in the world, and Jamaica has one of the best sprint teams. Iceland can beat Germany in handball, and Nigeria can beat them in football. However, these examples come from competitions in which economic and technological resources have a limited role. In high-tech equipment-based sports, such as motor racing, skiing and sailing, or where economic resources are decisive, such as in professional European club football, representatives from 'weak' systems seldom achieve success, if they ever get to participate in the first place.

7 The distinction between basic abilities and skills is by no means unproblematic, and the role of genetics in their development is not clear. For example, little is known about the genetics of motor development (Bouchard 1991: 302–3). Are we genetically disposed to develop certain general skills, such as those called in the literature basic loco-motor movement patterns (walking, skipping, running), non loco-motor patterns (pushing, stretching, balancing), and manipulative patterns (kicking, throwing, striking)? Or should we view all skills as pure products of the environment in the sense that we must be stimulated in a particular way in order for them to be learned and developed? Is the erect gait really something all normal people learn without special stimulation? The discovery of children raised among animals (for instance wolves) indicates the opposite; these people walk as if they had four legs.

8 These terms are explained with the help of the glossary in Atkinson *et al.* (1996).

9 Interestingly, this is in line with one of the basic ethical goals of the US Human Genome Project: to foster greater acceptance of human genetic variation (Bouchard *et al.* 1997: 11).

10 Carr (1999) argues that a common understanding of athletic performances as a product of merit is hard to justify. He considers such understandings as typical expressions of the egocentric and individualistic value system developed in liberal-democracies such as our own. Carr does not reject the meritocratic element of athletic performances but warns of exaggerations and recommends an education in sport in which athletes are taught to value the intrinsic rewards in terms of experiential qualities of these practices and not become preoccupied with ideas of individual merit and prestige. This is in line with my argument. The norms I have formulated acknowledge the influence of chance and reject the idea of competitions as purely meritocratic. Moreover, I have developed norms that are intended to reduce the influence of external systems and expertise, and to cultivate the role of athletes as moral agents with the potential for making voluntary choices. If the structure of the competitive sport system follows such

guidelines, there will perhaps be more room for the kind of proper modesty in sport that Carr advocates.

11   Indeed, performance-enhancing drugs can affect skills as well. Improved strength may affect the technical and tactical solutions of an alpine skier. She can increase the force applied through her outer ski during a turn and avoid skidding, and she can choose a tougher line through the course. Similarly, increased endurance helps a football player to keep up the pace in the important last fifteen minutes of the game. Still, the influence of bio-chemical manipulation here is limited. Sport-specific skills in technique and tactics are displayed as complex movement patterns that must be learned through experience and social interaction with others.

12   In addition, there are significant arguments in favour of a ban on performance-enhancing drugs linked to their out-of-competition negative social consequences. Lifting the ban would probably have significant long-term consequences for the status of sport in society. The most negative effects could perhaps be on recruitment and on the socialization of children and the young. In some sports, such as the 100-metre sprint and weight lifting, in which basic abilities for speed and strength are of decisive importance, it would probably be impossible to succeed without drug use. Would responsible parents let their youngsters take up a competitive sport in which bio-medical manipulation is almost a necessity to succeed? Further athletic performance could become less associated with individual talent and one's own efforts, and more dependent upon external expertise. Admiration based on identification with great performers could lose meaning and perhaps be replaced by admiration of strong bio-medical support systems. But would admiration of expertise systems be of similar intensity and quality as the identification with individual human beings as performers? I have chosen not to develop these kinds of arguments here, however, because my focus is on the just and good competition as such, and not on the role of sport in society.

13   What do we do, then, with all the grey areas in which we are not sure if a bio-chemical substance, a method, or a new technology should be banned or not? There is a clear parallel here to the discussion of equality. There I suggested a series of norms to restrict the role played by the 'system' in performance enhancement. The ban on certain performance-enhancing substances and techniques is another step in this direction and can be understood as rules to eliminate non-relevant inequalities. My demarcation criterion for equality is to eliminate or compensate for inequalities that have significant effects on performance but which individuals cannot influence and for which they cannot be held responsible. In advanced high-tech training regimes, athletes easily become a means of manipulation to secure the survival of the system. Together with the particular argument on drugs above, these are my guiding norms in the confrontation with all kinds of substances and techniques. The next step then is a case-by-case approach. For instance: even if the distinctions are not clear cut, a morally relevant difference between specialized and scientifically based diets and low oxygen chambers, as opposed to substances such as anabolic steroids and rEPO, is that the latter expose athletes to significant and (according to my argument) unnecessary harm. Even if some of us consider modern high-tech training environments over which athletes have little control a threat to their integrity and to the values of sport, a general ban seems unreasonable and difficult to justify. Here, some sports in which basic bio-motor abilities play a key role face a significant challenge. Will they turn into advanced, scientific experiments on human performance, or will they be able to keep a 'human touch', so that in which individual talent and efforts remain the key elements of good performance?

14 See Morgan (1988) and Breivik (2000) for discussions of the role of chance and luck in sports. Both authors seem to be sympathetic to what I have here called the rationalist position, but do not really examine in detail the consequences of such a view.

15 There is a significant body of philosophical literature on the aesthetic elements of sport. For a selection of essays, see Part VIII in Morgan and Meier (1995).

16 In practice, the distinction between intentional and unintentional violations is difficult to maintain. How do we know if a boxer's punch below the belt is a deliberate attempt to break the rules and get away with it, or just a matter of lack of skill and bad luck? How do we know if a team handball player in fact kicked the ball to gain an advantage or just had the bad luck of touching it with the foot? There are grey areas here as well, where actions do not fall clearly in one category or the other. How do we deal with recklessness? How do we deal with rule violations that are results of laziness in not learning the rules properly? Just practice depends upon honest athletes and officials with insight into their sport. Honest athletes and competent officials are the products of a good moral education in sport, and of years of training and experience. The task here is to develop a scheme of justice in which moral education and the sound development of talent in sport can take place. Discussion of the content and methods of moral education and applications of rules by officials are matters of the psychology, sociology and pedagogy of sport.

17 For complete formulation of the rule, see FIFA's homepages: www.fifa2.com/scripts/runisa.dll?s7.131602:gp:943789:67173+refs/laws/ milestones/90+E

18 We can of course discuss whether the advantage given for a victory really balances advantage given for a draw or loss of advantage due to a defeat. In general, however, the distribution of advantage in meta-competitions is the result of experience and trial and error, and seems to function with reasonable justice.

19 For a good literary example of the conflicts that can occur when competitions are threatened by unfairness and injustice, see Ernest Hemingway's short story 'Fifty Grand' (1927, 1961: 95–120).

4 Good sport competitions: play

1 Thanks are due to Claudio Tamburrini for his helpful comments on Chapter 4.

2 Obviously, there is another group of significance here at all levels of performance: people who are close to competitors, such as family and friends. In fact, they tend to be significantly affected. A bad loser is hard to deal with the night after a lost game of football. A runner's joy over a new 'personal best' on the track might have positive effects for the people close to her. The preferences of family and friends usually cohere with the competitors' own preferences. Family and friends wish us well. In my general argument on good competitors, I assume that the preferences of people who relate to each competitor and 'love' (and for that matter, 'hate') 'their' competitor are equal in number and strength among winners and losers and, therefore, pretty much even out.

3 Source: 'World Stadiums', http://homepages.go.com/-cikku/stadstart.htm

4 The devoted Chelsea supporter Sut Jhally provides another illustration. In 1997 he reacted strongly upon seeing the logo of the beer brewer Coors (known in the US for its support of the radical political right) on the chest of Chelsea manager and star player Ruud Gullit. To Jhally, that kind of cooperation was contrary to the values of football and the club he loved. In an emotional comment, he said the

situation was just as '. . . if Jesse Owens had been forced to wear Hitler's swastika' (Jhally 1998: 224).

5 For critical essays on spectator sport, see for instance Wenner (1998). For the history of sport violence and spectator hooliganism, see Guttmann (1986).

6 In game theory, players interact and choose strategies in the light of the strategies of other players. Two or more players influence each other's decisions. An alternative approach here would be to assume that competitors do not act consistently upon one predominant preference but are open to interaction. For instance, we could examine a 'tit-for-tat' strategy as an alternative action-guiding norm. The point then would be to adjust one's strategies according to one's competitors. This strategy is designed to maximize self-interest of the agent. Here I seek to establish norms that can be expected to maximize average preference satisfaction for all parties concerned. Hence, though more complex game-theoretical explorations would indeed be of interest, the first step must be the testing of various preference contents as ideals for acting in sport.

7 My examples here are based on two-person competitions. Most sports, from track and field to ball games and winter sports like skiing and skating, involve more than two competitors. Would my preliminary specification of norm 2 stay the same for competitions with many parties involved?

Let us hold on to the distinction between direct and indirect competitions explained in Chapter 3 and take direct n-person competitions like basketball, football, and volleyball, and indirect n-person competitions with many participants, like cross-country running races, as examples.

A 1' – The instrumentalists' competition
Imagine a competition A1' in which all competitors have external preferences. In a game of basketball, only one team can win. Average preference satisfaction will be as in A1: 50 per cent with probability p: 1. When it comes to the cross-country race, only one competitor can win. If we assume that preference satisfaction for all competitors depends upon being ranked number one, the average satisfaction will be very low. If there are 50 runners, we are talking in fact of an average of 1 : 50, that is 2 per cent. However, at least some of the runners will probably consider a ranking in the top ten best as satisfying their win-preference. If so, average preference satisfaction will increase to 20 per cent. In any case, in n-person indirect competitions of this kind, expected average preference satisfaction will not rise above 50 per cent with a relatively high degree of certainty, p: 0.75. The value of (vA1') will therefore never rise above 75.

A 2' – The mixed competition
Now imagine A2', involving competitors with both external and internal preferences. If the two basketball teams consist of players with external preferences and internal preferences respectively, we have the situation of A2. If the number of players with external preferences increases, there will be even lower probability that players with internal preferences will find the competition meaningful, so average preference satisfaction can be expected to decrease. If the number of players with internal preferences increases, the chance of experiencing a well-played game increases and so, we can assume, does expected average preference satisfaction. What can be said about the cross-country race? We are dealing here with an indirect competition in which there is no direct interaction – the performance of one competitor does not significantly influence others. Expected average preference satisfaction becomes a direct function of the number of runners with external and internal preferences. The greater the number of runners taking part with external preferences, the lower the expected average

preference satisfaction. This applies vice versa: the more runners with internal preferences, the higher the average preference satisfaction that can be expected. If the number of competitors with internal preferences is high, both direct and indirect competitions of the A2′ kind might rise above A1′ in average preference satisfaction. That is, vA2′ can exceed 75. But as long as there are runners with predominant external preferences, vA2′ will never reach levels such as those we find in A3.

A3′ – The players' competition
Finally, imagine A3′ in which all competitors have internal preferences. Again, provided we have players at a similar level of preference strength and performance potential, the situation is identical with A3 both for the basketball game and the cross-country race. We can expect full preference satisfaction of 100 per cent with probability p: 0.75.

    Hence, we can see that the results for the two-person competitions A1, A2, and A3, still stand, with one exception. In indirect mixed competitions where the number of competitors with internal preferences is high, A2′ might be ranked as the second-best solution. But this difference does not challenge my preliminary specification of norm 2. This condensed sketch of *n*-person competitions supports my conclusions.

8 In addition to the characteristics of play given here, Huizinga notes that play often promotes social groups of players who tend to surround themselves with secrecy and at times disguise, or in other ways underline their difference and 'otherness' from the rest of the world. This might seem a bit off target in a discussion of sport. Still, the socialization into and learning of the ethos of the sports in which we take part are in many ways initiations into practical, tacit knowledge of a group's view of their practice. Supporter subcultures cultivate the secrecy and the rituals of 'otherness' to an extreme, through songs, costumes, body paint, and the like.

9 For a collection of essays on this central topic in the philosophy of sport, see Morgan and Meier (1995), Part I.

5 Fair play in sport competitions: a moral norm system

1 Caillois (1988) divides play into four categories. In addition to *agôn* and *alea*, which will be explained below, Caillois talks about play with emphasis on *mimicry*: illusion and play-acting, and on *ilinx*: vertigo, giddiness and intoxication. Caillois also writes about the evolutionary development from unorganized play, *paidia*, to more rational and organized play with fixed rule systems, *ludus*.

2 In his use of the term, Kretchmar (1975) refers to Warren Fraleigh as its originator.

Bibliography

Aarnio, A. (1987) *The Rational as Reasonable. A Treatise on Legal Justification*, Dordrecht: D. Reidel.

Apel, K. O. (1988) *Diskurs und Verantwortung. Das Problem des Übergangs zur postkonventionellen Moral*, Frankfurt am Main: Suhrkamp.

Archetti, E. P. (1999) *Masculinities. Football, Polo and the Tango in Argentina*, Oxford: Berg.

Aristotle (1976) *The Ethics of Aristotle. The Nichomachean Ethics*, London: Penguin Books.

Armstrong, D. J. and Reilly, T. (1996) 'Blood Boosting and Sport', in D. R. Mottram (ed.) *Drugs in Sport*, London: E & FN Spon.

Armstrong G. and Gulianotti R. (eds) (1997) *Entering the Field: New Perspectives on World Football*, Oxford: Berg.

Armstrong G. and Gulianotti R. (eds) (1999) *Football Cultures and Identities*, London: Macmillan.

Arnold, R. K. (1986) 'Taxonomies of Motor Skills', in L. D. Zaichkowsky and C. Z. Fuchs (eds) *The Psychology of Motor Behaviour: Development, Control, Learning and Performance*, Ithaca: Movement Publications.

Atkinson, R. L., Atkinson, R. C., Smith, E. E., Bem, D. J. and Hoeksema, S. N. (1996) *Hilgard's Introduction to Psychology* (12th ed.), New York: Harcourt Brace.

Bannister, R. (1997) 'Human Performance in Athletics – Scientific Aspects of Record Breaking', unpublished paper presented at the IAF seminar in Budapest, 11–12 October, 1997.

Beamish, R. (1982) 'Sport and the Logic of Capitalism', in H. Cantelon and R. Gruneau (eds) *Sport, Culture, and the Modern State*, Toronto: Toronto University Press.

Beauchamp, T. L. (1991) *Philosophical Ethics: An Introduction to Moral Philosophy* (2nd ed.), New York: McGraw-Hill.

Beauchamp, T. L. and Childress, J. F. (1983) *Principles of Biomedical Ethics* (2nd ed.), New York: Oxford University Press.

Beisser, A. R. (1967) *The Madness in Sports. Psychosocial Obeservations on Sports*, New York: Meredith.

Best, D. (1978) *Philosophy and Human Movement*, London: Allen and Unwin.

Black, T. and Pape, A. (1997) 'The Ban on Drugs in Sport, the Solution or the Problem?', *Journal of Sport and Social Issues* 21(1): 83–92.

Bompa, T. O. (1994) *Theory and Methodology of Training. The Key to Athletic Performance* (3rd ed.), Iowa: Kendall/Hunt.

Bouchard, C., Malina, R. M. and Pérusse, L. (1997) *Genetics of Fitness and Physical Performance*, Champaign, Ill.: Human Kinetics.

Breivik, G. (1987) 'The Doping Dilemma – Game Theoretical Considerations', *Sportwissenschaft* 17(1): 83–94.

Breivik, G. (2000) 'Against Chance: A Causal Theory of Winning in Sports', in T. Tännsjö and C. Tamburrini (eds) *Values in Sport*, London: E & FN Spon.

Brohm, J-M. (1978) *Sport: A Prison of Measured Time*, London: Ink Links.

Brown, R. M. (1984) 'Paternalism, Drugs and the Nature of Sports', *Journal of the Philosophy of Sport* XI: 14–22.

Brown, R. M. (1990) 'Practices and Prudence', *Journal of the Philosophy of Sport* XVII: 71–84.

Bryant, J., Zillmann, D. and Raney, A. A. (1999) 'Violence and the Enjoyment of Media Sports', in L.A. Wenner (ed.) *Media Sport*, London: Routledge.

Burke, M. D. and Roberts, T. J. (1997) 'Drugs in Sport: An Issue of Morality or Sentimentality?' *Journal of the Philosophy of Sport* XXIV: 99–113.

Burke, M (1998) 'Is Boxing Violent? Let's Ask Some Boxers', in D. Hemphill (ed.) *All Part of the Game – Violence and Australian Sport*, Melbourne: Walla Walla Press.

Butcher, R. B. and Schneider, A. J. (1998) 'Fair Play as Respect for the Game', *Journal of the Philosophy of Sport* XXV: 1–22.

Butcher, R. B. and Schneider, A. J. (2000) 'A Philosophical Overview of the Arguments on Banning Doping in Sport', in T. Tännsjö and C. Tamburrini (eds) *Values in Sport*, London: E & FN Spon.

Caillois R. (1988) 'The Structure and Classification of Games', in W. J. Morgan and K. V. Meier (eds) *Philosophic Inquiry in Sport*, Champaign: Human Kinetics.

Carr, D. (1999) 'Where's the Merit if the Best Man Wins?', *Journal of the Philosophy of Sport* XXVI: 1–9.

Chick, G. and Loy, J.N. (1996) 'Definitions', in D. Venison and K. Christensen (eds) *Encyclopedia of World Sport: From Ancient Times to the Present* (vol. 1), Santa Barbara: ABC-CLIO.

CNN/Sports Illustrated (1999) 'Finally French. Agassi Fights Back to Capture First Title at Roland Garros'. Available at: http://sportsillustrated.cnn.com/tennis/1999/french.open/news/1999/06/06/french.final/index.html (18 January 2001).

Coakley, J.J. (1998) *Sport in Society: Issues and Controversies* (6th ed.), Boston, Mass.: Irwin McGraw-Hill.

Conzelmann, A. (1998) *Entwicklung konditioneller Fähigkeiten im Erwachsenealter*, Schorndorf: Karl Hoffmann.

Cooper, J. M. (1975) *Reason and Human Good in Aristotle*, Cambridge: Harvard University Press.

Cordner, C. (1988) 'Differences Between Sport and Art', *Journal of the Philosophy of Sport* XV: 31–47.

Crane, G. R. (ed.) (2000a) 'Liddel-Scott-Jones Lexicon of Classical Greek', in *The Perseus Project*. Online. Available at:
http://www.perseus.tufts.edu/cgi-bin/lexindex?lookup=e)/
qos&author=*2.0&lang=Greek&corpus=2.0 (23 January 2001).

Crane, G. R. (ed.) (2000b) 'Lewis and Short Latin Dictionary', in *The Perseus Project*. Online. Available at: http://www.perseus.tufts.edu/cgi-bin/lexindex?lookup=mos &display=&author=perseus&lang=Latin (23 January 2001).

Cratty, B. J. (1983) *Psychology in Contemporary Sport. Guidelines for Coaches and Athletes*, Englewood Cliffs, New Jersey: Prentice-Hall.

Csikszentmihaly, M. (1975) *Beyond Boredom and Anxiety: The Experience of Play in Work and Games*, San Francisco: Jossey-Bass.

D'Agostino, F. (1981) 'The Ethos of Games', *Journal of the Philosophy of Sport* VIII: 7–18.

Darwall, S. L. (1983) *Impartial Reason*, Itacha: Cornell University Press.

Davis, P. (1993–1994) 'Ethical Issues in Boxing', *Journal of the Philosophy of Sport* XX–XXI: 48–63.

de Wachter, F. (1985) 'In Praise of Chance. A Philosophical Analysis of the Elements of Chance in Sports, *Journal of the Philosophy of Sport* XII: 52–61.

Dixon, N. (1992) 'On Sportsmanship and Running Up the Score', *Journal of the Philosophy of Sport* XIX: 1–13.

Dreyfus, H. F. and Dreyfus, S. E. (1986) *Mind over Machine. The Power of Human Intuition and Expertise in the Age of the Computer*, Oxford: Blackwell.

Dubin, C. L. (1990) *Commission of Inquiry into the Use of Drugs and Banned Practices Intended to Increase Athletic Performance*, The Minister of Supply and Services Canada, Ottawa: Canadian Government Publishing Centre.

Eckhoff, T. and Sundby, N.K. (1988) *Rechtssysteme: eine systemtheoretische Einführung in die Rechtstheorie*, Berlin: Duncker & Humblot.

Elias, N. (1986) 'The Genesis of Sport as a Sociological Problem' in N. Elias and E. Dunning (eds) *Quest for Excitement – Sport and Leisure in the Civilizing Process*, Oxford: Basil Blackwell.

Elster, J. (1989) *The Cement of Society. A Study in Social Order*, Cambridge: Cambridge University Press.

Elster, J. (1992) *Local Justice. How Institutions Allocate Scarce Goods and Necessary Burdens*, Cambridge: Cambridge University Press.

Espy, R. (1979) *The Politics of The Olympic Games*, Berkeley: University of California Press.

FIFA (2001) *Milestones in the History of the Laws of the Game*. Online. Available at: http://www.fifa2.com/scripts/runisa.dll?s7.131676:gp:428622:67173+refs/laws/milestones/90+E (18 January 2001).

Finley, M. I. and Pleket, H. W. (1976) *The Olympic Games: The First Thousand Years*, London: Chatto and Windus.

Fraleigh, W. P. (1982) 'Why the Good Foul is not Good', *Journal of Physical Education, Recreation and Dance* 53(1): 41–42.

Fraleigh, W. P. (1984) *Right Actions in Sport. Ethics for Contestants*, Champaign, Ill.: Human Kinetics.

Frankena, W. K. (1963) *Ethics*, New Jersey: Prentice-Hall.

Føllesdal, D., Walløe, L. and Elster, J. (1996) *Argumentasjonsteori, språk og vitenskapsfilosofi* (6th ed), Oslo: Universitetsforlaget.

Gabler, H. (1998) 'Fairness/Fair Play', in *Lexikon der Ethik im Sport*, Schorndorf: Karl Hoffmann.

Galtung, J. (1969) *Theory and Methods of Social Research* (Revised Edition), Oslo: Universitetsforlaget.

George, A (1996) 'The Anabolic Steroids and Peptide Hormones', in D. R. Mottram (ed.) *Drugs in Sport*, London: E & FN Spon.

Gerhardt, V. (1993) 'Fairness – die Tugend im Sport', in V. Gerhardt and M. Lämmer (eds) *Fairness und Fair Play*, St Augustin: Akademia.

Gilberg, R. and Breivik, G. (1999) 'Hvorfor ble de beste best? Barndom, oppvekst og idrettslig utvikling hos 18 av Norges mest-vinnende utøvere', Oslo: The Norwegian University for Sport and Physical Education.

Glader, E. A. (1978) *Amateurism and Athletics*, West Point: Leisure Press.

Grupe, O. (1987) *Sport als Kultur*, Zürich: Edition Inferfrom.

Gruneau, R. (1999) *Class, Sports and Social Development*, Champaign, Ill.: Human Kinetics.

Guttmann, A. (1978) *From Ritual to Record. The Nature of Modern Sports*, New York: Columbia University Press.

Guttmann, A. (1986) *Sport Spectactors*, New York: Columbia University Press.

Guttmann, A. (1987) 'Ursprunge, soziale Basis und Zukunft des Fair play', *Sportswissenschaft* 1: 9–19.

Guttmann, A. (1992) *The Olympics. A History of the Modern Games, Urbana*: University of Illinois Press.

Hahn, E. and Remans, A. (eds) (1988) *Promotion of Fair Play*, Brüssel: International Stichting De Backer-Van Ocken vor de Strijd tegen het Gewelt in de Sport.

Hammond, J. S., Keeney, R. L. and Raiffa, H. (1999) *Smart Choices – A Practical Guide to Making Better Decisions*, Boston: Harvard Business School Press.

Hare, R. M. (1963) *Freedom and Reason*, London: Oxford University Press.

Hare, R. M. (1975) 'Rawls' Theory of Justice', in N. Daniels (ed.) *Reading Rawls. Critical Studies of 'A Theory of Justice'*, Oxford: Blackwell.

Hare, R. M. (1981) *Moral Thinking*, Oxford: Clarendon Press.

Heikkala, J. (1993) 'Discipline and Excel: Techniques of the Self and Body and the Logic of Competing', *Sport Sociology Journal* 10: 397–412.

Heinilä, K. (1982) 'The Totalization Process in International Sport', *Sportwissenschaft* 2: 235–54.

—— (1988) 'International Competition as a Test of Athletic Performance – the Overt and Covert Validity', unpublished manuscript, University of Jyväskylä.

Hemingway, E. (1961) 'Fifty Grand', in E. Hemingway *The Snows of Kilimanjaro and Other Stories*, New York: Macmillan.

Hill, C. R. (1992) *Olympic Politics*, Manchester: Manchester University Press.

Hoare, D. (2000) 'Birth Date and Basketball Success. Is There a Relative Age Effect?', unpublished paper presented at the 2000 Pre-Olympic congress in Brisbane, 7–12 September.

Hoberman, J. M. (1992) *Mortal Engines. The Science of Performance and the Dehumanization of Sports*, New York: Free Press.

Holt, R. (1989) *Sport and the British. A Modern History*, Oxford: Clarendon Press.

Hornby, N. (1992) *Fever Pitch*, London: Victor Gollancz.

Hortleder, G. (1978) *Sport im nachindustriellen Gesellschaft*, Frankfurt: Suhrkamp.

Houlihan, B. (1999) *Dying to Win. Doping in Sport and the Development of Anti-Doping Policy*, Strasbourg: Council of Europe Publishing.

Hudson, W. D. (1983) *Modern Moral Philosophy* (2nd ed.), London: Macmillan.

Huizinga, J. (1955) *Homo Ludens. A Study of the Play-Element in Culture*, Boston: The Beacon Press

Hyland, D. A. (1990) *Philosophy of Sport*, New York: Paragon.

IOC (2000a) *Olympic Movement Anti-Doping Code*. Online. Available at: http://www.olympic.org/ioc/e/org/medcom/pdf/doping_code.e.pdf (23 January 2001).

IOC (2000b) *The Olympic Charter*. Fundamental Principles. Online. Available at: http://www.olympic.org/ioc/e/facts/charter/charter%5Fintro%5Fe.html (23 January 2001).

James, W. (1958) *Talks to Teachers on Psychology, and to Students of Some of Life's Ideals*, New York: W. W. Norton.

Jamieson, D. (1993) 'Method and Moral Theory', in P. Singer (ed.) *A Companion to Ethics*, Oxford: Blackwell.

Jarvie, G. and Walker, G. (eds) (1994) 'Scottish Sport in the Making of the Nation: Ninety Minute Patriots?', in *Sports, Politics, and Culture*, Leicester: Leicester University Press.

Jhally, S. (1998) 'Free at Last – Sponsorship, Fanship, and Fascism', *Journal of Sport and Social Issues* 22(2): 224–26.

Jones, B. J., Wells, L. J., Peters, R. E. and Johnson, D. J. (1988) *Guide to Effective Coaching: Principles & Practice* (2nd ed.), Boston, Mass.: Allyn and Bacon.

Kamper, E. and Mallon, B. (1992) *The Golden Book of the Olympic Games*, Milan: Vallardi & Associati.

Keating, J. W. (1964) 'Sportmanship as a Moral Category', *Ethics* 75 (October): 25–35.

Kretchmar, R. S. (1975) 'From Test to Contest: An Analysis of Two Kinds of Counterpoint in Sport', *Journal of the Philosophy of Sport* II: 23–30.

Kukhatas, C. and Pettit, P. (1990) *Rawls: A Theory of Justice and its Critics*, Oxford: Polity Press.

Kupfer, J. (1995) 'Sport – The Body Electric', in W. J. Morgan and K. V. Meier: *Philosophic Inquiry in Sport*, Champaign, Ill: Human Kinetics (2nd ed).

Kymlicka, W. (1993) 'The Social Contract Tradition', in P. Singer (ed.) *A Companion to Ethics*, Oxford: Blackwell.

Lasch, C. (1979) *The Culture of Narcissism. American Life in An Age of Diminishing Expectations*, New York: W.W. Norton.

Leaman, O. (1981) 'Cheating and Fair Play in Sport', in W. J. Morgan (ed.) *Sport and the Humanities: A Collection of Original Essays*, Bureau of Educational Research Service, University of Tennessee.

Lenk, H. (1964) 'Values, Aims and Reality of the Modern Olympic Games', *Gymnasion* 4: 11–17.

Lenk, H. (1993) 'Fairness und Fair play', in V. Gerhardt and M. Lämmer (eds) *Fairness und Fair Play*, Sankt Augustin: Academia Verlag.

Lenk, H. and Pilz, G.A. (1989) *Das Prinzip Fairness*, Zürich: Edition Interform.

Liponski, W. (1988) 'Recognizing the Celts. Some Remarks on The British Origins of The Modern Fair Play Concept', unpublished manuscript, Budapest: Magyar Testnevelesi Föiskola.

Loland, S. (1989) 'Fair play – i idrettskonkurranser – et moralsk normsystem', Doctoral dissertation, Oslo: The Norwegian University for Sport and Physical Education.

Loland, S. (1996) 'Outline of an Ecosophy of Sport', *Journal of the Philosophy of Sport* XXIII: 70–90.

Loland, S. (1998) 'Fair Play Historical Anachronism or a Topical Ideal?' in M. J. McNamee and J. Parry (eds) *Ethics & Sport*, London: E&FN Spon.

Loland, S. (1999) 'Justice and Game Advantage in Sporting Games', *Ethical Theory and Moral Practice* 2, 165–183.

Loland, S. and McNamee, M. J. (2000) 'Fair Play and the Ethos of Sports: An Eclectic Philosophical Framework', *Journal of the Philosophy of Sport* XXVII: 63–80.

Lowe, B. (1977) *The Beauty of Sport. A Cross-Disciplinary Inquiry*, New York: Prentice-Hall Inc.

Loy, J. W. (1968) 'The Nature of Sport: A Definitional Effort', *Quest* X: 1–15

Loy, J. W., McPherson, B. D. and Kenyon, G. (1978) *Sport and Social Systems: A Guide to the Analysis, Problems, and Literature*, Reading, Mass.: Addison-Wesley.

MacIntyre, A. (1984) *After Virtue* (2nd ed.), Indiana: University of Notre Dame Press.

Mandell, R. D. (1984) *Sport. A Cultural History*, New York: Columbia University Press.

Mangan, J. A. (1981) *Athleticism in the Victorian and Edwardian Public School: the Emergence and Consolidation of an Educational Ideology*, Cambridge: Cambridge University Press.

Martin, D. (ed.) (1991) *Handbuch Trainingslehre*, Schorndorf: Hofman.

McBride, F. (1975) 'Toward a Non-Definition of Sport', *Journal of the Philosophy of Sport* II: 4–11.

McIntosh, P. (1979) *Fair Play. Ethics in Sport and Competition*, London: Heinemann.

McPherson, B. D., Curtis, J. E. and Loy, J. W. (1989) *The Social Significance of Sport: An Introduction to the Sociology of Sport*, Champaign, Ill.: Human Kinetics Books.

McNamee, M. (1995) 'Sporting Practices, Institutions, and Virtues: A Critique and Restatement', *Journal of the Philosophy of Sport* XXII: 61–82.

Meier, K. V. (1980) 'An Affair of Flutes: An Appreciation of Play', *Journal of the Philosophy of Sport* VII: 24–45.

Meier, K. V. (1985) 'Restless Sport', *Journal of the Philosophy of Sport* XII: 64–77.

Meier, K. V. (1988) 'Triad Trickery: Playing With Sport and Games', *Journal of the Philosophy of Sport* XV: 11–30.

Midgley, M. (1985) *Evolution as a Religion*, London and New York: Methuen.

Midgley, M. (1993) 'The Origin of Ethics', in P. Singer (ed.) *A Companion to Ethics*, Oxford: Blackwell.

Mill, J. S. (1863) *Utilitarianism*, London: Parker and Bourn.

Miller, R. B. (1996) *Casuistry and Modern Ethics – A Poetics of Practical Reasoning*. Chicago: University of Chicago Press.

Morgan, W. J. (1987) 'The Logical Incompatibility Thesis and Rules: A Reconsideration of Formalism as an Account of Games', *Journal of the Philosophy of Sport* XIV: 1–20.

Morgan, W. J. (1989) 'Chance, Skill, and Sport: A Critical Comment' *Journal of the Philosophy of Sport* XII: 62–63.

Morgan, W. J. (1994) *Leftist Theories of Sport: A Critique and Reconstruction*, Urbana: University of Illinois Press.

Morgan, W. J. and Meier K. V. (eds) (1995) *Philosophic Inquiry in Sport* (2nd ed.), Champaign, Ill.: Human Kinetics.

Mottram, D.R. (ed.) (1996) *Drugs in Sport* (2nd ed.), London: E & FN Spon.

Munthe, C. (2000) 'Selected Champions: Making Winners in the Age of Genetic Technology', in T. Tännsjö and C. Tamburrini (eds) *Values in Sport*, London: E & FN Spon.

Murray, T. H. (1983) 'The Coercive Power of Drugs in Sport', *The Hasting Center Report* XIII: 24–30.

Newcombe, T. M., Turner, R. H. and Converse, P. E. (1966) *Social Psychology. The Study of Human Interaction*, London: Routledge and Kegan Paul.

Nilsson, P. (1993) *Fotbollen och moralen. En studie av fyra allsvenska fotbollsforeningar*, Stockholm: HLS Förlag.

Norton, K. and Olds, T. (2000) 'The Evolution of the Size and Shape of Athletes', unpublished paper presented at the 2000 Pre-Olympic Congress in Brisbane, 7–12 September.

Næss, A. (1977) 'Notes on the Methodology of Normative Systems', *Methodology and Science* 10: 64–80.

Parfit, D. (1984) *Reasons and Persons*, Oxford: Clarendon.

Parry, J. (1987) 'The Devil's Advocate', *Sport and Leisure* Nov/Dec: 34–5.

Parry, J. (1998) 'Violence and Aggression in Contemporary Sport', in M. J. McNamee and S. J. Parry (eds) *Ethics and Sport*, London: E & FN Spon.

Patriksson, G. (1982) *Idrott och tävling. Idrottspedagogiska rapporter I, Göteborg: Institutionen för praktisk pedagogik*, Göteborg University.

Pearson, K. M. (1973) 'Deception, Sportsmanship, and Ethics', *Quest* XIX: 115–18.

Perelman, C. (1980) *Justice, Law and Argument. Essays on Moral and Legal Reasoning*, Dordrecht: D. Reidel.

Plato (1995) 'The Separation of Body and Soul', in W. J. Morgan and K. V. Meier (eds) *Philosophic Inquiry in Sport* (2nd ed.), Champaign, Ill.: Human Kinetics.

Purdy, D. A. and Snyder, E. E. (1985) 'A Social Profile of High School Basketball Officials', *Journal of Sport Behavior*: 54–65.

Rae, D. (1981) *Equalities*. Cambridge, Mass.: Harvard University Press

Rawls, J. (1971) *A Theory of Justice*, Cambridge, Mass.: Harvard University Press.

Reddiford, G. (1985) 'Institutions, Constitutions and Games', *Journal of the Philosophy of Sport* XII: 41–51.

Rescher, N. (1995) *Luck. The Brilliant Randomness of Everyday Life*, New York: Farrar, Straus, Giroux.

Rigauer, B. (1969) *Sport und Arbeit*, Suhrkamp: Frankfurt am Main.

Riordan, J. (1999) 'The Impact of Communism on Sport', in J. Riordan and A. Krüger (eds) *The International Politics of Sport in the 20th Century*, London: E & FN Spon.

Sartre, J-P. (1995) 'Play and Sport', in W. J. Morgan and K. V. Meier (eds) *Philosophic Inquiry in Sport* (2nd ed.), Champaign, Ill.: Human Kinetics.

Scanlon, T. M (1985) 'Utilitarianism and Contractualism', in J. Rajchman and C. West (eds) *Post-Analytic Philosophy*, New York: Columbia University Press.

Scheffler, S. (ed.) (1988) *Consequentialism and Its Critics*, New York: Oxford University Press.

Schiller, F. von (1988) 'Play and Beauty', in W. J. Morgan and K. V. Meier (eds) *Philosophic Inquiry in Sport*, Champaign, Ill.: Human Kinetics.

Schmidt, R. A. (1991) *Motor Learning & Performance. From Principles to Practice*, Champaign, Ill.: Human Kinetics.

Schneider, A. J. (2000) 'On the Definition of Woman in the Sport Context', in T. Tännsjö and C. Tamburrini (eds) *Values in Sport*, London: E & FN Spon.

Searle, J. (1969) *Speech Acts. An Essay in the Philosophy of Language*, Cambridge: Harvard University Press.

Simon, R. L. (1991) *Fair Play: Sports, Values, and Society*, Boulder: Westview Press.

Singer, P. (ed.) (1986) *Applied ethics*, Oxford: Oxford University Press.

Skillen A. (1998) 'Sport is for Losers', in M. J. McNamee and S. J. Parry (eds) *Ethics and Sport*, London: E & FN Spon.

Skirstad, B. (2000) 'Gender Verification in Competitive Sport: Turning From Research to Action', in T. Tännsjö and C. Tamburrini (eds) *Values in Sport*, London: E & FN Spon.

Spà, M. de M., Rivenburgh, N. K. and Larson, J. F. (in cooperation with researchers from 25 countries) (1995) *Television in the Olympics. International Research Project*, London: John Libbey & Company Ltd.

Suits, B. (1973) 'The Elements of Sport' in R. G. Osterhoudt (ed.) *The Philosophy of Sport*, Springfield: Charles C. Thompson.

Suits, B. (1978) *The Grasshopper. Games, Life and Utopia*, Toronto: University of Toronto Press.

Sutton-Smith, B. (1974) 'Towards an Anthropology of Play', *The Association for the Anthropological Study of Play Newsletter* **1–2**: 8–15.

Tamburrini, C. (2000) *The 'Hand of God'? Essays in the Philosophy of Sports*, Göteborg, Sweden: Acta Universitatis Gothoburgensis.

Tangen, J. O. (1985) 'Defining Sport: A Pragmatic-Contextual Approach', *International Journal of Physical Education* **22**: 17–25.

Tangen, J. O. (1997) *Samfunnets idrett: en sosiologisk analyse av idrett som sosialt system: dets evolusjon og funksjon fra arkaisk til moderne tid*, Norway: Telemark College.

Tännsjö, T. (1998) 'Is Our Admiration for Sport Heroes Fascistoid?', *Journal of the Philosophy of Sport* XXV: 23–34.

Tännsjö, T. (2000) 'Against Sexual Discrimination in Sports', in T. Tännsjö and C. Tamburrini (eds) *Values in Sport*, London: E & FN Spon.

Tranøy, K. E. (1986) *Vitenskapen – samfunnsmakt og livsform*, Oslo: Universitetsforlaget.

Tuxill, C. and Wigmore, S. (1998) 'Merely Meat? Respect for Persons in Sport and Games', in M. J. McNamee and S. J. Parry (eds) *Ethics and Sport*, London: E & FN Spon.

Verroken, M. (1996) 'Drug Use and Abuse in Sport', in D. R. Mottram (ed.) *Drugs in Sport*, London: E & FN Spon.

von Wright, G. H. (1963) *The Varieties of Goodness*, London: Routledge.

von Wright, G. H. (1983) *Practical Reason. Philosophical Papers*, Volume I, Oxford: Blackwell.

Walzer, M. (1983) *Spheres of Justice*, Oxford: Basil Blackwell.

Webster's *New World Dictionary* (1984), New York: Warner Books.

Weinberg, R. S. and Gould, D. (1999) *Foundations of Sport and Exercise Psychology*, Champaign, Ill.: Human Kinetics.

Wenner, L. A. and Gantz, W. (1998) 'Watching Sports on Television: Audience Experience, Gender, Fanship, and Marriage', in L. A. Wenner (ed.) *Media Sport*, London: Routledge.

Wetlesen, J. (1986) *Forelesninger over etikkens historie*, Oslo: University of Oslo.

Whannel, G. (1998) 'Reading the Sports Media Audience', in L. A. Wenner (ed.) *Media Sport*, London: Routledge.

Williams, B. (1985) *Ethics and the Limits of Philosophy*, Cambridge: Harvard University Press.

Weinberg, R. S. and Richardson. P. A. (1990) *Psychology of Officiating*, Champaign: Leisure Press.

Wischmann, B. (1962) *Die Fairness*, Frankfurt: Wilhelm Limpert-Verlag.

Wittgenstein (1953) *Philosophische Untersuchungen – Philosophical Investigations* (transl. by G. E. M. Anscombe), Oxford: Basil Blackwell.

Young, R. (1993) 'The Implications of Determinism', in P. Singer (ed.) *A Companion to Ethics*, London: Blackwell.

Index

abilities 67–9, 71

advantage
  and athletic performance xiv, 84
  and disadvantage xiv, xv
  distribution of xiv, 84, 91
  gained through rule violations 99, 128
  informal 85–6
  and luck and merit 87–92, 94–5, 145, 148
  sport-specific 85–6, 88, 90, 92, 94

aesthetic criteria for sport 92–4
  analytic (objective) criteria 94

Agassi, Andre 109, 135

age, classification by 59–60

aggression 108, 121

agon 148

alea 148

amateur sport 1

amateurism 62–3, 107

anabolic steroids 79, 81

Andersen, Anja 116

Angola 62

Apel, K.O. 3

Archetti, E.P. 119

Archimedes 12

Argentina 119

Aristotle 11–12, 19, 29, 30, 33–4, 39, 75–6,
  108, 147

athletes
  goals of 113
  as moral agents 57, 74–5, 76
  Olympic 12
  rights of 79–80

athletic performance
  and advantage xiv, 84
  description 30, 66–8

  and drug use *see* drug use
  and environmental influences 60–5
  inequalities in 34, 45–6, 54–6, 65–76
  interpretation of 71, 77–8, 83, 91, 145,
  measurement of *see* measurement,
    comparison and ranking and merit
    153–4*n*
  and morality 71–8, 153*n*
  potential 125, 133–4, 135–6, 137, 141
  and talent 83, 87

Australian Open (tennis, 2000) 48

autotelic activities 14, 138–9, 141, 149

badminton 96, 106

ball games 46–7, 52, 97, 101, 135
  see also basketball; football, etc.

bandy playing 61

Bannister, Sir Roger 69

Barcelona, football team 61

base-jumping 77

baseball 11, 93, 123

basketball 3, 5–6, 8, 55–6, 83–4, 56, 86, 90,
  93, 95, 96, 101, 116, 131, 136, 156–7*n*

Bayern München 61

Beamish, R. 82

Beisser, A.R. 119

Bentham, Jeremy 19, 26–7, 112

Best, D. 92

beta-blockers 79

bio-motor abilities 58, 59, 68, 75, 79, 81–2

body contact, severe 77

body size 54–7, 60, 67

Bompa, T.O. 58, 70

Bouchard, C., Malina, R.M., and Pérusse,
  L. 72

boxing 3, 9, 23, 52, 54–5, 56, 77, 95
Breivik, G. 80, 82, 116
Brohm, J.M. 108
Bryant, J., Zillmann, D., and Raney, A.A.
    121
BSkyB 120
Butcher, R.B. and Schneider, A.J. 14

Caillois, R. 148
Cambridge, University of 13
Camp, Walter 118
capitalism, and sport 108, 138, 140
Carr, D. 153–4n
casuistry 34
Celts 12
chance 88, 91–2,
    acceptance of 145
    in beach volleyball 102
    cynical position 89–90
    influence on performance 72–5, 92, 101,
        148
    in knockout competitions 100
    player's position 90–1
    rationalist position 90
    in series 101
    see also luck
chariot racing 12, 46, 85
cheating 93, 94, 96–7, 106, 127, 131
Chelsea football team 61
chess 139
children and play 139
children's and youth sport 1, 57, 59, 154n
China
    Cultural Revolution 10–11
    swimming 80
Christie, Linford 48
clarity, in norm system 34–5, 144
classification
    according to body size 56, 153n
    by age and sex 57–60
    for inequalities 56–7
    of teams 135
climatic conditions 60
climatic inequalities 49–50, 52
climbing 9
coaches 114, 117
Coakley, J.J. 108

cognitivism 20
combat sports 55, 77
commercial entertainment sport 1
communities, sport 120
competence 33–4
competitions
    cups 99
    definitions 1
    direct 47–50
    as experiments 44–6
    fair play in 143–50
    goals xiii
    home and away 48–9
    indirect 50–1
    instrumentalists', mixed and players' 124,
        127–9, 130–2, 138, 156–7n
    knockout 99, 100, 103
    knockout and series combined 101
    and merit 94–5
    mini-series 101–2
    moral goal 147–50
    and norms for fair play 34, 35, 37–8, 41,
        105
    and preferences 26–7
    raison d'être 12
    and rational self-interest 25
    as rule-governed practices 2–4, 31
    series 99, 101, 103
    and sport-specific advantages 86, Fig. 5
    structural goal of 10, 15
    with many participants 156–7n
    see also good sport competitions;
        meta-competitions
competitive advantage 45
competitive sport, origins 113
competitors
    families and friends of 155n
    preferences 114, 115–16, 122
completeness, in norm system 35, 144, 147
connoisseurs 118–19, 130, 133
consensus 7
consequentialism xiv, 19, 25–7, 38–9, 111,
    143, 145, 151n
consistency, internal, in norm system 35,
    144–5, 147
constructivism 20
contract theory
    ethical 37

non-consequentialist 30–1
Conzelmann, A. 59
Coors (brewers) 155*n*
critique of sport 108, 140
Csikszentmihaly, M. 107
cycling 4–5, 79, 80

D'Agostino, F. 5–6, 7–8
Davis Cup (1988) 103
de Wachter, F. 88
decision theory 124–7
decision-theoretical model (decision tree)
    132
deontic logic 20, 33
determinism 22
discus throwing 79, 85
disqualification 97
diving 2
Dixon, N. 137
doping *see* drug use
Dreyfus, H.F. and Dreyfus, S.E. 67, 116
drug use 18, 27, 28, 66, 78–83, 117
    banning of 28, 63, 83, 154*n*
    negative effects of 154*n*
Dubin report 18
Durocher, Leo 11

East Germany 80
easy wins 137
Edberg, Stefan 131
egoism 38
    rational 24–6
El Salvador 114
Elias, N. 13
entertainment value (of sport) 121, 131–2,
    133, 136
environmental influences on performance
    60–5, 67
    and development of skills 69–71
    relevant or non-relevant 72–6
equal opportunities xiv, 14
    prospect-regarding and means-regarding
    152*n*
equality 46–65
    in external conditions during
    competitions 51–3
    in initial external conditions 47–51

norms for 53
    in person-dependent matters 53–60
    see also inequalities
equipment standards 63
error, sources of 45
erythropoietin (rEPO) 79, 81, 82, 154*n*
ethical inquiry, levels 21, Fig. 1
ethical theory
    mixed xiv, 29, 111, 143, 145
    teleological and deontological 151*n*
ethics 17–31
    applied 20
    consequentialist and
        non-consequentialist 19
    descriptive 18, 20, 21–2
    normative 18–22
ethos conformity 124
ethos of sport xiv, 6–9, 15, 23, 31, 41
    criteria 9
    shared (just) xiv, 65, 84, 103–4, 112, 128,
        129, 130, 132, 135, 137, 139, 141,
        144–5, 147
    see also norms, shared
eudaimonia 19, 26, 147
fair play
    in competitions 143–50
    current understandings and definitions
        xiii–xiv, 13–15
    formal 14, 41, 143
    historical background 12–13
    informal 14–15, 16, 143
    theory of 36, 144–9
fairness 41–106, 110
    and justice 16
    see also justice; norms
fans 120–1, 122, 130, 136
fencing 63
FIFA (Féderation Internationale de
        Football Associations) 64, 98, 103
    Law XII on Fouls and Misconduct 98
'Fifty Grand' (Hemingway) 106
figure skating 92, 93, 94
Finley, M.I. and Pleket, H.W. 12
first-order moral beliefs 36, 39, 82, 104, 111,
        143, 147
football 1, 2, 3, 7, 9, 11, 46, 52, 58, 61, 64, 69,
        76, 77, 88, 90, 91, 93, 96, 97–8, 99, 100,

football (*cont.*)
  101, 102, 103, 104, 112, 114, 115, 119,
  120, 123, 131, 154*n*
formalist position 5–6, 7–8
fouls 97
Fraleigh, Warren xv, 45, 97, 106, 149
Frankena, W.K. xiv, 29, 111
freedom, practical 22, 138
French Open tennis tournament (1999) 109

Gabler, H. 14
game theory 112, 156*n*
gender equity programme 58
genetic predisposition 57, 68–9, 71
Gerhardt, V. 14
German Democratic Republic 61
Germany 153*n*
gladiators 30
global thinking 115
goals
  external 62, 130, 140
  intentional xv, 10–11, 15–16, 17, 25, 45,
    65, 74, 77, 91, 102–3, 109–10, 122, 137,
    140, 141, 144–5 *see also* preferences
  moral xiii, xv, 11–12, 38, 65, 74, 102–3,
    147–50
  and rules 8
  sport–specific 8, 9–10, 15, 66
  structural xiii, xv, 9–10, 65, 72, 74, 91,
    102–3, 109, 123, 135, 147
  and winning 2
golf 3, 58, 66, 88
  'unplayable lie' rule 84
good
  common 14, 82
  definition 26
  moral 16
  ultimate 11–12
good sport competitions xiv–xv, 20, 34,
    107–42, 149
  norms for 137–8
  as playful competitions 138–40
  as realization of intentional goals 109–10
good sport experience, phenomenological
    structure 91, 149
Grand Prix track and field meetings 99
Green Bay Packers 11

Gretzky, Wayne 67
growth hormones 79
Gruneau, R. 108
Gullit, Ruud 155*n*
Guttmann, A. 118
gymnastics 56, 92, 93, 113, 117

handball, European 13–14, 86, 95, 101, 102,
    116, 124
happiness 11, 26
Hare, R.M. 24, 28, 111, 122
harm and injury 76–7, 77, 98
Harrow (school) 13
hedonism 26
height and weight 54–7
Heinilä, K. 6, 8, 61, 80, 116, 117
Hemingway, Ernest 106
Hewitt, Lleyton 48
high jumping 87
Hoare, D. 59
Hobbes, Thomas 24–5, 30, 140
Hoberman, J.M. 74
Homo Ludens (Huizinga) 138
Honduras 114
Hortleder, G. 108
Huizinga, J. 107, 138, 139, 140, 141, 149
human agency 21, 22, 38
Human Genome Project 74, 153*n*
Hume, David 24
Hyland, D.A. 108

ice hockey 36, 67, 77, 97, 106, 123, 124, 131,
    136
Iceland 153*n*
identification and identity construction
    119, 120, 130, 131
ilinx 157*n*
inequalities
  acceptability of 50
  in access to resources 61–5
  in athletic performance 65–76
  basis for 78
  in body size xiv, 54–7, 67
  climatic 49–50, 53
  due to rule violations 95, 99
  elimination or compensation for 62–5
  in environmental influences 60–5, 67

in external conditions 67
in genetic predispositions 57, 68–9
and meta-competitions 99, 102–3
non-relevant and relevant 34, 36, 39, 45,
    51, 84, 144
in performance potential 134–5
in person dependent matters 53–60, 67
and unequal treatment in competitions
    83–104
see also equality
injury and harm 76–7, 98
instrumentalists 124, 127, 129, 131, 132,
    139, 156n
intentionality 95
FIBA (International Basketball Federation)
    62
ICSSPE (International Council of Sport
    Science and Physical Education) 14
IOC (International Olympic Committee)
    1, 14, 80
    and amateurism 62
    Anti-Doping Code 78
    sex testing regime 58
intra- and inter-subjectivity 45

Jahn, Friedrich Ludwig 113
Jamaica 153n
James, William 149
Jarvie, G., and Walker, G. 119
javelin throwing 88
Jhally, Sut 155n
Jones, Marion 119
Jordan, Michael 93, 116
jumping 50
justice
    Aristotle on 29, 30, 39
    and casuistry 34
    and chance 91
    and cheating 93
    in competitions 105
    formal, distributive and procedural 43–4,
        49, 50, 55, 80
    interpretations of 14, 29, 43
    and chance 91
    non-consequential theories of 20, 29
    and performance-enhancing substances
        79–80
    social 31
    see also fair play; fairness; norms, fairness
        (justice)
Juventus 61

Kafelnikov, Yevgeny 48
Kant, Immanuel 2, 12, 19, 23, 29, 30
karate 77
Keating, J.W. 12
Kenya 153n
kickboxing 77
King John (Shakespeare) 12
knights errant 12
Kretchmar, R.S. 134, 135, 157n

Lake Placid Winter Games (1980) 87
lane allocation 47–8, 51
Lasch, C. 118–19
Lenk, H. 14–15
Lewis, Carl 48
Liponski, W. 12
Lithuania 62
Liverpool Football Club 108
Locke, John 22
Loland, S. 6, 7, 8, 14, 91
Lombardi, Vince 11
long jumping 85, 87, 95, 97
lots, drawing 50–1, 52, 53
'lottery, natural' 88
lottery system, in knockout competitions
    100
luck 88–92, 94
ludus 157n
lusory attitude 138, 148
lusory and prelusory goals 151n

McEnroe, John 131
McIntosh, P. 12
MacIntyre, Alasdair 14, 19, 113
Manchester United 61, 120
Maracana football stadium, Brazil 118
Maradona, Diego 58
martial arts 52
Martin, D. 66
mass media Fig. 6
matching, even, of competitors 135, 136,
    143, 148

Matthews, Stanley 59
measurement, comparison and ranking
  athletic performance 60–5, 72
  competitors 135
  difficulties in 111
  and distribution of advantage 84–5
  and fairness norm 1, 145
  levels of measurement 84–5
  and luck 94–5
  and meta-competitions 99
  in series 103
  as structural goal of competitions 15,
    44–6, 51, 53, 90, 109, 125
  of systems 61
Medvedev, Andrei 109, 135
Meier, K.V. 3, 4, 15, 107, 140
meta-competitions 99, 102–3
meta-ethics 19
meta-norms 37, 38, 39, 111
Midgley, M. 25
Mieto, Juha 87–8
Milan football team 61
Mill, John Stuart 19, 26
Miller, R.B. 34
mimicry 157n
mixed procedures 51, 53
mixed theory xiv, 29, 111, 143, 145
Moore, G.E. 26
moral agents, athletes as 57, 74–5, 76
moral education 24, 155n
moral realism, soft 37, 39
moral reason (rationality) 23–5, 38
moral thought, critical level 122–38
moral truth 37, 39
moral value (of sport) 115, 118–19
moral wrongness 152n
morality xiv, 16, 17–39, 32, 145
  and ethics 17–31
Morgan, W.J. 4, 5, 8, 15, 108, 119, 148
motor development, genetics 153n
motor-cross 51–2
mountain climbing 81
Munthe, C. 74
Murdoch, Rupert 120
Muscular Christianity 13
Muths, Guts 113

naive realism 36
narrow equilibrium 152n
NBA (National Basketball Association,
  USA) 1, 55, 62
natural duties and obligations 32, 41
neo-Aristotelians 19, 21, 29
netball 52
Newcombe, T.M. *et al.* 6
Nicomachean Ethics (Aristotle) 29, 33–4, 104,
  147
Nietzsche, Friedrich 18
Nigeria 153n
Nilsson, P. 6, 8
non-consequentialism xiv, 19, 29, 39, 77,
  143, 145, 151n
norm systems 34–8
  external justification 35–8, 39
  fair play as 144–7
  internal requirements 34–5
norms
  absolute 33
  consequentialist and
    non-consequentialist xiv, 25–9, 30, 33,
    36, 37, 38, 39, 110, 143
  distributive 43–4, 52, 90
  for fair play 34–5
  fairness (justice) xiv, xv, 41, 79, 83,
    103–4, 109, 143–7, 148
  for good competitions 137–8
  meritocratic 46, 48, 86, 90, 91–2, 148
  moral xv, 17–18, 20, 31–3
  for non-injury and non-harm 3, 41, 78,
    81, 104
  for play 140, 141, 143–7
  'real' or proper 107
  shared 6–8, 15, 18, 23, 25–6, 30–2
  statements 32
  for unequal treatment linked to rule
    violations 99
Norton, K. and Olds, T. 54
Norway
  bandy playing 61
  elite athletes 116
  football cup 99
  taxation system 44

obligations, conflicting 33

officials, preferences 114, 116, 122, 130, 133
Olympic Charter (1974) 62
Olympic Games 48–9, 61, 91, 118
    (1896, Athens) 114
    (1984, Los Angeles) 48
    (1992, Barcelona) 58, 62
    (1998, Calgary, Winter Games) 62
    (2000, Sydney) 102
    ancient 10, 12, 85
    Summer 120
Olympic Movement 107, 113
    ideology 62
orienteering 115
original position 31, 41, 53
outdoor sports 50
Oxford, University of 13

paidia 157*n*
parachute jumping 81
Parfit, D. 151*n*
Parry, J. 77
Pele 58
penalties 95, 97, 98, 102
performance-enhancing substances
        see drug use
philanthropic movement 113
pistol shooting 86
Plato 107, 149
play acting ('taking a dive') 97
play theory 138–40, 149
play tradition 107–8
playing to win 124, 128, 129, 134, 135, 137,
    139, 145, 149
polo 119
Popper, Karl 30
positions, changing of 52
power sports 55
power-lifting 9
practical reasoning (rationality) 33–4, 108–9
predictability 147–8
preference content 114–21, 145
    competitors 114, 115–16, 136
    support systems 117–8
    spectators and the mass media 118-21
preference satisfaction
    average 27–8, 30, 39, 110, 112, 114, 125,
        126, 131, 137, 140, 156–7*n*

and evenly matched competitors 135
in instrumentalists' competitions 127
the mixed competition 127–8
the players competition 128–9
for spectators 130–1
preference strength 121–2, 125, 133–6, 141,
    144
preference-utilitarianism 110
preferences
    external 113, 117, 118, 130–1, 134, 135
    internal 112–13, 115–16, 117, 119, 130
    laundering 26–7
    winning, external and internal xv, 123–4,
        127–8, 144, 145
probabilities 125–6, 127, 129
professional foul 7, 18, 97–8, 127
professionalization 1, 62
public races ('folkerace', motorcar rallies)
    64
public school system, British 13, 113
Puerto Rico 62

quantification (of average preference
    satisfaction) 126–7

Rae, D. 152*n*
rationality, and self-interest 24–5
Rawls, John 27–8, 301, 32, 36, 38, 41, 43,
    53, 75, 147, 149
Real Madrid 61
reason, as slave of passions 24
recreational sport 1
refereeing scandals 93
reflective equilibrium 36, 39
relativism 20, 36, 130
reliability 45
rEPO (erythropoietin) 79, 81, 82, 154*n*
Rescher, N. 88
resources, material, human and economic
    60–5
respect for opponents 14
restoration of initial fair situation 96, 97, 99
Rigauer, B. 108
'right' as concept 41
risks, of harm and injury 76–7, 81
Romans, ancient 12
rough tackles 98

Rousseau, Jean-Jacques 113
rugby 8, 77
rule violations
    acceptable and non-acceptable 5–6
    and drug use 28
    elimination and compensation for 23, 84,
        104
    inequalities due to 66
    intentional 96–8, 99, 102, 127–8
    in meta-competitions 102
    sanctions incurred by 32
    tactical 97–8
    and unequal treatment 99
    unintentional 95–6, 102
    and winning 121
rules
    auxiliary 3
    consensus over 7, 14
    constitutive and regulative 2–5, 8, 15, 86,
        124, 138
    definition of disadvantages 84
    interpretation 6
    of skill 3
running
    and age 59
    average preference satisfaction in 156–7n
    and fairness 104
    goal 9–10
    home and away 51
    inequalities in 12, 47–8, 84, 87, 92
    long-distance 48, 51–2, 54, 66–7
    in marathon 84
    and resources 153n
    see also sprinting

safety 3
sailing 48, 63
Sartre, Jean-Paul 107
Scanlon, T.M. 31, 38, 152n
Schiller, Friedrich 107
Searle, J. 2
seeding 101–2
self-interest 24–5, 82
sex, classification by 57–8, 60
Shakespeare, William 12
Shankly, Bill 108
shooting 58, 79

shot-putting 56
Simon, R.L. 12, 58
simplicity, in norm system 35, 144
Singer, P. 20
skating, speed 52
ski jumping 3, 92, 93, 94
    V-style 93
skiing 4, 9, 49, 60, 152n
alpine 50–1, 52, 60–1, 87, 88, 101, 112, 117,
    154n
    bases and preparation of skis 63
    crosscountry 51, 59, 63, 79, 87–8, 99
    downhill 50, 81, 147–8
Skillen, A. 118
skills
    and abilities 67–8, 75
    and environmental influences 69–71
    sport-specific 154n
    technical and tactical 58, 70
slalom racers 4, 9
snowboarding 1
social contract 24–5
social discrimination 107
social logic 5, 15
social union 149
socialization 24
Soviet Union 61
Sparta 113
spectators 114, 118–21, 122, 130–2, 136
The Sporting Magazine 13
sprinting 47, 48, 51, 54, 65, 75, 85, 90, 91,
    93, 97, 153n, 154n
standardization 46–7, 75
    of equipment 63–5
steroids, anabolic 79, 81, 154n
stress management 70–1
success 117, 118
Suits, B. 3, 4, 15, 108, 138, 148, 151
support systems 114, 117–18, 122, 130, 134,
    137
supporters 119–20, 122, 130, 136, 137
    subcultures of 157n
Sweden 60
swimming 9, 47, 75, 80

tactical violation (professional foul) 7, 18,
    97–8, 127

talent
    and development of abilities 68–9
    as part of athletic performance 67, 71, 72–6, 83, 87, 104
    realization of 78
    and unequal treatment 78
Tamburrini, C. 58
tango 119
Tännsjö, T. 58, 108
Tärnaby, Sweden 60–1
team sports 92
technique 70–1
telos 19
tennis 2, 4, 48, 54, 60, 66, 86, 88, 90, 91, 100, 101, 103, 131
    stress management in 71
tension xv, 136, 148–9
testing families 134, 135
throwing events 50, 87
traffic control 4–5
Trevino, Lee 88
Tuxill, C. and Wigmore, S. 14
TV, sport on 120–1

UEFA (Union des Associations Européennes de Football) 64
uncertainty of outcome xv, 91, 100, 112, 121, 135, 136, 139, 149
unequal treatment *see* inequalities
UNESCO (United Nations Educational, Scientific and Cultural Organization) 14
USA
    leagues 136
    in Olympic Games 61
universities 13
utilitarian analysis 114–15, 124–7, 140, 145
    and preference strength 122
utilitarian calculus 110–12, 132–3, 136, 140, time frame 111–12
utilitarianism xiv, 19, 20, 25–8, 29, 39, 137, 138, 151*n*
    act 28

alternatives to 27–9
    applied 110–12
    rule 28
utility theory 112
value statements 32
virtue 19
volleyball 55–6, 70, 101
    beach 1, 99, 102
voluntary choice 22–3, 38, 53, 62, 65, 75, 109–10, 138, 152*n*

Waitz, Grete 66–7
war, sport as kind of 108, 130, 138, 140
warrior ethos 12
Wassberg, Thomas 87–8
weather conditions 49–50, 52, 53, 86
weight lifting 55, 85, 87, 154*n*
weight training 82
Weinberg, R.S., and Gould, 10
Weinberg, R.S., and Richardson, P.A. 116
Wenner, L.A., and Gantz, W. 120
Whannel, G. 121
Wilde, Oscar 122
Williams, B. 20
Williams, Venus 109, 135
win-win situation 129
windsurfing 49
winning 2–3, 4, 123–4
    definitions 3, 8, 9
withdrawal, prudent 106
Witt, Katarina 93
Wittgenstein, Ludwig 6
women in sport 1, 56, 57, 58
    discrimination against 82
World Championships
    (1982), football 103
    athletics 48, 119
    (Helsinki, 1999), figure skating 93
World Cup (football) 98, 114, 118, 120

Zhang Shan 58